The Navy Gave Me Shoes

Douglas A. Bryant, ENCS (SS) USN (Ret)

And

Jeff Wignall

ISBN – 10: 1544869657

Dedication

I wish to dedicate this volume to my late wife, Virginia, who so willingly accepted the burden of becoming a Navy wife during the early years of what would come to be our marriage of 58 years. As beautiful a lady as she was on the outside she was perhaps more so on the inside, and I miss her greatly.

In addition I would like to add the members of my family, both the living and the departed, and the great submarine sailors, the shipmates I sailed and served with. I learned so much from them and could not be the man I am today without the accumulated knowledge that was passed on to me by them. Regrettably nearly all are now gone, but I owe them all my deepest gratitude. A special thanks to my daughter Maureen with whom I remain very close - I rely on her for advice in all of my decisions involving my life – and to my special friend Joanne Frate for her assistance in preparing my story.

Doug Bryant, ENCS (SS) USN (Ret), Middleton, Massachusetts 2017

Foreword

Doug Bryant is a close friend and fellow submariner. He is a retired USN Senior Chief Engineman and a product of the Great Depression, and has written this story of his life in those times. Doug was born in 1926 and his book covers his life from then until his retirement from the Navy in 1967. His first Navy assignment as a teenager was to the USS Seadog (SS401) in WWII. He made five war patrols, endured depth charging and participated in "Operation Barney" with eight other submarines as they threaded their way through a minefield into the Sea of Japan in the closing months of the war. Sea Dog was the lead submarine and sank the most enemy ships during that operation.

Doug joined the Navy in 1943 at the age of 17. He served on five submarines, attended the USN Deep Sea Diving School in 1947 and was a First Class hard hat diver. He also attended Underwater Swimmer's School in 1955 at Key West, Florida to become a SCUBA diver, and served as an instructor at the Submarine Escape Training Tank in Groton, Connecticut, where he taught submarine escape and SCUBA diving.

He is a Veteran of WWII, Korea, Vietnam, and the Cold War, and retired from the Navy with credit for 25 years of service.

At a young 90 years of age at the time of this writing, he lives on his own and drives and travels extensively. He remains very active and has put time into his book every day since beginning it a year ago. He feels he has a great story here, and since I know it, I know he does.

Dan Crovo, US Navy Submarine Veteran, Bradford, Massachusetts, 2017

Preface

My role in producing this volume is mainly that of editor although I will own to having used my crayons here and there, and I did have a limited knowledge of the printing options available to get it published – we hope.

Otherwise this is a memoir by Senior Chief Doug Bryant, USN (Ret). Doug had been working for some time on a manuscript that detailed his experiences growing up in Northern New Hampshire during the Great Depression, and his subsequent 25 year career in the US Navy - from WWII and on into the 1960s - and was looking into ways to move it forward. He felt it was worth telling and perhaps more so that it be written. I not only totally agree but further suggest that all others who have played their seemingly small parts in large events take note.

My involvement came about in a roundabout way. Doug was meeting with a group of fellow submariners from the area in a local pub and it came about that a group of local schoolteachers gathered there on that particular afternoon.

Fast-forward about 15 minutes and the two groups were in mutual conversation. I couldn't say if that was a Navy thing, or Doug, I wasn't present, but either works. When it became know that Doug was a Veteran of WWII he was asked if he might be willing to speak to their students as Veteran's Day was approaching. Doug of course was quite willing, and that event took place in due course.

During the arranging and the doing, Doug had made it known that he was trying to put together a book about his experiences, and asked if they knew of anyone who could assist him.

One of the teachers is a neighbor of mine who was aware that I had *some* experience (please note the italics) with the process, and approached me about it.

I walk my dog in the morning but my afternoons are free, so I contacted Doug and the rest is – this book.

This is Doug's story and the content exclusively his. However, it was his feeling that my assistance be recognized by my being a co-author. I can "aw, shucks" that, but frankly feel honored to have been able to help him get his fascinating story into print – and proud to see my name associated with his on the cover.

His story looks at some things relative to both the Depression and the War that are in some instances little known and in others largely forgotten. My mission, and I chose to accept it, is to help prevent the latter in particular from happening.

At the risk of overly extending, I would like to say a few words about the authors that have no home elsewhere.

Doug Bryant's formal education was interrupted at 10 years. That was far more the norm in his day than now, and "there was a war on." But in terms of *Life Experience* credits, Doug can sit confidently at any table. Longevity alone might qualify him, but it need not. He is from a disappearing group that made their way successfully in life with more grease under their fingernails than ink in their pens. That said, Doug is a highly articulate man and his manuscript details a fascinating account of his Depression upbringing and a Navy career that spanned four periods of conflict.

For my part, I have one book in print, *Farebersviller 1944 - Amazon.com* for anyone interested. My *professional* qualifications arise only because a few copies were sold and some money changed hands. As a first book it has its flaws, perhaps from proximity to the subject. In this volume I was able to be more objective and the result, I believe, more satisfactory. I am personally non-military although something of a military historian, and from a family that has seen many members in uniform. My more direct involvement ties to my nearly 30 years of involvement with the 80th Infantry Division Veterans Association in which I am now a Past National Commander, which is to say a small fish in a shrinking pond, but I do take pride in it.

Jeff Wignall, Peabody, Massachusetts 2017

Introduction

My name is Doug Bryant – in some circles Bryant, Douglas A. ENCS (SS) USN (Ret) and in others, Chief. I wear the latter with pride, but will answer to all especially if it involves a refill.

I retired from the US Navy in 1967, credited with 25 years of service as a Veteran of WWII, Korea, Viet Nam, and the Cold War. At my present age – and I will leave the math to the reader since it changes annually – my uniform hangs pressed and ready in my closet for wear when occasions demand, and they still do despite my being on the beach for 50 years – and counting.

This is my story. No point in going into details here as they follow immediately except to say that the book is a memoir of my growing up during the Great Depression of the 1930s, and my career in the US Navy. The historic events of the time are well known, but where I fit in as an enlisted submariner is unique and hopefully will be of interest. I felt it should at least be recorded. Life during the Depression years was far from unique but largely forgotten now.

Individuals whose assistance and encouragement have carried my story into print have been noted elsewhere but I would like to include these lines from the motto of the US Submarine Veterans Association to address a larger purpose: *To perpetuate the memory of our shipmates who gave their lives in pursuit of their duties while serving their country. That their dedication, deeds, and supreme sacrifice be a constant source of motivation toward greater accomplishments.*

Also needing a mention are my primary sources of reference, "Hellcats" by Peter Sasgen, Penguin Books, NY, NY, 2010, and "Hellcats of the Sea" by Admiral Charles A. Lockwood and Hans C. Adamson, Chilton Co., Philadelphia, 1955. These books have helped inspire me to make my own contribution to the history of the WWII submarine fleet, and have been a source of information about aspects that I had forgotten, and in some cases never knew about.

My thanks also to Peter J. Koester, ET2 (SS), and National Historian of the US Submarine Veterans Association, for his suggested additions.

Douglas A. Bryant, Middleton, Massachusetts, 2017

Timeline

1926 - 1931 - Newburyport - Amesbury, MA

1931 - 1936 - Snowville - Eaton, NH

1936 - 1942 - Madison, NH

1942   - National Youth Association (NYA) - trade school - ME

1942   - Boston Naval Shipyard - mechanic learner - MA

1943   - Wooden Heel Factory - Conway, NH

1943   - Enlisted U.S. Navy - Boot Camp - Newport, RI

1943   - Motor Machinist - Mate Diesel Engine School - Richmond, VA

1943 - 1944 - Submarine School - Submarine Diesel School - New London, CT

1944   - USS Sea Dog SS401 - (New Submarine) - Portsmouth, NH

1944 - 1946 - USS Sea Dog SS401 - 5 War Patrols WWII, 9 ships sunk

1946 - 1947 - USS Spinax SS489 - City of Lynn Ship - MA

1947   - Deep Sea Diving School - Washington, DC - 6 month course

1947 - 1950 - Diver, Torpedo and Mine Testing Range - Solomon Island, MD

1950   - USS Sunbird ARS15 - (Diver) Submarine Rescue Vessel

1950 - 1955 - USS Sea Owl SS405

1955   - Underwater Swimmers School (Scuba Diver) - Key West, FL

1955 - 1958 - Submarine Escape Training Tank - Submarine Base - Groton, CT
                  Instructor - Submarine Escape Training and Scuba Diving course

1958 - 1960 - USS Entemedor SS340

1960   - Commander Submarine Force - Leadership Instructor

1960 - 1961 - USS Crevalle AGSS291

1961 - 1964 - Squadron II Staff - Engine Overhaul Shop

1964 - 1967 - USS Sea Dog AGSS401 - Naval Reserve Training Center - Salem, MA

1967   - Transferred to Fleet Reserve - Credited with 25 years service

In anticipation of questions that may be asked - a few key facts about submarines in the Pacific during WWII:

288 US submarines were available for duty in WWII.

263 were engaged on war patrols.

Approximately 30,000 men served in the submarine fleet (about 1.6% of total Navy personnel).

About 16,000 served on war patrols (and 3505 were lost).

A total of 52 submarines were lost (41 while on patrols), about 1 in 5.5 boats or 18% of the fleet. 48 were lost in the Pacific.

51 submarines remained in the Pacific after Pearl Harbor to carry on the war until production of new vessels caught up.

Initially enemy targets were capital ships, later merchant ships to cut off supplies, then destroyers to weaken the protective screens around capital ships, finally tankers to cut off fuel supplies.

A submarine could run submerged (on battery power) for up to 36 hours at very low speed, but only about 30 minutes at maximum speed.

Oxygen replacement and CO_2 removal was required after 12 -15 hours submerged.

Early boats could submerge to about 250 feet; later about 400.

Crews on the early (smaller) boats averaged 55 officers and men, later 72.

Of approximately 9 million tons of Japanese shipping sunk by the entire Navy about 5 million were sent to the bottom by submarines; nearly 55% of the total (by 1.6% of the Navy). An additional 700,000 tons of Japanese naval Vessels were sent to the bottom amounting to 30% of the total. This included 8 aircraft carriers, 1 battleship, and 11 cruisers.

504 downed airmen were rescued by submarines on lifeguard duty.

The rumors about serious problems with our torpedoes – despite denials from officials – were true. For various reasons many missed their intended targets while others failed to detonate on impact. This was not only unproductive but exposed crews to greater danger.

At least one submarine sunk itself when a torpedo with a flawed guidance system caused it to run in a circle.

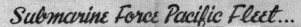

Submarine Force Pacific Fleet...

extends to

Douglas Almon Bryant, MoMM2

membership in the distinguished order of...

Mighty Mine Dodgers

a small band of brave men of high courage who have completed with skill, ingenuity and tenacity a task that required transit of the most dangerous of war waters, through enemy minefields and penetrating what the Emperor of Japan considered his inviolate waters.... the Sea of Japan.

No weapon of Dai Nippon could halt these determined men. They did wilfully and with due knowledge of the dangers involved, carry out their assigned task to emerge with incontrovertible proof of the success of their daring, thus becoming members of the Mighty Mine Dodgers and entitled to all the rights and privileges thereof.

Let all men who read this scroll be forever grateful and respectful of those heroic American submariners who went in and especially to those who gave their lives in this operation. The job was superlatively "well done."

M. Fenwood
VICE ADMIRAL U.S.N.

★ ★ ★

JUNE 1945

NAVY DEPARTMENT, BUREAU OF NAVAL PERSONNEL

SERVICE   SCHOOLS

UNITED STATES OF AMERICA

This certifies that

BRYANT, Douglas Almon, MoMM2(DO), 573 25 09, USN

has satisfactorily completed the prescribed course of study at the U.S. Naval School (Deep Sea Divers), NavGunFact., Wash., D.C. with a mark of 82.3. Maximum depth reached 300' on air; 320' on HeO2, *this* 27th *day of* February , 19 48

I. V. BAILEY,   G. G. MOLUMPHY,
Ensign, USN,   Commander, USN,   *U.S. Navy, Commanding.*
Assistant Officer–in–Charge   Officer–in–Charge

BNP 674
(Revised October 1942)   U. S. GOVERNMENT PRINTING OFFICE   16—30559-1

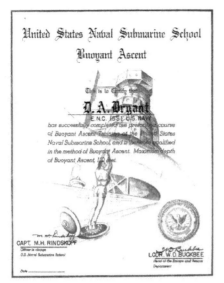

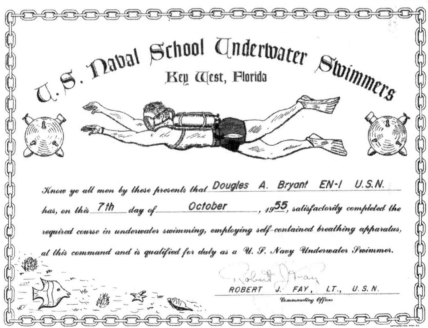

Preceding: Achievement Certificates awarded to author during his Navy career.

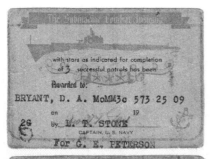

ID Cards, Left to confirm legitimacy of wearing Submarine Combat Insignia if challenged by proper authority. Right identifies the bearer in the event of a medical emergency as noted. Latter doubled as the only thing at hand to note the name and address of the young lady who would eventually become Mrs. Bryant.

The Navy Gave Me Shoes

By Douglas Bryant & Jeff Wignall

A close friend of mine, Vinnie Messina, a former ship's cook, served on submarines as I did during World War II. I think he's always been a little jealous of the fact that I stayed in the Navy and drew a pension, while he, somewhat to his regret, did not. Vinnie likes to get even in a sense by relating his version of how I joined the Navy - and how I came to stay for the long haul - whenever a suitable audience is present.

As Vinnie tells it, a Navy recruiter came to Madison, New Hampshire, and while looking over candidates for enlistment noticed me - with no shoes on. He pulled me aside and told me if I enlisted in the Navy they would give me a nice new pair of shoes to wear. I supposedly jumped at the offer and signed up for the duration. When the war ended and I was being processed out, I was told I had to turn in my shoes. Naturally I was very reluctant to do that (and return home barefoot). They advised me that my only option was to re-enlist, and that's why I stayed in the Navy.

The story never fails to get a good laugh – at my expense, but all in fun. The fact is that like most good fiction there's a lot of truth in it. We really did grow up going barefoot much of the time in those days in rural New Hampshire (as many did in other places as well) - whenever the season permitted - in order to extend the life of our valued shoes and keep them looking good for school and such. It was what we used to call a *druther*: we'd ruther go barefoot.

So while in reality I did have shoes to wear – and of course wore them when I enlisted - the Navy did present me with a nice new pair of shiny black shoes to go with my new blue uniform.

And, no, they didn't ask for them back. I re-upped for other reasons as will be seen. That's just Vinnie taking his best shot.

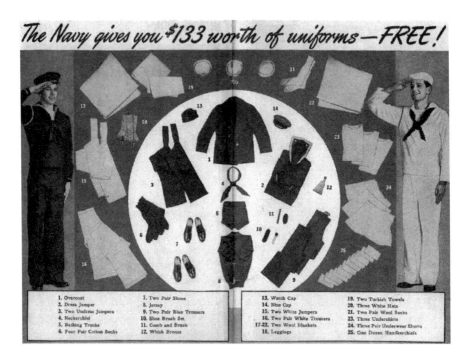

Actually two pairs of shoes – as of 1942.

Recollections of the Great Depression

I was born in 1926 at the Anna Jacques Hospital in Newburyport, Massachusetts. At that time my family – my father, Almon, born in Eaton, NH in the late 18oo's, my mother, Edith, born in Nova Scotia in 1898, and my brother John (but always Jack), born in 1925 - lived in the nearby Merrimac River town of Amesbury.

My father worked in the automobile body shops in Amesbury. There were several shops there at that time, some producing completed cars and others building custom bodies for vehicles being produced elsewhere. Amesbury had been known as the "Carriage Capitol of America" for its production of horse drawn carriages for over a century. Many vehicles from the early 1900's were little more than carriages with a gasoline engine replacing the horse.

By 1931, the height of the Great Depression, the industry, like so many others, had collapsed, and my father was out of a job and unable to pay the rent on our apartment. He was not a man who could live on charity – the nearest thing to welfare at the time. So he packed the family up and moved us to Snowville (part of the town of Eaton) in northern New Hampshire, where he was born and grew up. He knew of an abandoned house badly in need of repair that we could live in rent-free in exchange for doing the repairs to make it livable. There was no electricity, running water, or central heat, and no bathroom. This was long before TV, and we didn't even have a radio for a long time.

My father had grown up here, and his return from the better life he had hoped for in Amesbury represented a *strategic retreat* to a life that he felt – correctly as time would show - would insure his family's survival in the bad times that had befallen the country. He knew the land and he knew the people, and he knew he could *get by* here for as long as it would take for conditions to improve.

No one could foresee how long that might be, nor could anyone have imagined the event that would bring it about.

For the long hours of darkness we had two kerosene lamps for the house and one other for my parent's bedroom. My brother and I were not allowed under any circumstances to touch the lamps as a precaution against burning the house down.

There was a small barn with a few animals, a couple of cows, a pig, and some chickens and rabbits. A lantern would be used to light our way into and out of it but the animals were left in the dark through the long nights. Lanterns were more durable – mostly metal – but lamps, as used in the house, pretty fragile. Glass chimneys were easily broken, rendering a lamp useless, and the breakage of a glass oil reservoir could be disastrous.

Our water came from a hand-dug well located some distance from the house. My year-older brother Jack and I shared the chore of providing water to the kitchen for our mother to use for cooking, cleaning, and laundry. More was needed on Saturday nights that would be heated on the wood-fired stove in the kitchen for the Saturday night baths in a big tub on the kitchen floor- close to the stove for the added warmth.

Heat for the house came from the kitchen stove and another wood-burner in the living room. The bathroom, well, as I said, we didn't have one. We had an outhouse, and while a lot could be said about that perhaps it doesn't need to be. The previous year's Sears Roebuck catalog was kept out there. Sometimes, if my mother could save a little extra change from shopping, she would indulge herself with real toilet tissue, but that was reserved for her personal use.

My father appeared to have made one mistake in doing too good of a job restoring the house since it wasn't long before the owner sold it and we had to move to another. As I recall we went through that process three times from 1931 to 1936 so possibly it was part of the deal.

I wonder now how anyone survived in those years. Jobs were scarce and paid less than two dollars a day. My father did have a friend named Snow, from the family whose name was attached to the town,

Family photos: Top left about 1924 above with father, Almon at left.

Top right, Almon and sister – Aunt Jessie.

Group below in Snowville 1930: Mother 3rd from left rear, author, Uncle Frank, and Jack. Aunts Eva and Loretta in foreground.

who owned a woodlot in town, and my father would cut firewood for him for $2.00 a cord. Cutting a cord of firewood – a stack of four foot logs eight feet long and four feet high was considered a day's work in those days – and it was all done with hand tools; axes and saws – and files to touch them up. I've often thought it may have been a charitable gesture by his friend to help someone out that possibly resulted in stacked piles of logs rotting away back in the woods over time, but wood was the primary source of heat in the area in those days.

The Bryant family of Eaton-Snowville goes back to the early 1800's in Snowville and to the 1700's in Maine. The family history says that the first settlers in the area were the Bryant and the Snow families following the War of 1812. The Snows settled on Foss Mountain and the Bryants in what is now Snowville. At some point the families traded houses, the Bryants moving to Foss Mountain and the Snows to the village that would eventually take their name. They opened a store there and acquired a lot of the surrounding land, and eventually became very well off.

My father was a hardworking man who could do almost anything. Reveille for him would usually be about 4:00 AM to allow time for taking care of the animals before breakfast at 6:00. Breakfast was normally a full meal such as fried pork and potatoes. When employed he would be at work at 7:00 AM. In the 1930's the workday was typically 9 hours long, 6 days a week, with Saturday ending at noon for some. During the week he would be home by 6:00 for another session with the animals. My mother would serve the evening meal at around 8:00 PM. After dinner my father would sit in his favorite chair and read the Boston Globe (2 cents in those days) then retire at about 9:00 with no problem falling asleep. Today when I hear people talking about being "stressed out" I think of my father. Such words were not in his vocabulary.

Much that I have to say about my father provides the best way to describe what it was like living in Eaton during the Depression. A typical year began in early spring when the snow melted and it was time to clean all the manure from the barn to spread on the garden. Plowing and planting would follow as the weather warmed. We didn't have a horse for plowing but my father had among his friends two unmarried brothers from a neighboring farm who had a team and would plow our garden. No money was exchanged, but at a later time my father would do some work for them when needed. This was called "changing works" back then.

As a boy of 6 or 7 I can remember going to their farm with my father and brother. If it was in the evening after dark when we arrived in their yard all that could be seen was a dim glow in the kitchen window from the lamp on the kitchen table. The windows were so dirty you could barely see through them.

From time to time my father would take them to *town* (Conway) to shop, usually at the package store for beer and whiskey. I hated to ride in the car with them because their body odor was so strong. They also had hard cider and home-brew beer at the farm, possibly why my father was so close with them.

I have to say I think my father drank too much. If he was *flush* (had money) he drank bourbon or gin. Not so flush, it was port wine or home-brewed beer.

In the fall he could always find free apples on old farms. My brother and I would go along with him to pick them and gather the drops, and take them to the cider mill to have them pressed. After a couple of months the cider would turn hard and be ready for consumption. He had a 50 gallon barrel that he allowed to go hard and a smaller, 15 gallon barrel that would have beet juice added (for color), sugar, and grapes to boost the alcohol content.

To get back on course – with the planting done it was time to cut hay for the animals. We didn't have enough land to provide the hay we needed so had to look elsewhere for it. When found, it was cut and raked by hand, and hauled to the barn on a trailer pulled by my father's car.

He owned two during the decade of the 1930s which would seem at odds with our economic situation, but both - Model A Fords - were well used and cheap. Since he owned them outright there was no problem about the cost. He did all the maintenance, and their use was limited to necessity so the fuel cost was kept low. There were no Sunday drives and insurance not an issue back then.

The garden required continual attention - hoeing to keep the weeds down - until harvest time. Then my mother would be busy canning things for the winter. If my father had found any regular work, the farm chores, aside from the daily attention to the animals, fell to evenings and weekends for as long as the job lasted, and more and more to Jack and me as we got older.

No rest followed the end of the gardening season. Then it was time to bring home the 10 or more cords of firewood cut the previous fall and stacked to season for a year that would be needed to get through the winter. The four foot lengths had to be reduced to 16" to fit the stove, split, and stacked in the wood shed. Then the cutting for next year would begin. Even at six and seven years of age, my father always brought Jack and me with him. We would drag the brush away as he trimmed the branches. As time passed we began alternating taking an end of the two-man saw with him on the other to reduce the felled logs to four feet.

Butchering for the winter's supply of meat was also done at this time of year when the weather became consistently cold enough to help with preserving the meat. All we had in the way of a freezer was winter. We always had a pig to butcher, and, one year, an injured milk cow whose time had come. Much of the meat was cooked and canned to preserve it as we only had a small *ice box* for food storage, and that was not adequate for lengthy storage in any case. A lot of the hog fat was cut up and preserved in a wooden barrel packed with salt. When times were tough, usually as spring approached and we started to run out of things, we would be getting by on salt pork and fried potatoes.

Butchering was a two man job. Whoever was brought in to help was paid either with a portion of the meat or possibly just the return of the favor.

By the time we moved to Madison my father felt I was old enough to help. The pig was kept in the lower level of the barn where the horse and cow manure was kept – to be spread over the garden in the spring

The pig was to be let out through the side door of the cellar where my father would shoot it with his pistol. When the pig went down, I was to step in and grab its front legs to prevent the kicking that usually followed. This would allow my father to safely move in with his well sharpened knife and cut the pig's throat to bleed it. Without the pig being held firmly my father faced the risk of injury either from the knife or the thrashing hooves.

However, the sudden sound of the shot and my basic fear of the pig caused me to freeze, and I was powerless to do as I had been instructed. My father was very angry with me and I expected a licking, but he calmed down when the job was done without injury. I guess he understood my fear - may have gone down that road himself at an earlier time.

My mother was a great cook and as long as we could afford flour, sugar, and chocolate she made homemade bread, biscuits, cakes, cookies, pudding, and apple pies if we had leftovers from the cider making. We always had homemade beans on Saturday night, with hot dogs if the budget had room. Bananas were a great treat. When over-ripe they sold for 4 pounds for a quarter. This was the only time we had them.

Shortly after President Roosevelt was elected a relief program was started and surplus food was distributed to needy families. Much of this food was quite good but many Republicans in town refused it because it was "Democrat food."

With things shut down for winter there would seem to be time for skating or skiing, but no, this was the time to go to the lake and clear the snow from the ice to cut blocks to be stored in the ice house for use in the *ice box* when spring arrived. And at first we didn't own such things as skates and skis. We could make snowmen; no money needed for that.

That briefly was my father's (and our) routine for a year in rural New Hampshire in hard times. I don't wonder that he needed to drink some.

When we moved from Amesbury to Snowville in 1931 I was 5 years old. I lived for a time with my aunt Jessie, my father's sister, near the Snowville School. I expect this was to keep me out of the way while the house was being worked on. Aunt Jessie was a great lady and well liked in town. She had a son and daughter, both grown and married.

I was allowed to attend the school, but I think as sort of a mascot. If I got out of control the teacher would send me back to Aunt Jessie's house just up the hill from the school.

The school was a single room with an entrance coat room that had a 5 gallon crock of drinking water and a box mounted on the wall with cubby holes for each student's tin cup. There was electricity, but no indoor plumbing. A large wood stove in the center of the room provided heat when needed. A two seat outhouse was attached to the back of the building with a wall separating the boys and girls sides, each with its own door. With no running water, there was no hand washing. Lunches were brought in lunch pails or lunch boxes - by those who had one to bring.

About once a month a projector was brought in and we got to see a short film. It's difficult now to understand what a major event that it was: Moving Pictures! It's not so much that they were new - they had been around for some time and there were even *talkies* by this time - but pretty rare for us!

There were eight grades with about 25 students and a single teacher whose only relief was the assistance given younger students by the older ones. I believe there was another similar school in town, but smaller.

There was no high school in the town of Eaton so students were bussed to Conway High School, also known as the Kennett High School. Apparently the Kennett family had offered to build the school and wanted their name attached to it. The town wanted it called Conway, but since the school was badly needed eventually agreed to the name Kennett.

The old Snowville School is now a private residence.

My father told me that when he was a boy the meadow across the road from the school extended about a mile to the Conway road and would be mowed by a team of six men with hand scythes. They would line up at one end, mow to the other and be rewarded with a drink of hard cider, then work back for a similar reward at the starting point. As a Bryant I've wondered if the land was former Bryant land acquired by the Snow family in the house trade years before.

One family whose children attended the Snowville School lived some distance away and they did not own a car. Their father brought them to school in a horse drawn buggy, and, in winter, in a sleigh. Their route home was in the same direction my brother and I traveled and we attempted once to stand on the rear runners and hold on to the back of the rear seat. This worked well as the horse labored up the hill, but as they sped up on the downhill side the older boy beat on our fingers forcing us to let go and tumble into the road. Returning home with torn clothes and bruises, and the threat of a switch to the rear end looming convinced us not to try again.

In winter, roads were plowed but with no particular urgency, and the surfaces would remain coated, slick and slippery so the few cars that moved about all had chains on their wheels to give them traction to move forward, and with a bit of praying, to stop.

The main roads through Eaton and Snowville were only paved in the town centers. To either side the roads were gravel and not very smooth - sometimes described as washboard roads. In early spring the backroads in northern New England become quite muddy. The region officially recognizes a fifth season called Mud Season when the rapidly melting snow cover turns any exposed earth to seemingly bottomless mud. My father always carried tools in the car to use in case he became stuck. These included an axe to quickly cut a small tree to lever a wheel out of the mud. My brother and I would throw rocks or anything solid that could be had under the wheel as he raised it. One of the reasons for his preference for the Model A Ford was its spoked wheels that made lifting easier with the lever inserted between the spokes.

When blueberries ripened my mother and father would find some time - usually on a Sunday - to pick berries on Foss Mountain near our old home. At times we could fill a washtub plus a couple of pails. My mother then had the job of cooking and canning the berries, and making pies. She made great pies with perfect crust, not an easy thing in a wood fired oven.

The third house we lived in - for only a short time - had a shallow, muddy pond on the land and my father made us a raft that we could use on it with the aid of a long pole. He had a favorite pond of his own well away from the road in the woods that was a great place to catch *horned pout* (a freshwater catfish). The best time to catch them was at night with a fire on the shore to attract them. We would often fill a couple of water pails, and if lucky add a couple of eels.

Eaton had a nice lake called Crystal Lake where we would sometimes go on a Saturday night for a swim and a bath. Soaping up in the lake was acceptable in the 1930's but certainly not today.

This last house was in Eaton about a mile from Eaton Center. However, we were then about three miles from the Snowville School so transportation was provided by a man who had a contract with the town using his own car. There were only 4 or 5 students, but he may have had other routes.

We moved to this house in either 1933 or 34 when I was 7 or 8 and Jack 8 or 9. We had no other kids to play with so were very close.

When we were not with our father or doing assigned work in the garden we could always find things to do. I remember constructing a mini-road at the edge of a field with a tunnel and a bridge built with scrap lumber. We made cars from blocks of wood using large buttons from our mother's sewing basket for wheels. My father would let us use most of his tools - all hand tools.

If my father needed material for a rabbit pen or other small structure he always seemed to know of a collapsed building where he could salvage lumber for the project. This would be hauled home on a trailer attached to his car where Jack and I would have the job of pulling the nails and stacking it. The used nails were not thrown away. We had a favorite rock in the yard we could lay the nails on and straighten them with a hammer. Our fingers and thumbs took a beating until we got good at it. Jack was always better at most of the chores. He was older and stronger than I, but I think he also paid more attention to what he was doing so could always do a better job. I think he also had more patience than I did.

In the fall some of the used boards would be staked about a foot away from the foundation of the house and the space filled with sawdust – available free from the local sawmill. This blocked cold air from blowing into the house making it much warmer through the winter. In the spring it would all be removed.

At about this time we got our first radio. It required two dry cell batteries and a 6 volt car battery to run. The car battery needed frequent charging which was not possible at home as we still had no electric service. Our father had recently been elected to the Board of Selectmen so had access to the town garage where the plowing tractor was kept – along with a battery charger. Use of the radio was restricted to the evenings when my father was home until later when we moved to a home with electricity.

We had an older half brother and sister from our father's previous marriage who were about a dozen years older than we were. After the divorce his son Merton lived in Amesbury with us but later went back to Snowville to live with his grandfather. His daughter Dorothy had remained with her mother. Both had married and had children, and visited frequently. Jack and I were always happy to see them when they visited since they always brought us each a bag of candy. We remained friends over the years.

Christmas was not a big day for us. Our parents could not afford turkey or roast beef. We would have something like a stuffed hen with cranberries and sweet potatoes, and a couple of our mother's pies. Presents would usually be winter clothes. One Christmas I got a jackknife, and another an orange. I don't think we felt neglected because all the families we knew were in the same boat.

On Saturday nights we would go to Conway for the few store-bought groceries we needed for the week, with a stop at the State Liquor store for my father's *beverages*. My brother and I were in the habit of asking for a nickel each to spend, but one Saturday when I was 8 or 9 I made the mistake of asking him while he was talking to a friend and was told to never do that again. I don't know that I ever asked for - or received - the nickel again.

During those years in Eaton my mother would occasionally go to Boston to visit her sisters. She was at times quite nervous and needed a week or so away to recover. During those stretches my father would hire a live-in woman to cook and care for Jack and me. It appears that a relationship developed between my father and one of them. Over the next few years following a verbal altercation with my mother - usually on a Saturday night and possibly timed - my father would dress and go out for the evening. I recall one incident that involved my mother chasing him with a kettle of boiling water from the stove. At that age I had no idea of her intentions or the reason behind it but later suspected an apparent attempt to decommission a critical part of his anatomy to curtail his tomcatting.

Moving from Amesbury to the woods of Snowville was very difficult for my mother. To move from a house with all the conveniences of the day to a subsistence life in the backwoods of northern New Hampshire would have required a considerable adjustment. In addition, she was a devout Catholic and there was no Catholic church in Snowville. The nearest was in Conway and impossible for her to attend until years later when my brother became old enough to drive her.

I do not wish to be overly harsh on my parents. They were each in their own right good people with many friends, but they were not compatible in marriage. As a Catholic, divorce for my mother was out of the question so she just carried on, with her escapes to Boston from time to time as a restorative. Someone may note the irregularity of her marrying my father who was a non-Catholic *and* seemingly a divorcee, but it was found that his first wife had never been baptized thus the marriage was considered invalid. I think the matter of attending church was a significant issue with my mother, and later with her mother when she lived with us, particularly in regards to Jack and me. Our upbringing was to have been in the Catholic Church, but our instruction was limited to what my mother provided and we had little direct church experience.

In 1936 we were still deep in the Depression. My father was working on a government *make work* program designed to combat the gypsy moths that had invaded the local forests. The larvae fed on the leaves and damaged the trees. The nests were quite visible and the workers cut them down with long poles with a cutter on the end. After accumulating a pile of nests they would be burned to kill the caterpillars inside.

The crew worked in several towns in the area and seemed to schedule their work to place them near a farmhouse at lunchtime. They hoped they might be invited in, especially in the colder weather.

One day in the town of Madison, three or four miles from Eaton, the crew was working near the home of George Kennett and invited in to eat their lunch and warm up. George was in his sixties and lived alone since he had no close relatives. He apparently was looking for a family that would move in and care for him in exchange for the lodging. More than one family had taken his offer but friction always developed and he would end up asking them to leave. My father arranged to bring our family to meet with him, and warned my brother and me to be on our best behavior. That was no particular problem as we were trained to keep our mouths closed when adults were talking. The meeting went well and it was decided that they would meet with a lawyer to write a contract that would prevent our being thrown out in the event of trouble.

1745   MADISON TOWN HALL, SILVER LAKE, N. H.

Madison

During the summer of 1936 we moved in. Although the house was not in perfect shape it certainly was a palace compared to where we had been living. The house had electricity, running water, and wood stoves in the kitchen and living room. There were five bedrooms on the second floor. The first floor had a kitchen, bathroom, and living room, and another bedroom. While we did have the bathroom, the septic system was not in good condition, so we generally used the outhouse located in the barn, much warmer than the outdoor version we had used in Eaton.

Things started well. Mr. Kennett was a huge man and loved to eat. My mother was a great cook and with the extra money provided by Mr. Kennett we all ate quite well. There were always desserts as he loved his sweets.

My brother and I were enrolled in the Madison Corner School. This was also a one-room school, with six grades taught by one teacher.

We faced a culture shock the reverse of what our mother had experienced in the move from Amesbury to Snowville. Madison was a more affluent town than Eaton. It did have some families that *lived on the other side of the tracks* as the saying went. Looking back, I guess we were one of them.

In Eaton it seemed everyone was poor, however my father served on the Board of Selectmen because of the family roots going back to the early 1800's, and we were a *prominent* family there.

When we arrived at school in knickers and home style haircuts, and with biscuit sandwiches rather than bread, we were made fun of. Being Catholic and Democrat when the only church was Baptist didn't help.

Author, Doug Bryant with year-older brother Jack and father, Almon, 1929 to 1939.

Coming from the fifth grade in Eaton, I don't think I was quite at the level of the fifth grade in Madison. I was not a particularly good student, and did not get good grades.

One difficulty developed when I was called on to read the bible passage that began each school day along with the Pledge of Allegiance. Being a Catholic my mother felt I should not read from a non-Catholic bible, but the teacher required it and was not a favorite of mine as a result.

In later years when I visited my parents when on leave from the Navy, I would often be in the company of former school-mates and her name would come up. I would always make sure to mention my dislike of her. She had her favorite students, and many thought very highly of her. Looking back, I put equal blame on my mother - they should have worked together. What was the big deal about reading from a Protestant Bible? But it was a different era.

After moving into Mr. Kennett's place, things went quite well. He was very pleased with the work done by my father. My brother and I were well behaved, but a lot of pressure was put on us to cater to Mr. Kennett. One of the things we did for him (since he was such a heavy man) was to put on his slippers every evening.

In addition to the large house, there was a barn, a carriage house, and a woodshed. Mr. Kennett also had a horse. With the horse, the field for the garden was plowed and planted. A mowing machine my father had owned before he went to Amesbury was brought over and used to cut hay for the animals. He also built an ice house to store ice for the summer.

With electricity at hand it would seem that we would have a refrigerator, but it would have taken several weeks of income to pay for one. Also, electricity was expensive compared to my father's cash income - and not all that reliable at times.

My father did manage to purchase a 100 acre tract of woodland and meadow at a tax sale for $15. This provided cord wood for cooking and heating the house, and a supply of meadow grass that was considered an important food source for cows.

Our family situation was considerably improved. My father and mother were getting along much better. Although she had a lot more work to do I think she felt she had more purpose in her life. And the amenities of the Kennett house were far more to her liking.

Work at the Wooden Heel factory in Conway had picked up and my father was working steady. Since Madison was a more affluent town they did not want the neighbors seeing the government food truck at our house as it was in Eaton.

Now that he was working regularly at the heel factory, Jack and I had more time for the fun things in life such as swimming, fishing, hunting, and ice skating. One might think we *had it made,* but not quite, especially during the summer. On most days we were assigned jobs in addition to our regular chores. During the growing season we had specific areas of the garden to be hoed or weeded each day. Although Jack was older, bigger, and stronger, so *capable* of doing better work, he didn't do well with jobs he didn't like - such as working in the garden - so my father leaned on him more than he did me.

Another assigned job was storing the winter's supply of firewood in the wood shed. This had to be stacked neatly to get the maximum amount in there.

We did not put sawdust around the foundation here as in Eaton, possibly because it simply wasn't needed for the better constructed house, but I think also, since we were on the main road through town, it was a matter of appearances - much as with the food truck.

Mr. Kennett had a large lawn that he was quite proud of. We were not allowed to play on the grass. Before we had moved in, Mr. Kennett had hired a boy named Earl to mow the lawn with a reel type mower. Supposedly, Earl mowed the lawn for two summers and was rewarded with a pair of used clamp-on ice skates. I believe Jack and I were paid 25 cents for each mowing, maybe inflation, possibly the Depression nearing its end. Earl and his family became close friends of mine.

One day Jack and I, and I think one other kid, were out in the field playing with a football. Somehow the ball wound up on Mr.

Kennett's lawn. He came out of the house with a knife, intending to get the ball and cut it. I did not realize at the time, but I believe he was showing signs of dementia – what was often called *hardening of the arteries* back then. He was not able to get the ball – probably prevented by his bulk – so went back into the house and came out with a gun - a .32 caliber revolver he kept in a desk drawer (and, yes, we knew about it). My mother had come out to see what was going on and he began waving the pistol in her face. She being a spunky person - and left handed - hit him on the nose with her left hand, hard enough that her wedding ring left a mark, then wrested the pistol away from him. He began crying and she consoled him, and took him into the house to bath his face. But my parents agreed it was the right time to contact the sheriff and he came and took possession of the gun.

First examination of the revolver suggested that it could not have been fired because of its corroded condition, but a test by the sheriff proved otherwise.

It was probably good that there was a contract covering our tenancy or we might have been thrown out of the house after that episode, but they made up and things returned to normal.

I did not know much about Mr. Kennett's background. He may have been related to the Kennetts from Conway; there were a lot of them in that area, but if so he was not from the rich side of the clan. I believe he ran a livery service at the Portsmouth Naval Shipyard at one time, carrying passengers, baggage, and freight back and forth from the Yard to the railway station with a horse and buggy. He received a pension, so evidently had been a Shipyard employee in some capacity.

1937 was a much better year than 1936. By that time I had made a lot of friends in the neighborhood. I have mentioned attending the Madison Corner School. There was a second school in the town, the Silver Lake School, also a single room school with six grades. We lived about midway between the two schools. Most of our friends attended Silver Lake, and for some reason we were assigned there in 1937. I never knew if it was merely to balance the number of students in each, or if it was somehow arranged by my not-so-favorite teacher, but it certainly was a favor for me!

Our teacher there, Mrs. Whiting, was a great teacher and a wonderful woman. She had two daughters in the class. I remember one day we were playing with a deck of cards in class, so she invited us to her house for a party where we could play cards with the girls. That was an event! A perfect example of *leadership*, a subject I will return to later in the book. During my later visits home I would always call on Mrs. Whiting.

By 1937 Jack had acquired a pair of skates, but I don't know where they came from. I still had none. My father had a few summer residents that he did work for - cutting lawns, painting, and such. There was one, a nice lady with a daughter - I don't remember where they came from - who gave my father a beautiful pair of women's figure skates. He thought they would be too big for me, so he gave them to my brother who wore them a couple of times, but he had his own so passed them on to me. Probably one of the nicest things I had ever received.

Jack also had come by a pair of skis, poles, and boots – used - and I don't know the source of those either. He was really interested in skiing. I eventually wound up with a pair of skis with no bindings (but no boots – needed for use with bindings) that attached to any boot or shoe I had with small straps. It was a workable arrangement and far more common, but I was never really much interested in skiing.

There was a nice ski tow in Madison. I think it was built by local people. It was not on a mountain but a pretty good sized hill. There was a gasoline engine at the bottom and a series of pulleys carrying the rope to the top. At one time there was a jump; I never used it, but Jack did.

In 1938, at age 12, I was back at Madison Corner in the one-room junior high, seventh and eighth grades, in a building next to the grammar school. I had a good teacher and met a lot of new friends.

Mr. Kennett had passed away in bed one night back in October of 1937 - I believe from a stroke. It is possible that my mother contributed to his passing. In the 18 months since we had moved in she continually provided him with all the sweets and rich foods that he enjoyed. The terms of the contract covering our living there conveyed the property to us, giving us a permanent home.

Turning the property over required "settling up" Mr. Kennett's final expenses which included five doctor's visits (house calls) in the month leading to his passing (at $5 each!) and funeral expenses of $215.00 including a headstone. The $5 paid to Ernie Ames for digging the grave (by hand) was over and above that but did include filling it in. And of course an inheritance tax was due to the state.

In the fall of 1938 my grandmother (on my mother's side) moved in with us. Her name was Margaret Alexander and she had been the mother of 13 children. She had spent some summers with us in Eaton, and would stay with one of the other daughters during the winter. With Mr. Kennett gone there was plenty of room. She was a very religious lady and spent much of her time in her room saying prayers – at least it was her activity whenever I was present, maybe to convey a message. She loved Jack and me and would watch over us if our parents were away shopping. Nothing we ever did on her watch ever got back to them! She also made a patchwork quilt - possibly at my mother's suggestion to give her something to do - that I have to this day on my bed. I think given the work involved a good deal of her time was also spent with a needle and thread in addition to praying. All of her work was done by hand. The years have taken their toll on it, and it has recently been restored although the material is now fragile and its use limited. She was certainly a great lady in our eyes.

The next year, eighth grade at Madison Corner, was an interesting year. A Mrs. Helen Parker bought the old Bryant homestead on Foss Mountain at *Pedlar's End*. Family lore says the location name came from the fact that the house was located at the end of a long road and when the traveling peddlers of the early days reached it, they could go no further. This does not fully explain the spelling issue, but the early settlers up there were better at speaking than spelling.

She planned to use it as a summer home. The roads were not plowed in winter so she would be unable to use it then, but it was a beautiful and very private location for a summer place.

But the house - a center chimney colonial now over a century old - was very rundown. Mrs. Parker inquired about someone who might be able to restore it and my father was recommended as a possibility as he had been born there and would know as much about it as anyone would.

The house had been built about 1819 and came into the possession of John Bryant in 1822 as a result of the land swap with the Snow family. He did not take up residence there until sometime after 1850. Prior to that, the Bryants had live in a house on Bush Road.

She contacted my father and he agreed to take on the job. She asked if he would need to hire any additional help and he answered to the effect that, "I have two boys as good as any man," and he would be happy to use them on the job. I don't know how much he was paid for the job - I expect something like $3 or $3.50 a day - but my brother and I were to get $1 a day for each day we worked.

When we first went up to see it, it was in very bad shape. The sills were completely rotted out - typical of those early houses that were always too close to the ground. The house had to be jacked up to replace the sills, and be made level. All the windows had to be replaced with new ones, and the roof re-shingled. It was quite an experience to watch the house being raised and the old sills removed – some as long as 16 feet and 12 by 12 inches thick. Stock that size had to be special ordered from the local sawmill and brought in by truck because of the size and weight. Each had to be notched along its length to receive the randomly spaced wall studs – all done by hand with a two-handed drill and chisels to clean out the corners.

The chimney was a monstrous affair with three fireplaces in it, one in the living room, one in the kitchen, and the third in what might have once been the master bedroom. We worked along with my father who was an excellent teacher and we learned a lot. That likely was his main reason for wanting us on the job although cheap labor probably figured in. We were approaching the time when decisions about our futures would need to be made and no one was thinking much about our involvement in the trouble that began in Europe later in the year much less the changes that would come from it. For all that anyone knew we would be making our way in the world in the same manner our father had.

Grandmother Margaret Alexander

When fall came Mrs. Parker asked if we could continue working through the winter. My father said, yes, he could do it, but he would have to charge based on leaving and returning home since it was so difficult to get there. I recall that he quickly acquired a small sheet iron stove - not the usual and heavier cast iron. This one he was able to carry on his back and my brother and I walked with him to Pedlar's End. We installed the stove in a second floor bedroom with a southern

exposure. Our first daily chore was to build a fire in that stove so we would have a warm place to eat lunch or get warmed up while working.

We never missed school to work up there, so our time was limited to weekends, but our father would continue during the week.

Re-shingling the roof was an interesting job. Mrs. Parker wanted the house restored to its original condition. The original roof had been done with cedar shingles, so the replacement was done with cedar shingles.

The entire job took for about two years as I recall. The only other help involved came from that of an old time stone mason who was hired to repair the fireplaces and chimney. That required the specialized skills of a mason, but we assisted by mixing and carrying mortar for him.

In 1940 I was a freshman at Madison High School where at the age of 14 I learned to smoke - if *learning* is the right word. The process as I recall was just a matter of doing it until I stopped coughing. At opportune times during the day - recesses and lunch (weather permitting) - we would jump the back fence for a smoke. If we were flush it was Lucky Strikes at 15 cents a pack; if *tight* it might be Sensations at 10 cents per, or sometimes King Size Wings, also 10 cents but being longer could be cut in half to get more cigarettes. (More *butts* also, so maybe not such a good deal after all.) We also had Bugler - roll your own - which was harder to figure as 10 cents bought a package of loose tobacco that made a lot of smokes. Bugler offered a neat little machine that would do the rolling for you, but it

Top: Pedlar's End, birthplace of my father and restored by him about 1938.

Bottom: the Kennett House where our family lived from 1936.

wasn't something we could carry with us so we learned to do it by hand. One member of our gang was from a poor family that was on Town Relief. They received a food order at the local food store that always included top-shelf cigarettes. Another friend would always be *bumming* cigarettes from him, and when asked about it would say, "Our fathers and mothers are paying for them."

I was able to enjoy the luxury of smoking because - despite our general condition of being poor - I actually had some income from the dollar a day our father was charging for our services at Pedlar's End. No, we didn't get the whole dollar. This was still a time when any earnings by a family member were family income and it all went into the pot, but our father was fair in handing some of it back to us for our own use. Smoke 'em if you got 'em. Not the smartest use of my money as I was fortunate enough to learn early on.

A smarter purchase was the used bicycle I bought after saving up five dollars. This had a large basket attached to the handle bars that allowed me to carry sweet corn to summer folk over on Silver Lake. Sometimes one of my customers would have a small job of painting or cleaning up their property. The corn money went to my father since he knew about it, but the odd job money I kept (because he didn't). I also had a favorite uncle in Canada who would occasionally send me a dollar when an American bill came into his hands.

But spending money for cigarettes says I didn't have my priorities in order, although it was the times. Everybody smoked.

I finally quit smoking when I was 29. That brings to mind a conversation I had with our diving medical officer years later in the Navy who told me, "The human brain does not fully develop until you reach the age of 27." I guess I was a couple of years behind in the development of mine.

The high school had one large room where the students had their desks, a smaller one for classes, and a laboratory. There was also a basement area used for special purposes. We ate lunch there, and the lunches were stored there on an overhead support beam until needed.

The teaching staff consisted of the principal and one teacher.

I could have been a better student if I had studied a little more and put more time into my homework. I did *get by* and I liked my teachers well enough, but I just wasn't cut out for *book learning*.

Sports didn't interest me much either. We didn't have enough students for a football team. We did manage to field a baseball team, but our equipment was lacking. There was no glove available for a left hander – like me. With budgets tight as they always are, I can understand it, but having to pull off my righty glove to throw the ball usually got a laugh - and didn't help my game. I did play a little basketball.

I think it was this year also - possibly the next - that a fellow in town named Robert Chick started a Boy Scout troop. He was older than any of us, and a very nice guy from a prominent local family. He had no family of his own and had graduated from either college or a technical school and worked in the family business. He did a lot for us, helping us study the Scout Manual and learn our knots and other things needed for advancement. With a few volunteers he took us mountain climbing and on local trips in the summer. Although most of us were about 14-15 he didn't seem to be troubled by our smoking.

Most of us could not afford a complete Boy Scout uniform. I believe I had only a cap and neckerchief. We had a tent and some other gear for camping that was probably surplus from WWI that was available to Boy Scout troops from the government.

One summer our troop attended a Jamboree at Hampton Beach. Bob took us down on a Sunday, helped us with our tent, and saw to it that we had food and supplies for a few days. He came back in the middle of the week to check on us. We had been on our own with no supervision and must have looked like a real ragamuffin group.

Some of the adults at the beach gave us a bad time about the smoking. Apparently we didn't project the proper image for the BSA. After the war Bob offered me a job in his business, but as will be seen, I stayed with the Navy.

When we lived in Snowville and Eaton we made maple syrup in my aunt's *sap house* (more often now *sugar shack*). In Madison we had only a few trees located across the road. Jack and I had the chore of collecting the sap each morning and evening of the run for my mother to boil down on the kitchen stove.

From time to time when on leave I would go up to Foss Mountain to check on the state of Peddler's End. It declined steadily over the years as I believe it passed through the hands of several owners. Recently however I was in the area and found that someone had made the investment to restore it once again.

Cars were always a significant part of my life. I was always very attentive when my father was driving or making repairs on our car. At about this time if the car was in the barn and my father not at home I would start the car and practice driving in the driveway. My mother never told my father. I believe she was looking forward to the day when I could drive her around.

1927 Ford Model T Coupe

A friend of my father had a 1927 Model T Ford Coupe with a damaged front tire. I guessed a new tire (if he could find one) would cost more than the car was worth. Jack and I bought it for $5.00 and drove it home on the flat tire. I can't recall who drove, likely my father as steering with a flat can be tricky. Eventually we found a wheel with a hard rubber tire that fit the car. This became a great toy and we drove it in the fields and woods whenever we could come up with the 19 cents for a gallon of gas.

At 15 I began to notice girls - and learned to dance. During the winter on most Saturday nights there was a dance at the Town Hall with a local band playing barn dance (old fashioned) music. The proper dress for boys was ski boots and ski pants - something my parents could not afford. A friend from a more affluent family had been given a new pair of boots the previous Christmas and offered me his old pair for $5.00 which solved that part of the problem, so I grabbed them. As for the pants, Mr. Kennett had a couple of old steamer trunks in the attic filled with old clothes. Searching through them, I found a pair of black *peg leg* pants, in style in the early 1920s, and with my mother's help converted them to what passed for ski pants. I thought I was pretty sharp!

One thing that stands out about the dances was the occasional appearance of a sailor named Smith in his uniform - including his blue flat hat bearing his ship's name, USS Arizona. To his good fortune he was making a transition to the Submarine Service and had left the Arizona before it was sunk at Pearl Harbor on December 7th. I later became friendly with him and he was the inspiration for my joining the Navy and volunteering for submarine duty myself.

I have commented on the good and not-so-good things about my father, but I remain grateful for all that he taught me, perhaps foremost his willingness to work. Seemingly he was harder on my brother than on me. I guess that's common with the eldest - the one parents learn on. One day while we were working in the field - and I can still recall the exact spot after all these years - he was giving Jack a bad time about something, and Jack, 15 or 16 at the time and now bigger than he was, grabbed him by the shirtfront and pulled him face to face. "Bud and I are all through taking your shit," he yelled at him. From that time on my father started treating us like men, only right since we were doing the work of men by then. If they had come to blows, I like to think I would have stepped in on Jack's side. Fortunately it did not and I was never forced to make a choice like that. I think that's when *whuppings* came to an end. They were infrequent but painfully effective. Our mother favored a *switch* while our father grabbed anything at hand. That made him arguably more dangerous, but Mother was more effective.

In late spring or early summer the main road through the center of town was sprayed with hot tar and sanded. There were never enough men to handle the job, so the town would take on retired men who were still able and high school students for the job. The pay was about $3.00 a day - big money for us students, but it was hard work. Piles of sand were dumped from a truck at intervals along the road and as the tar truck moved along we would shovel the sand into it. The old timers knew how to pace themselves. The job of loading the truck reminded me of batting in baseball where you might bat left or right, and sometimes either. Usually a new hire could only throw the sand one way, and if an old timer spotted it he would place him on the opposite side to force him to learn to throw in the other direction.

One day I was working a different detail with an older man named Ward, smoothing an embankment at the side of the road, and I had a sudden need to answer a call of nature. I quickly found a suitable spot behind a nearby tree and with equal speed transacted my business and got back to my job. Mr. Ward liked me well enough but seemed to enjoy embarrassing me at any opportunity. On my return he said to me, "Hey kid, do you know what you just did?" Being embarrassed by his drawing attention to me, I did not answer immediately, and he continued saying, "Well, you just did a rabbit shit. You know what that is, don'cha?" I was forced to reply, "No," as I had no idea. "Well," he said, "Ef you seen a rabbit hoppin' along in the woods n' he stops to unload, he drops some n'en he hops a short piece and does it ag'in. You wan't there long enough - be goin' ag'in shawtly." He was right, and it turned out I had to, but I couldn't see his call for making anything of it except hayseed humor designed to cause me some embarrassment.

In the towns where we lived most of the household water came from hand-dug wells, some as much as twenty feet deep. Most people would use a *dowser* (someone with the ability to find water) to fix the location of their well. My father had that ability, and I remember watching him walking properties with his forked-stick, sometimes with quite an audience. There would always be some disbelievers snickering in the crowd. That was embarrassing to me, but after helping him dig some successful wells over a few years' time I became a believer in the *divining rod*.

In one instance a pair of elderly ladies with a summer residence on Foss Mountain approached my father about locating a vein of water with enough water to supply a well. He asked where they might want it, and they said as close as possible to the house. The house was situated on the side of a hill, so he said the best location would likely be at the top of the hill, but they were reluctant to have it so far from the house. He explained that since they did not have electricity to run a pump, having the well at the top of the hill would allow the water to flow through a pipe by gravity right to the house, and they thought that a wonderful possibility.

The stick - in the hands of a gifted dowser - seemed not only able to locate the water but determine the strength of the flow and its depth. In this case I recall he estimated about 14 feet.

To safely dig to this depth without a cave-in our hole was begun with a 14 foot diameter opening and tapered to about 5 feet at the bottom. The digging went easily to a depth of about 8 feet. From that point we could no longer shovel the dirt directly out and had to build a small staging platform and transfer it to the surface. The digging became more difficult when we struck hard pan.

One morning we arrived on the job and discovered a couple of small holes at the level we had reached. We suspected a small animal had done it, but a while later the ladies came up to the site and told us they thought we were not making much progress so went down and tried digging themselves. They now understood why things had slowed down.

When we reached the predicted depth, the water rushed in. The next job was to collect stones from around the farm to stone up the well. This was heavy work, but this was New Hampshire, so not difficult to find plenty of stones.

We used a horse and dump wagon for this part of the job. Since we lived about six miles away, my father built a small shelter for the horse to stay at night until we finished.

My father loved doing well work and was always elated when he hit water. I was on Foss Mountain some 70 years later and went by that particular well and found it still in good shape and being regularly used.

We needed a vehicle of some sort to haul the cord wood home from our wood lot. Seemingly a truck would be the logical choice but an old car could be bought for under $25 and a truck would have been twice as much. The answer proved to be a 1928 Buick at a cost of $5.00 that had been converted to a small truck. By then I had often driven my father's 1929 Model A Ford, and of course our own 1927 T, better than my father - *maybe* - and I really enjoyed hauling our wood home in the Buick.

In June Jack turned 16 and got his driver's license which made my mother very happy as she now could be driven to church in Conway on Sunday.

Jack set an example for me that year - good or bad as you see it - by quitting high school. That was more common than not in those days when only a small percentage finished high school and only a very few went on to college. A job and cash money was far more important. He got a job cutting timber at a sawmill owned by a friend's stepfather and also received room and board at his friend's mother's house. In the evening before bedtime the family would gather for a snack, but Jack was never invited to join in. I don't recall all the jobs he had. He drove a bus for a short time, and in the fall of 1941 went off to a NYA (National Youth Association) trade school in Berlin, NH, to train as a machinist. This was a government run program much like the CCC (Civilian Conservation Corps) of that time.

Of course, in December we were attacked by Japan and things began to change rapidly. Day to day life went on during the war years much as it had because of the restrictions on goods. But the end of the war was going to bring changes we couldn't have imagined, and our old way of life would soon disappear.

1942 saw the country mobilizing for a total war unlike anything ever seen before. The Depression had been slowly disappearing and suddenly was over, and there were plenty of jobs at good wages and lots of overtime becoming available. Relocating was frequently necessary and conditions at the new locations not always the best - at first - but people who had weathered the privations of the Depression for a decade managed it.

Members of a Madison family that had been involved in aviation in the early 1930s were executives at Pratt and Whitney United Aircraft in East Hartford, Connecticut. Through this connection three of my friends had been hired there. The one closest to me told me he was making over $100 a week with the overtime, and bought a 1940 Buick Super Convertible for $1,000. That was a lot of money for that time! A weekly wage of $25 (five days and a half day on Saturday) was typical for the time (although not in places like Madison, NH). At $40 a week a worker was doing really well and $50 was still something to dream about. $100 a week was like striking it rich in a gold rush!

With my fascination with money and cars (something you do when you don't have either), I realized I too would have to leave Madison to make that kind of money. The best I could expect to earn in the area was 37 ½ cents an hour, close to the minimum wage at that time.

Even though I wanted to get out of Madison and start making some real money, I had set my sights on the Navy because of Smith.

At the age of 15 when Pearl Harbor was attacked I don't think I had a full understanding of the war. But with the draft in place since 1940 and several local men already in the service, everyone was very patriotic and I could hardly wait until I was 17 to sign up.

In April I found out from a friend that the Motor Vehicle Department didn't ask for a birth certificate. I thought I'd try lying about my age. It worked and I got my driver's license a few months early.

I turned 16 in August and started the school year as a junior at Madison High School in September. I wanted to quit and go to work at Pratt and Whitney but found out they wouldn't hire me at that age. I did learn that I could get hired at the Boston Naval Shipyard, so quit school that fall, packed my clothes, and took the train from Silver Lake to Boston. My aunt Eva was my mother's sister, the one she would periodically visit when she felt the need to get away from life in Snowville. She and my uncle Bill lived in Dorchester. They never had children of their own and at one point when things were looking pretty bleak in our family they had proposed adopting me. I did spend time with them occasionally in the summers when I was younger. I knew the subway route to their house on Tolman Street, and that I would be welcome there – for a short time at least - until I could find a place of my own.

I had no difficulty getting hired at the Navy Yard, and was put on as a Mechanic Learner. Within a few days they found me a room on West Newton Street in Boston proper where a woman my uncle knew had a room available for $2.75 a week.

My job was to tighten the hull bolts on one of the destroyers being built there. My boss would tell me which seam of bolts to tighten, and if I finished too soon would tell me to loosen them and do them again. I guess I was too dedicated to the war effort; maybe it was the work discipline that my father had instilled in me to do a job well and quickly, but I was uncomfortable with that kind of attitude, particularly from a boss.

The restroom building was set up with two rows of toilets along each side with a door at each end. When a door was opened cold air would blow down the length of the room so the practice was to keep the door on one side locked and use the toilets on the opposite side to avoid the cold. This meant that men would stand around waiting for an open toilet on the now-limited warm side, which to me was a complete waste of valuable time. ("Don't you know there's a war on?") When I found it necessary to use the facilities I would immediately go to the open "cold" side but nearly always someone would make a crack like, "They'uh used to a cold seat up in Cow-Hampshuh." Well, I was, but still …

I guess all the *meatheads* weren't up country.

I had taken the job at the low rate of 37 ½ cents an hour unaware that overtime was not available in that position. After paying my room rent, eating meals in a cafeteria, and doing my laundry I was lucky to have enough left for a couple of shows. After about two months I realized I wasn't learning anything and was certainly not getting ahead financially, so I went back to Madison. My father got me into the Wood Heel factory where he was working. I worked in the shipping department as a packer with an increase from my shipyard pay of $15 to $21 a week. I could now save a little and my parents were happy to have me at home to help out with chores.

During my time at the wood heel factory I became friendly with Dave Phinney who was older than I was - but not yet 21. Dave decided I needed a few days of vacation so called a girlfriend in Hartford to see if she could fix me up with a date. In a nice way he told me I would need to update my wardrobe for the trip. I guess he knew about my second hand ski boots. So I bought a new outfit: top coat, shirts, pants and shoes.

I don't remember much about my date. It couldn't have been all that great as I don't remember her giving me her address.

We stayed at the Bond Hotel in downtown Hartford, had some good food and saw a couple of movies. Dave appeared older than his age and had no trouble buying a bottle. This was not my first experience drinking; over the years my father had allowed me a taste, and I would drink beer with my friends. But this was the first time I really drank whiskey and of course became quite sick. I was glad when we checked out the next morning and put it behind me.

Dave really wanted to join the service but for some reason could not pass the physical. One day while discussing our futures we decided we would quit our jobs and join the NYA as my brother had in 1941. What was offered to us was the Quoddy Reservation at Eastport, Maine. We lived in apartments that had been built for the workers and their families who were to work on the proposed Quoddy Dam to harness the tides to generate electric power. It was one of President Roosevelt's projects from the early 1930s that never got started.

We left in the late fall, rode a bus to Portland and a train to Eastport. Our room and meals were provided and we were paid $10 a month for spending money. I enrolled in the aviation engine class and Dave the machinist class. After a couple of weeks, because of my lack of math, I transferred to the machine shop. I did much better there; the machine shop was coed - maybe that's why (although it seems it should have been the other way).

A girl in the shop - a couple of years older - took a liking to me. We spent some time together and on one dark night she put a kiss on me. Although I had kissed a girl before I never had a kiss like she put on me!

43

I believe this was my first real introduction to the ladies. She came from Hartford and I thought it was a shame I didn't know her on my trip there with Dave. Might have saved me a terrible hangover.

The food at Quoddy was awful! We ate a lot of potato soup. They didn't bother to cut the black spots out of the potatoes. Out of our $10 pay we would try to buy something better to eat - for the least amount of money. That turned out to be a loaf of bread and a jar of peanut butter.

We usually saved a couple of dollars for our visits to Eastport. Dave would buy a couple of quarts of Canadian Ace Ale and we would drink them under one of the waterfront piers.

Within a few months the NYA program was shut down due to a lack of funding from the government. Looking back, I learned the basics of being a machinist from a good instructor that helped me later during my Navy career. As for the food experience, I don't think I ever complained about Navy chow.

My first love never gave me her address. A shame with all the time I spent at the submarine base at New London. After I had matured some we might really have gotten serious.

When Quoddy closed Dave and I were given train and bus tickets for our trip home. We also received a few dollars owed to us from back pay. We must have had a discussion about what to do with our windfall bucks. We didn't need bread and peanut butter since we would be at home in the evening. So it was Canadian Ace for the train to Portland. Arriving in Portland on a particularly cold night we were told that the next bus to Conway - where Dave lived - was at 10:00 AM the next day. I suggested that we go to the police station for a night's lodging. Dave was the leader and not in favor of the idea but because he couldn't come up with a better suggestion, he agreed. At the station the jailor was not very sympathetic to our request for food and lodging. He finally told us that food was not available but that we could spend the night in a cell. However he was required to lock the cell door. This was better than a night outside, so we were each issued a blanket and locked in.

Our bus ride the next day delivered us to Dave's house at about noon. After 40 hours without food the homemade beans in the refrigerator were about the best beans I'd ever eaten.

This turned out to be the best lesson I could have had on handling money before joining the Navy. We both returned to the Wood Heel factory doing our previous jobs.

Jack joined the Navy at about this time, but after a few weeks was discharged for medical reasons. They said he would not be able to perform in combat. A year later he was drafted into the Army and eventually served in the 5th Division in Patton's Third Army in Europe. He received a Purple Heart and was awarded the Combat Infantryman's Badge and later a Bronze Star because of the CIB. He served in Korea also, was a Prisoner of War for a short time, and was awarded a second Purple Heart there. Army and Navy physical standards both were very high at first but were loosened considerably as the war went on and more and more men were needed as casualties grew.

Now that I had a driver's license - and an income - I was enjoying life much more. My father would let me use his car occasionally, and I had a few friends with cars. We were able to attend the local dances, go bowling, and see a few movies.

One morning in February 1943 before my father and I left for work, he checked the temperature on our outside thermometer. The lowest reading printed was 40 degrees below, and our reading was below that mark. Workers at the factory said it had been 55 below in Conway that morning.

One of the workers, we thought because of all the extra clothing he had worn, had his arm pulled into the cutters of his machine when he started it. When I saw him he was standing up, but with the lower half of his arm missing. He was surrounded by workers who had no idea of what to do, and it was my father who stepped in, got him to the floor, and administered first aid. He always seemed to know what to do in a crisis.

Across the street from the factory there was a large thermometer on the building that housed *Ed's Lunch*. At 10:00 AM, and with the sun on it, it read 40 below.

I have related this many times over the years to general disbelief. But I still have in my possession a clipping from the Boston Globe giving the five coldest days on record. February 9, 1943 - the day of the accident - was noted as 18 below *in Boston,* the coldest day since records were kept starting in 1872. And Madison, in the White Mountains of New Hampshire, is a few latitudes closer to the North Pole than Boston!

Boston's five coldest recorded days

The National Weather Service records dating back to 1872 lists the following five coldest days in Boston's weather history:

18 below — Feb. 9, 1943
17 below — Dec. 29, 1933
15 below — Dec. 30, 1933
14 below — Feb. 15, 1943
13 below — Jan 24, 1882

The last day it was below zero in Boston prior to being 3 below this morning was on Jan. 16, 1994, when it was 1 below.

One fall day a friend and I went out bird hunting. We each had single barrel shotguns loaded with birdshot rounds, but my friend had pocketed a few buckshot rounds, "In case we see a deer."

A little later we did see one and quickly exchanged the birdshot loads for the buckshot loads in our guns. He fired first and I immediately after, and we both hit the deer. We then had a small, dead deer on our hands, but there was a complication. It wasn't deer season.

Now, a lot of up-country folks have no problem with that - as long as they don't get caught. They'll take a deer anytime they can, up to and including with a jack-light. But my friend came from a broken home and lived with his grandparents, and he was certain that his grandfather would *kill* him for taking a deer out of season. And I well knew my father felt the same way, but since the deer was dead he would take the meat before wasting it.

We went to my house and my father returned with us to the woods, loaded the animal into the car, and returned home to our cellar for the butchering. My father gave my friend a few dollars as his share and everyone was satisfied although my father something less than happy about the incident.

Years later my friend told his grandfather the story, and he replied that he too would have accepted the meat since the deer was already dead, and that his family had been more in need of it than the Bryants.

I've never been much for hunting since then, but then I've generally had a commissary or a supermarket to fill my food list.

I should mention that I have used very few names in my account. I was concerned that I might omit someone important or possibly attach the wrong person to an event. So I will collectively mention the names of friends and families I was particularly close to in my early years: Frost, Gagnon, Hurd, Jones, Meader, Nickerson, and Ward, and hope I haven't overlooked anyone. I remained in touch with many of these folks over the years - and they have become long years.

After his release from the Navy my brother Jack worked in a machine shop in Union. I visited him a couple of times on weekends and we would go into the *big city* of Rochester for entertainment.

In the spring of 1943 while on a noon lunch break one of my fellow workers told me that a Navy recruiter had parked a short distance from us on Main Street. I immediately *beat feet* to his truck. I told him I wanted to join up, but that I was still only 16. He asked when I would turn 17 and I told him, August. He said he could do all the paperwork and, provided my parents would sign for me, I could enlist on my 17th birthday. They were both willing to sign thinking the Navy would be better for me than remaining in Madison.

With my brother no longer at home and me leaving in just a couple of months, my father made plans to reduce the size of the farm and the number of animals since it would only be necessary to support two people.

Thinking back on it I'm fairly sure that if I had lied about my age - as I had for the driver's license - I would not have had to wait out the three months.

While he was in town I saw the recruiter on the sidewalk. He seemed to have an odd way of walking with a rolling motion to his body. Someone I mentioned it to at the factory said it was probably the result of a lot of time at sea. But after spending time at sea myself - and acquiring my own *sea legs* - I realized that it was really just the result of his round shape.

Shortly before August 23, 1943, I received my orders and a bus ticket with instructions to report to the Navy Recruiting Station in Manchester on Monday, August 25th. I had hoped to mark the event by joining on my birthday, but the Navy was closed on Saturday; I would have to wait until Monday to get my shoes!

Stand by to dive! Men on submarine duty see plenty of exciting action. And they get extra pay.

The extra pay part got my attention!

REQUIREMENTS FOR ENLISTMENT IN THE NAVY AND NAVAL RESERVE

There are two branches of the Navy — the Regular Navy and the Naval Reserve.

Enlistment in the Regular Navy is for six years. Enlistment in the Naval Reserve is for two, three or four years. And, in addition, Naval Reservists will be released to get back to their jobs as soon as possible after the national emergency is over.

In the Reserve, your pay, your training, your chances for promotion are the same as in the Regular Navy. And you get this extra advantage — if qualified, you can choose the type of work you want to do before you enlist.

Here are requirements for both branches of service:

1. Age — In the Regular Navy, 17 to 31. In the Naval Reserve, 17 to 50. If under 21, you must have the written consent of parents or guardian.

2. Citizenship—Native-born American. If not native-born, you or your parents must have naturalization papers. You must show written proof of citizenship.

3. Height — At least 5 ft. 2 in. Weight, in proportion.

4. Eyes—Requirements now modified. You can qualify with combined vision (both eyes) of 15/20, not less than 6/20 in worst eye.

5. Physical — You must pass a physical examination to show you are in sound health. In the Reserve, requirements are less strict than in the Regular Navy.

6. Education — There are no specific educational requirements. You will take a simple intelligence test to show your ability to read, write and think clearly.

7. Character — The Navy wants men of good character. When you enlist, you will be asked to furnish two references.

8. Marriage—In the Regular Navy only unmarried men with no dependents are accepted. In the Naval Reserve married men may enlist. They must be able to support their dependents.

IMPORTANT NOTICE TO MEN WHO EXPECT TO ENTER MILITARY SERVICE

Even though you have received your orders to report for induction under Selective Service, you may still volunteer for the Navy right up to the moment of your induction. After that you can no longer choose your service. Remember, if you want to get in the Navy, you've got to volunteer before you are inducted. Don't wait till it's too late.

Requirements of 1942

The Chain of Command

Admiral - Leaps over tall buildings with a single bound. Is more powerful than a locomotive. Is faster than a speeding bullet. Walks on water. Gives policy guidance to God.

Captain - Leaps short buildings with a single bound. Is more powerful than a small engine. Is just as fast as a speeding bullet. Walks on water if the sea is calm. Talks with GOD.

Commander - Leaps short buildings with a running start. Is almost as powerful as a small engine. Is slower than a speeding bullet. Walks on water in indoor swimming pools. Talks with GOD if special form is provided.

Lieutenant commander - Barely clears little huts. Lose tug of war with small engine . Can fire a speeding bullet. Swims well. Is occasionally addressed by GOD.

Lieutenant - Crashes into buildings trying to leap over them. Is run over by small engines. Can sometimes handle a gun without inflicting self injury. Dog paddles. Talks to animals.

Lieutenant Junior Grade - Cannot recognize buildings. Recognizes small engines two or three times. Is not issued ammunition. Can stay afloat if instructed in Mae West. Talks to walls.

Ensign - Falls over doorstep when trying to enter a building. Says"Look at the Choo-choo" when locomotive passes by. Not allowed elastic for his slingshot. Plays in puddles. Mumbles to himself.

Chief Petty Officer - Lifts tall buildings and walks under them. Kicks Locomotives off tracks. Catches Bullets in teeth and eats them. Freezes water with a single glance. He is GOD.

The Navy

I have included the foregoing (Command Structure) for a couple of reasons, firstly to continue my story with something light - not always the case from here on - and I'm told a good thing for a "speaker" to open with. It does in its way say a lot about the pecking order in the Navy (and the Army has its version as well) but mainly it points out that skippers are not in the habit of sharing their innermost thoughts with white-hats. I am telling my story as much as possible as I saw it, but the fact is that much of it requires information that submarine crew members, ordinary seamen in any assignment for that matter, would not have had at the time.

Our training was to do our assigned job – with speed and accuracy, and without question. We understood our positions as part of a team - part of a machine - in which any error or failure to perform as directed could have serious and possibly fatal consequences to all hands. Our duties were carried out in isolated sections of the boat, mainly by routine, but when necessary in response to commands from the bridge, and we would be otherwise unaware - as a rule - of things going on elsewhere.

That said, the command structure on a submarine is described as *broad,* with a small number of chiefs and a large number of Indians - perhaps not the best analogy due to the use of the term *chiefs* (a good many Chiefs in the Navy) but makes the point. Most skippers will keep their crews informed about as much as possible in the interests of good morale - far more important on a submarine than elsewhere. But mission orders will usually be known only by those with the *need to know*, and of course in periods of action there is no time for news bulletins.

So I have relied on sources compiled later to fill in "the rest of the story" where it was necessary for a reader to understand certain events.

For those unfamiliar, the prevalent use of the term, *boat* may seem strange. Traditionally in the Navy a boat is a vessel carried on a larger vessel. Historically that was the case with *submersibles*. They were basically weapons designed to deliver a destructive device to the underside of enemy ships, and were in fact carried on board larger seagoing vessels. As they developed as tools of war, submarines were designed that were independently seaworthy - although at first (and during WWII) they continued to require the services of *tenders* for support; maintenance, fuel, and supplies.

As the boats became more independent from surface vessels, so did the submarine service, and in order to mark the distinction the term *boat* was retained while for all purposes today a submarine is a *ship*.

One other point to keep in mind that goes to life on board a WWII era sub is that of its being a delivery system for, generally, torpedoes. Submarines were designed with *that* as a priority - provision for crewmembers was secondary (or more so). Accommodations for the crew were worked into existing spaces that resulted in some strange sleeping arrangements, particularly for those at the bottom of the totem pole forced to share bunks with 3000 pound torpedoes.

Bunkmates

Basic Training

On Monday August 25, 1943 I reported to the Navy Recruiting Station in Manchester as ordered. After a physical we were sworn into the United States Navy, some of us into the regular Navy for a set period of time and others into the Naval Reserve for the duration of the War plus 6 months. Since both the Naval Reserve and the regular Navy would be doing the same jobs, I chose the Naval Reserve. My thinking was that if the war ended in less time than the enlistment period I would be free to go my own way earlier. As things turned out, it would not have mattered.

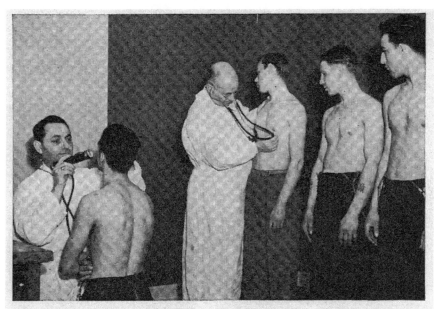

Any man in normal health should be able to pass his Navy physical exam with flying colors.

In the afternoon we were taken by bus to the Fargo Building in Boston MA. The Fargo Building was the receiving station for the 1st Naval District. We were given our evening meal and a bunk to sleep in for the night. After breakfast the next day we were bussed again to the Naval Training Station at Newport R.I. (boot camp) for eight weeks of basic training. Our company was #190 and had about seventy men. About 3/4ths of us were under twenty years of age; the rest around 40. They probably had been on deferment and finally the draft for military service caught up with them.

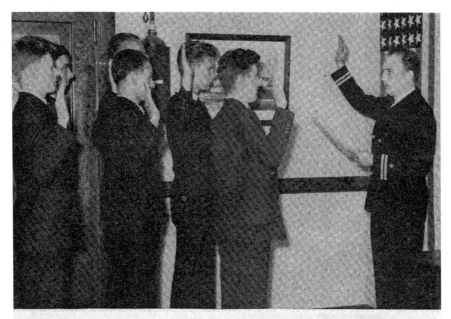

It's a proud moment when you raise your hand and swear to serve your country in the Navy.

Something I was not previously aware of then was that the Submarine Service was far more selective than I had realized. Less than 10% of those who applied - and that turned out to be about 22,000 out of 250,000 during the war - were accepted, and of those, 25-30% never made it through training. The fact that the submarine service experienced the highest rate of loss in the Navy would not be made known until the war ended and the numbers made public. Submarines constituted about 2% of the Navy in WWII – and sent about 30% of the Japanese Navy to the bottom, including 8 aircraft carriers. But 52 boats would be lost - and 3506 men.

Many applicants were experienced rated sailors, and many either had college time or were graduates. Our mental and physical abilities were continually tested, but success in the end depended a lot on the psychological factors that would get a man through some very difficult situations.

The Navy at that time had seven enlisted grades: Apprentice Seaman, (referred to as *lower than whale shit which is found on the bottom of the ocean*); Seaman 2nd Class; Seaman First Class; Petty Officer 3rd Class; Petty Officer 2nd Class, Petty Officer First Class; and Chief Petty Officer.

At the beginning of the war the pay rate for an Apprentice Seaman was $21 a month, but by the time I joined it had been increased to $50. In addition to that, as a member of the Submarine Service there was an extra 50% of the current pay rate added, and another 20% for sea duty. I didn't fully understand what I was getting into, but I knew I was going to be well paid for it.

I don't remember how many companies were in training at the same time, probably eight with the Senior Company graduating each week. As the incoming junior company, I remember the taunts we received ("You'll be sorry!") from those ahead of us.

Our company commander's name was Koson. He was a 2nd Class Boatswain Mate, and with a couple more promotions would be a Chief Petty Officer. The company was split into two platoons. Kosan picked two platoon leaders who would be in charge at times when he was not with us. Naturally he picked from the older recruits for this job.

We were issued all of our clothes (and shoes!) plus a hammock, mattress and a sea bag. Two stencils were issued to each recruit; one with the last name punched out and the other the initials punched out. These were used to mark all our articles of clothing, hammock, mattress and the sea bag. The large stencil was used to mark anything that would remain in a specific location. Small items such as the handkerchief and *skivvies* (mainly things that would require laundering) were stenciled in a designated place with initials added. White paint was used on blue backgrounds and black paint was used on white backgrounds.

We were shown how to make up our hammock and mattress, roll all of our clothing and tie the various articles with *clothes stops* - foot long pieces of light rope. By doing this all the clothing would fit in the sea bag. After this was done the rolled hammock and mattress could be formed into a horseshoe shape to encase the sea bag. These two items could then be lashed together. The purpose of all of this was that on being transferred to another ship or station all of the gear was in one package and could be hoisted to the shoulder and carried. If reporting aboard a ship that did not have a bunk or locker available, the hammock could be used as a bunk and a sailor could live out of his sea bag as he learned to do in boot camp. At seventeen and weighing one hundred and thirty three pounds, this was quite a lift for me.

Also, we were issued the Blue Jackets' Manual of the United States Navy (Tenth Edition), printed in 1940. This was our bible; it consisted of 784 pages and 59 Chapters covering (but not limited to) subjects such as:

The Navy as a Career, Clothing, General Information such as Cleanliness, Medical Service, Gambling, Profanity, Moral Turpitude, Rules and Regulations, Discipline and Good Behavior, Marching, Boats under Oars, Knots and Splices, the Compass, Signaling, How to Swim, What the Navy Offers, Service Schools, Academy and Promotions, Reporting for Duty Aboard Ship, Pay and Accounts, Navy Customs, Saluting Officers, Ships of the Navy, Personal Hygiene and First Aid, Painting, and Marlinespike Seamanship.

And we were expected – over time – to learn it all!

We were also to learn a lot about what it takes to be a "Leader of Men."

Our Company Commander, Koson, was well respected. When we compared him to other commanders we felt we had the best. He was not easy in training, but we felt he was fair. One day at morning inspection, one of our recruits had a dirty undershirt on. Koson grabbed the front of his undershirt with such force that I thought it was coming off without going over his head. I am sure this undershirt could not have been used again. In a short time, he was gone. The rumor that went around our company was that a wet spot and stains were found on his mattress cover. Self- gratification? He probably received an undesirable discharge from the Navy. One might wonder if that had been his plan all along.

Before joining the Navy I heard stories about how terrible the Navy dentists were and how bad the food was. To take care of the dentist fear I used some of my hard earned savings to have my teeth fixed by a civilian dentist in Conway. This turned out to be a mistake. The Navy dentists found a lot more work to be done - and redone - in my mouth, including some of the fillings I had paid my own money for. One could also wonder if maybe I was being used as a training aide for the young dentists coming into the Navy. Whatever the answer, I still have good teeth and I thank the Navy for that. The food, compared to what we were fed at the National Youth Association, was quite good.

Every Saturday morning all companies had inspection and marched in review at the parade grounds. If a company did not do well, it could expect a visit from the Company Commander at about 3:00 AM with orders to lay out sea bags for inspection. Luckily, our CO, Koson, had trained us well and we always looked sharp on the parade grounds.

After 5 or 6 weeks in boot camp we were rewarded with a few hours liberty in Newport. Following inspection on Saturday morning, with our hair cut to the scalp and only one thin stripe on the cuffs of our uniforms we went into town - where everyone knew we were boots. The Shore Patrol would take great pleasure in picking one of us up and hauling him back to the station and the brig for any infractions - real or perceived. Most of us were too young to drink; about the only thing we could do was have a meal and go to the movies.

BEFORE   AFTER

Author, Fireman 1/c Motor Machinist Mate School, 1943 Richmond, VA

Sea Dog, 1944, Portsmouth, NH

The Boot on guard duty (note the leggings) and the boot home on leave with proud mother looking on.

As we progressed through our eight weeks of boot camp, we were given aptitude tests to see what schools we might qualify for. Since my father had taught me a lot about automobile engines, along with what I learned in Machine Shop Training at the N.Y.A., I think I did quite well in mechanical aptitude. Before we graduated a selection process took place by our Company Commander and our two Platoon Leaders to decide who would be picked to fill billets required by the Navy. About half of our company would go to ships in the fleet as deck hands. But I was going to Motor Machinist Mate School (Diesel Engines). Prior to World War II Machinist Mates performed the maintenance and repair of diesel engines as well as their other duties involving high pressure boilers, refrigeration, air conditioning and many other systems. Now that we were building ships to make landings on foreign beaches and the landing craft were powered by diesel engines, the Navy created a new rate for specialization in diesel engines called Motor Machinist Mate, abbreviated MOMM. Later, about 1948, someone in the Department of the Navy must have realized that the word *motor* usually referred to electric motors, not diesel engines, and Motor Machinist Mate was changed to Engineman.

I got along very well with my platoon leader; he was a father image to me and I have always been thankful to him for his part in recommending me for that school.

About the middle of October 1943, we graduated from boot camp with a big ceremony at the Parade Grounds. We were all advanced in rate to Seaman Second Class. We were still as *low as whale shit* but we were *starting to float toward the surface*. My pay as a Seaman Apprentice was $50.00 per month, but as a Seaman Second Class it went to about $60. With clothes, room, and board I was doing better than living in Madison.

We had about ten days leave (vacation) after graduation. One of the older recruits had a car and gave me a ride from Newport to Boston with plans to pick me up at the White Tower Hamburg Place for a return ride to Newport. Another nice guy.

Returning to Madison via the Boston and Maine Railroad, I was met by my mother and father. I was quite proud of my uniform - as was my mother. I visited my high school to see one of my favorite teachers. I also visited the other well-liked teacher that I mentioned earlier, but not the not-so-favorite teacher. I also visited my Aunt Jessie and all of my friends. When my leave was up I was happy to get back on the train to Boston. Although it was nice to see my parents, friends, and my brother Jack, I was anxious to learn about diesel engines.

My mother had a very sharp eye. I could put a lot of things over on my father, but not my mother. She could spot and pull a four leaf clover from a bunch of clover while I could look all day and not find one. When I came home at the end of the war, I picked up my Blue Jackets Manual and as I thumbed through it, I came upon a four leaf clover that my mother had apparently inserted sometime after my first submarine sailing. Before leaving, I had left all my extra things at home. I still have the book, and the clover is still there where its green coloring has left an imprint on the page. I am quite sure my mother believed it would bring me home safely.

And it did.

General Motors Diesel engine above, Fairbanks-Morse below

Richmond

I met my friend as planned at the White Tower for the ride back to Newport. The next morning I received my orders and train tickets to report to Richmond, VA to begin training at the MOMM School.

I rode the train to Richmond, but didn't repeat the mistake of spending all of my money for beer as I did the year before in Maine.

What a change from boot camp. We had a nice barracks to sleep in, the food was much better, and we could go to town on nights or weekends when we didn't have the *Duty* (watches to stand). To keep in shape we ran a one mile course every morning before breakfast. One of the older guys in our class - as in boot camp - was assigned to be our Section Leader and luckily he liked me and treated me well. We worked with several types of diesel engines. We also learned a lot about different fuel systems, and the difference between a two stroke and a four stroke engine. We disassembled some of these engines, then reassembled and tested them. Our instructor was a Second Class Petty Officer, or, in Navy language, an MOMM 2/c. I don't think he had much time in the Navy, but because of his civilian diesel background he came into the Navy as a 2nd Class Petty Officer. We liked him. When we had to study from a Navy training manual and could not understand the procedure to accomplish a specific task, his favorite saying would be, "This is shit for the birds. This is how you do it." And he would proceed to demonstrate.

Richmond was a nice city. At that time I believe Virginia was a dry state. In order to drink liquor you had to belong to a bottle club, and that was not possible at seventeen years of age. The downtown Main St. in Richmond sold a lot of peanuts and also gave out a lot of free samples. Many stores also sold a cheap Raisin Wine. If we wished to drink one of the older students in our class would buy it for us. Cheap wine with peanuts produced a terrible hangover.
There were always social activities to attend in Richmond and a lot of nice girls - probably from the local college. At times on the weekends we could rent a car for twenty dollars to drive around the

country side; split between four or five riders it was cheap entertainment.

As we neared the end of our eight week course, my section leader informed me that two billets for Submarine School would be available from our class. He also said if I wished to volunteer for one of these billets, I would be his choice. (Submarine duty was a voluntary service.) Once again I was taken care of by my section leader. Looking back over seventy years, I have to wonder, was I an ass kisser at that time? I don't really think so. I had been raised to be respectful (or else!) and was truly interested in what I was learning. There was an added incentive in knowing it was all for a deadly serious purpose. As I would learn later as an instructor, instructors are appreciative of that attitude and respond to it. It is hard today for many people to understand the seriousness that everyone - people at home included - applied to the war. About one person out of every eight wore a uniform during the war so nearly every family had someone in the service. Everyone had a personal stake. There were always a few *foul balls* of course, there always are, but the seriousness of what we were doing was a motivator as strong as my mother's switch - maybe more so.

One of my close friends was picked for the second billet and we were looking forward to continuing to work together. He came from Meriden, Conn., not too far from the Submarine Base at New London. But he was very nervous and later flunked the Submarine Escape Training. I was very sorry to see him go.

On 17 Dec. 1943, I graduated from Diesel Engine School. The following day I received my orders to report to the base at New London on 26 December. This gave me a week's leave at Christmas time before reporting in.

I used it for a trip home to visit my parents in Madison for the holiday. Nothing exciting took place up there at that time of the year. I should have just reported early to the submarine base and saved the week of leave for later.

Submarine School

I got to the train station at New London in the late evening of December 26, 1943. A Navy bus made pickups at various times at the train station, and a limousine service was available that was inexpensive if all the seats were filled. I choose the limo; I think my first ride in one. With my orders in hand I checked in at the main gate. I was instructed to report to the receiving barracks and told how to find it. No transportation was offered. So with my sea bag on my shoulder I walked to my assigned barracks - about a quarter of a mile away.

Before attending Submarine School, many physical tasks had to be performed and numerous tests taken to qualify. Each morning over a thousand candidates would fall in for muster when we would receive our schedules for the day.

Our group was known as Spritz's Navy.

Jacket patch from later years to denote those (un)fortunate enough to have belonged.

Charles Spritz, enlisted in the Navy about 1922 and retired about 1938 as a Chief Torpedo Man under the 16 Year Bill. At that time the Navy was cutting back and a sailor could retire at 16 years. Spritz was qualified in Submarines and also was a Deep Sea Diver, some sources say Second Class, others say Master but it's unlikely. He was recalled from the Fleet Reserve to active duty in about 1940 and ordered to duty aboard the submarine S24 at New London. The Captain thought with his background he would be a great asset to his command, so he was made the Chief of the Boat. However he was so hard on the crew - including the other Chiefs - they were all ready to go *over the hill*.

So the Captain had a problem: what to do with Chief Spritz?

At that time hundreds of sailors were coming into the base from basic training. Initially they were quartered at the Receiving Barracks while preparing for admission into the Submarine School. This required both physical training and academic coursework relating to submarines, and culminated in qualifying in the submarine escape tower. Controlling all the daily - and nightly - activities of so many men in this hectic environment called for someone with an iron hand to be in control. Spritz appeared to have all the needed qualifications.

The Commanding Officer of the S24 happened to be a personal friend of the Commanding Officer of the New London base and arranged with him that Chief Spritz be given the job of supervising these sailors - as many as 2000 men at a time at the height of the war. They became known as Spritz's Navy. It was a big job but Spritz was the man for it and deserves a lot of credit for what he achieved.

The origin of his story is somewhat in question, as is his supposed service as a New York City cop (in the Bronx as one account had it) during his inactive time. I had a close friend, a shipmate on the submarine Sea Dog, who had served with Chief Spritz on the S24 in 1940, who told me that Spritz had been a guard on the shipping piers on the East River, which would not be the Bronx. But Spritz legend in New London is well confirmed, and that's the part that counts.

He was hated by everyone for his oppressive ways, and everyone did anything possible to avoid contact with him! As a young sailor at that time, if I was on a sidewalk and saw Chief Spritz approaching on his bicycle on the same side of the street, I would make a quick 90 degree turn to the opposite side.

Spritz had no direct involvement in our schooling but had complete control of our lives otherwise, and had the power to transfer a man out of submarines and back to the fleet for infractions. He is best described as the Navy version of a Marine Drill Instructor. If anyone got into trouble he never seemed to forget the name or face.

A qualified submariner coming from the war zone for assignment to a new boat would be treated considerably better than a recruit. Spritz loved cats and kept a few in his office. I think they were treated better than we were. He seldom went ashore for Liberty in New London, but if he did he would be accompanied by some of his strong arm assistants. I believe he was afraid he might be beaten up by the sailors ashore. One story held that he never took liberty at all.

While in Spritz's Navy, we were given an advanced physical by a Diving Medical Officer before taking our fifty pound pressure test in the pressure chamber. This was the equivalent of being at 112 ft. of sea water. Some sailors would flunk the test because they couldn't pop their ears (to equalize the pressure). Others might fail because they were claustrophobic.

Before taking the pressure test we heard a lot of stories about how bad it was and how your ears would bleed and you could have your ear drums broken. And either can happen, but rarely does. But these stories were nothing compared the ones told about our next test. This one involved the use of the Momsen Lung for making escapes in the submarine escape training tank. This tank was 120 ft. tall with a diameter of 18 ft. and held a column of water 110 ft. deep and had an elevator to carry instructors and trainees to the top - or to the escape locks along the way. We first received a classroom lecture about how the Momsen Lung worked and how to use it. We were also shown how to go through the escape hatch (with the use of a mock-up) into the tank of water and safely make our assent to the surface. To do this a rope was positioned outside of the escape door.

(In Navy language a rope is a *line*). We would place our hands and feet around the line and the buoyant Lung would safely take us to the surface while we breathed in and out of it. After our mock-up training we were taken to the top of the tank and mounted ladders with the water level up to our chests. We then put our lungs on and continued down the ladder until our heads were under water while breathing into the lung. On my first attempt it felt uncomfortable and I raised my head above the water. One of the instructors shoved me underwater again and held me there. I panicked and they took me out of the water. I had failed and was back working for Chief Spritz, sure that my submarine career was over.

I felt then - and now - that a better instructor would have re-assured me when I raised my head instead of merely shoving me back down and I would have been fine. It was a lesson I applied as an instructor myself a dozen years later

But in less than a week I was sent back to the tank for another try. I went through the same mock-up training as before and probably did a better job listening to the instructor since I knew what was at stake. Up at the top of the tank for ladder training - where I had previously flunked - there was no problem this time. Maybe I just had a better instructor the second time, maybe just from doing it a second time. That day, our group of eight or ten students made a 12 ft. escape from the roving bell, an 18 ft. escape from the 18ft. lock, and a 50 ft. escape from the 50ft. lock. The next day we made our escapes from the 110 ft. compartment at the very bottom of the tank.

The *roving bell* mentioned above is a large cylinder closed at the top and open at the bottom that can be raised and lowered as needed within the tank on stainless steel cables connected to an electric motor in the cupola. It is a very old concept that works by trapping air inside much as a drinking glass would if turned upside down and lowered into a tub of water. Air is supplied from above to maintain the amount of air at a constant level and purity.

If during an exercise a student should panic, or should be seen not to be exhaling properly, an instructor could quickly guide him into the bell. There he could breathe normally, and while standing on the platform beneath it be returned to the surface. The Officer in Charge controlled the movements of the bell from above.

A few days later we returned for free assent training. In this type of escape we didn't have a breathing device. We carried enough air in our lungs to slowly carry us to the surface. However, as this air was expanding we would have to blow a continuous small stream of bubbles from our mouth to get rid of the expanding air.

I may not have covered the training at the escape training tank in as much detail here as I could. Little did I realize when I flunked out on my first try at the tank that I would someday be an instructor there myself, and later in the book, as an instructor, I will go deeper into the tank training. (Do I have to say, "No pun intended?")

Now that I had completed my escape training, I was no longer in "Spritz's Navy." I packed my sea bag and relocated to better quarters to attend Submarine School.

I was still too young to have understood then what Spritz had done for me, but in time, I would, as did so many others he had trained and tyrannized. He understood what we would be facing, and prepared us extremely well for it. He demanded perfection in everything, and said often that, "There's room for anything on a submarine but a mistake."

What I remember most about Submarine School was our first trip to sea. Our instructor marched us in formation from the upper base, where the class room building was located, to the lower base where the school's boats were tied up at the piers. The hatch we used to enter the submarine was located above the galley and crew's mess compartment. Once in the mess hall, we noticed 5 gallon cans of milk and Table Talk pies stacked to the overhead on one of the mess tables. Our chief said we could have all the milk we could drink and also stated that we could have a whole pie if we wished. This was really something compared to the food I received at the National Youth Trade School a year earlier.

The submarines we trained on were the O and R class built in 1917, 1918, and 1919. Since this was 1944 the question arises as to why we were training on submarines built during WWI? The reason was that all of our newer up to date submarines were fighting our Japanese enemy in the Pacific.

In our class rooms on the upper base we learned about how a submarine dives and surfaces, all of the piping systems for salt water, fresh water, fuel oil, lubricating oil, and the hydraulic systems. We were required to make schematics of all of these systems - and commit them to memory.

I didn't do to very well in Submarine School. Well enough to pass, but I didn't graduate in the upper half of my class. I think if I had asked more questions, I would have done better. I blame some of this on my upbringing. Growing up in my day, children were *to be seen and not heard*. I was never told to ask questions if I didn't understand something.

In addition to learning everything to be known about submarines in the class room, then going to sea on the obsolete submarines where we stood watches on most of the stations on the boats, we received training in other subjects such as first aid, fire-fighting, airplane and ship recognition, standing lookout watches, and night vision training. My night vision was excellent and this information must have been entered into my service record because when I served on my first boat my assigned battle station was lookout because of it.

Although I had gone to Motors Machinist Mate School in Richmond, the engines used on the newest submarines had not been taught in that course. After graduating from Submarine School I went on to the submarine diesel school - a part of the Submarine School itself. That course taught the General Motors 16 cylinder, 1600 horse power, 2 cycle diesel engine used on about one half of our newer submarines. It also covered the Fairbanks Morse 10 cylinder opposed piston, 1600 horse power, 2 cycle diesel engine used on the others. We also covered the basics of air conditioning and refrigeration.

Submarines only had the capacity to carry 4000 gallons of fresh water. This was not enough for long periods at sea. To provide a continuous supply we were equipped with two Kleinsmith stills to convert saltwater to fresh water that could each produce 750 gallons a day. These stills were located in the forward engine room and were operated by the motor machinists, so we were taught their operation and maintenance as well.

Our instructor was an elderly Chief Machinist Mate. He had probably been retired from the Navy and recalled for the war emergency.

He was a good guy and treated us well. After more than seventy years I can still remember him as Chief Mac, but I can't remember his last name. (Mac will re-appear later.)

I loved working on the diesel engines. Chief Mac would let us *kids* start and stop these big engines, remove the cylinder heads, take out the valves, remove the pistons from the cylinders, check all the bearings, replace the piston rings, and re-assemble the engines for a test run. Chief Mac never took the tools out of our hands; he let us do everything.

The officer in charge of the Diesel School was a lieutenant who looked older than my father. He had probably served in WWI. He never smiled and we students gave him a wide berth. Chief Mac was a portly guy, and a comic. He usually had a small cigar in the corner of his mouth.

One day I received a message through the office from my mother that her brother had passed away and she hoped I could attend the funeral in Newburyport, Mass. The funeral was on a work day in the middle of the week, and I knew it was almost impossible to get the day off in the middle of WWII. I decided to ask Chief Mac. Chief Mac said I would have to fill out a special request chit that he would sign for me, but then I would have to take it to Lt. Adams for final approval. He also had some advice for me. Chief Mac said of Lt. Adams - quote - "That old son of a bitch doesn't have his morning shit until noon, so my advice to you, kid, is to wait until he has his shit. Otherwise he'll turn you down." I followed Chief Mac's advice and my special request chit was approved.

Shortly before we finished submarine school, we received our dream sheet, our *wish list* of assignments. This was a list of all the new submarines being constructed in the various shipyards in the United States. The boat that took my eye was the USS Sea Dog. I thought that was a very salty name. My buddy liked the USS Sea Devil. Both were being built at the Portsmouth Naval Shipyard at Portsmouth N.H. We were both lucky we got our requests - and both boats survived World War II.

After graduation, I advanced to Fireman First Class. My pay was now about sixty-five dollars per month. I don't remember the exact amount, but somewhat better that my ten dollars a month at the N.Y.A. And the food was far better.

After successfully completing Submarine School sailors would be transferred to a boat presently in the fleet or a new submarine under construction in a shipyard - Portsmouth (NH) Navy Yard, Electric Boat Co. in Groton, Conn, Mare Island Navy Yard, Vallejo, Cal., or Manitowoc Shipbuilding Co. in Wisconsin.

I received my orders to report to the Portsmouth Naval Shipyard on 1 May 1944 to report aboard the USS Sea Dog (SS401) detail.

Navy Yard, Portsmouth, N.H.   Submarine School Enlisted Class   June 1, 1944   Reg No 537- #4

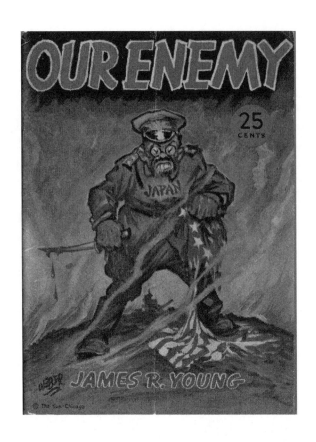

USS Sea Dog (SS401)

I don't recall my transportation back to Portsmouth, probably a train to Boston and bus from there to Portsmouth. On reporting in, I was directed to the Sea Dog barge. This barge had a couple of offices and a large work area where we performed our duties while waiting for the construction of the Sea Dog to be completed. Our sleeping quarters as well as our meals were in the submarine barracks.

I first met the Chief of the Boat, a Chief Gunners Mate (a *Right Arm* rate: Seaman Branch – involved with ship operations). I next met the Chief Motor Machinist Mate (a *Left Arm* rate: Artificer Branch – mechanics and craftsmen) who was in charge of the engine rooms and for whom I would be working. I also was introduced to our captain, Commander Lowrance, a very impressive Naval Officer. This was the first time I had the privilege of shaking hands with a Senior Officer.

Commander Lowrance wore the Navy Cross that he earned as the commanding officer of the U.S.S. Kingfish (SS234) earlier in the war.

I don't know how many submarines were under construction at one time, but I do recall that about every ten days a new one was commissioned and left to join the fleet in the Pacific.

Although I would be at Portsmouth for less than two months, a lot of work was required by the crew of the Sea Dog.

Before leaving for the war zones, several crews of the new submarines being built would be at the Navy Yard and using the facilities in the barracks at one time. I would guess about six. This required that each submarine furnish the mess cooks, and compartment cleaners to provide services for them. Other than the Chiefs and Officers, the remainder of the crew was in three section liberty which meant that in addition to the normal working day every third day each man had the duty for the full 24 hour period. This also applied to the weekends.

As I remember, I was usually assigned as a fire watch for one of the shipyard welders working on the Sea Dog. This was an important job; should a welder be in one of the tanks welding and fire started from the arc of his welding rod. Because of the welding helmet he wore, he might not realize he was in trouble. My job was to stay with the welder and extinguish any small fires with a CO_2 fire extinguisher.

One of the welders always asked for me to be his fire watch when I had the duty - I thought at first because he thought I was the best fire watcher. Not so. He had a daughter he wanted me to meet. He invited me to his house, but from the smell of the food he ate at lunch time, I was afraid I might be offered the same at his house so always had an excuse ready.

My brother Jack was living in Rochester and working as a machinist in Dover. He was usually my excuse, but I really did spend quite a lot of time with him. But I don't believe I ever passed up a date again in my Navy career because of what was in the father's lunch box.

Portsmouth was a nice town to visit for a meal and a movie; but at 17 and 18 we could not drink at the bars.

We spent a lot of time in the evenings studying the piping systems on the submarines being built in preparation for earning our dolphins, the prized insignia of the Submarine Service. We were also required to attend a course at the New Construction Submarine School located at the yard. This was a valuable course for learning about the boat we were going to sea in. As mentioned earlier, the submarines we had originally trained on dated back to WWI.

The USS Sea Dog (SS401) was commissioned on the morning of 3 June 1944. This was a great day for the crew. It meant we would start receiving our submarine and sea pay. Submarine pay amounted to 50% of base pay, and sea pay was 20% of the total amount, so nearly an additional 80% pay increase.

As part of the commissioning ceremony, we were rewarded with a party. This was a gala event that took place at a large function hall located a few miles south of Portsmouth, known as Ham's Place.

For some time the Walt Disney Studios had been producing patch designs for submarines and other military units. The Sea Dog logo was a Bull Dog modified for sea duty. Two of my shipmates, Parker and Wright, located a bull dog belonging to a farmer in Maine. He agreed to lend his dog to my shipmates to attend the commissioning party. When asked about the dog's temperament, the farmer told them, "You may have trouble keeping him awake." But the dog certainly was the star of the show.

It was a great event, with an orchestra, plenty of booze (the drinking age requirement for the State of New Hampshire not enforced), and several young ladies from Portsmouth, surrounding towns, and the University of New Hampshire in attendance. I spent the evening with a girl from Haverhill, Mass. She gave me her address and I promised to send her copies of the pictures taken. For some reason I failed to follow up; what a mistake! Two years later I was back at Portsmouth for another commissioning and party and wishing I had stayed in touch with her.

Late in the evening my fireman buddy from the engine room was found outside of Ham's Place, drunk and naked. One must assume that some nice lady was going to give him something nice before he went to war. I hope it worked out for him but it appeared she got more than he did. After searching the area we could not find a trace of his clothing, or the lady, or car that he might have been in. I sometimes wonder if there might be a great- grandmother in her nineties in the Portsmouth area that has a WWII sailor's uniform tucked away in a bottom drawer. I would like to tell her that he made it home safely at the end of the war on the Sea Dog.

But we had a big problem. How to get a blond, blue eyed, naked sailor, with no identification, and one who could easily be mistaken for a German spy, through the main gate of a Navy Shipyard guarded by Marines? Our Chief of the Boat informed our Captain of the problem. The Captain asked the COB if he had any suggestions and he told him that he himself was probably the only one who could transport this nude sailor back to the base without a search. So a tablecloth was snatched from one of the tables, our shipmate loaded into the back seat of the Captain's car, covered with the table cloth and driven back to the barracks by our Captain and Chief of the

Boat. I don't believe any disciplinary action was taken on the matter. Best for all concerned to just forget the whole thing.

Another shipmate, Red, also in a drunken condition, fell down the long set of entrance stairs and received a lot of cuts and bruises on his face. The next morning at quarters on the Sea Dog the Executive Officer, Mr. Lynch, noticed the damage to Red's face. He assumed he had been fighting and passed it off with the comment, "There's one on every ship."

My Father was able to attend the ceremony. I took him below decks and gave him a tour of the submarine. He also met Captain Lowrence. He told my father he would take good care of me. My Father was quite proud and I'm sure told the story many times back in Madison.

With a new submarine and a new crew, many of whom had never served on a ship or submarine in their time in the Navy, a lot of training was required. This began with dock trials. While tied to the dock and with all stations manned, we would operate the submarine (as nearly as possible) as we would at sea. We also conducted fire, flooding, collision, man over-board, battle stations, and torpedo and/or gun action drills. We did make a few trips to sea with key Navy Yard personnel aboard to fix any problems that might be detected.

Submarines were essentially surface ships with the capability of running submerged. When surfaced the air quality was good and mechanical ventilation distributed fresh air throughout the boat. Submerged, the air would remain good for several hours but would deteriorate during extended dives. A boat of WWII vintage moving slowly to conserve the power in her batteries could stay down for about 48 hours. As the oxygen supply became depleted, odors from stored diesel fuel, heads (toilets), the galley, unwashed bodies (one shower a week if needed or not!), and tobacco smoke would begin to dominate the heavy CO_2 laden atmosphere.

Smoking was permitted on board - probably the lesser of two evils. It relaxed people, particularly when under stress whereas not-smoking would magnify stress among smokers and nearly everyone

Officers And Chief Petty Officers Late Of 20¢ Sqd. Rsc (Paris) In Constantinople At Kort And Photographers.

Commissioning Party for Sea Dog, June, 1944.

smoked. Those who didn't actually were - they just didn't realize it. Smoking generally was encouraged by the very low cost of cigarettes - and pipe tobacco - on military bases exempt from the taxes that determined the civilian cost. As the air quality became worse during a prolonged dive, the cigarettes themselves became difficult to keep alight.

I've often wondered why I wasn't subjected to some sort of pulmonary problem long before now as a result of that exposure. Maybe just a base of good clean New Hampshire air growing up.

On about 10 July 1944 we left Portsmouth and made our way to Gould Island, off Newport, R.I., for torpedo exercises. Then on 12 July, 1944, we proceeded to New London for further training and final loading and fueling.

Loaded to capacity with fuel, stores, and torpedoes, the Sea Dog was declared "ready for sea" on 24 July 1944. We sailed the first leg of the long voyage through the Panama Canal to the battle areas of the Pacific.

Almost the entire run down the coast to the Canal Zone was made in moderately rough weather. All hands acquired their *sea legs* of necessity in a hurry. During this passage, veterans and novices alike were on a high state of alertness as the boat was passing through waters still frequented by German U-Boats.

Our normal watch at sea was 4 hours on, 8 hours off. If I was on watch from 8 am until 12 pm, my eight hours off period could be used for sleeping, studying, or whatever else I wished to do – within the obvious limitations of the boat. However, since this was a new submarine we still needed a lot of training. On most days from 8 am the worst watches were the 4 am to 8 am and the 4 pm to 8 pm. It was like standing a 16 hour watch.

I was an oiler in the forward engine room when the submarine was on the surface. When submerged, I would be on the diving planes or the trim manifold in the control room. Submerged, the boat would be powered by its electric motors and the diesel engines shut down.

Interior views: Galley, Engine Room, Fairbanks-Morse Engines

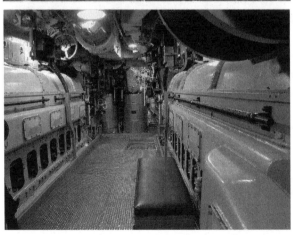

On 2 August, the Sea Dog entered the Gatun Locks and began her passage of the Panama Canal. Once inside the locks we were in Gatun Lake. This was a fresh water lake created by the Gatun Dam. The lake occupied about 164 square miles, and the distance through the canal was 51 miles.

As we made our way through Gatun Lake at a relatively slow speed, we noticed the flow of water around the submarine escape trunk located in the superstructure would provide a nice place to take a fresh water bath. Several members of the crew who were not on watch took advantage of this endless supply of warm fresh water, something in limited supply on the Sea Dog. I don't remember any of our Officers taking advantage of the opportunity. In those days it would have been improper for an officer to be seen in the nude by enlisted men.

In the afternoon, the Sea Dog was moored alongside the USS Icefish at the US Naval Operating Base, Balboa, Canal Zone. In checking some of my sources for this book, I find that the Icefish was also a new submarine commissioned on June 10th, a week after the Sea Dog, at Manitowoc. The route to the war zone for the submarines built in Manitowoc would be down the Mississippi to the Gulf of Mexico.

I had a friend, shipmate, and mentor on the Sea Dog. His name here will be Willie. Willie was about five or six years older than I was. He joined the Navy in 1940 before the war began and had been on the submarine Trigger earlier in the war. The Trigger had a good war record and sank a lot of Japanese ships in the early months. To provide trained qualified submarine sailors for the new submarines being constructed at this time, experienced men would often be transferred back to the States to a new boat. As I remember the story, Willie was transferred from the Trigger to a new construction vessel and the Trigger was lost on its next patrol.

Willie was a self-described lover and drinker, and I'm not sure in what order.

When he reported to his new boat at the Navy Yard, his routine physical disclosed he had a venereal disease - usually referred to as the *clap* (gonorrhea) in the Navy. This required a stay in sick bay in a section called the *clap shack*. Having a venereal disease was considered misconduct and pay was forfeit for the period of time spent in the clap shack. This could amount to several weeks. By the time Willie was released from sick bay his new submarine had been completed and gone to sea. Although I do not have the name of that boat, as the story goes, it too was sunk. Two and 0 for Willie. I guess being a lover and a drinker worked out for him.

Willie then got a new set of orders to the Sea Dog. This was my first contact with him. As a young sailor of seventeen, I was not a leader. I was a follower. Maybe I was his yes man. He took me under his wing.

We had arrived at Balboa. We spent about four days there and this was the first time many of us had set foot on land outside the continental United States.

Willie took me ashore to tour the gin mills. Drinking was not a problem here at seventeen; no I.D. card was required for anything. He took me to a beautiful night club - I still remember the name today, "The House of Love." There must have been at least fifty beautiful women dressed in evening gowns. This was a far bigger culture shock than moving from Eaton to Madison, N.H. in 1936! After over seventy years, I am unable to remember my priorities in Panama, whether the liquor or the ladies? I hope it was the ladies.

On 6 August, we got underway from the Canal Zone to Pearl Harbor, where we were assigned to Commander Submarine Force Pacific Fleet, (COMSUBPAC). After the long months of building, fitting out, and training, the Sea Dog was at last in the war.

Our routine at sea in the war zone was surprisingly quite easy unless we were in an engagement with the enemy.

When operating on the surface - generally at night - the routine would be 4 hours on watch at the duty station (for me, the engine room) and 8 hours off. If submerged, my watch station was either the Trim Manifold to maintain the proper buoyancy for the designated depth, or the Stern Diving Planes to maintain the proper angle of the boat. The same 4 hours on, 8 hours off schedule applied.

After leaving port for a patrol we ate quite well at first. However, food stocks gradually depleted and deteriorated. Milk (if we had it) would go first, then - pretty much in order - fresh fruit, ice cream, fresh vegetables, potatoes, and eggs (again, if available, but not in most ports). These items could only be kept refrigerated for a relatively short time before spoiling.

We had a large freeze locker stocked with plenty of frozen meat and seldom ran short unless the patrol was very long. Canned goods were never a problem as there was a large storeroom, and excess - until consumed - was stored in the torpedo compartments.

As patrols neared their end we ate a lot more rice, and Jell-O for desserts.

One of the cooks would be assigned - on rotation - as the baker, and would usually work in the nighttime hours when there was less traffic in the galley. It was comforting to know we had a competent baker aboard who could turn out good rolls, bread, and pies. I think it was Napoleon who said, "A navy floats on its stomach," - or something like that.

Although we had the stills to convert fresh water from seawater the capacity was limited, so we were limited to a single - quick - shower each week. The comment, "Needed or not," usually gets added to that, but it went without saying.

We had a small washing machine, and a crew member would be designated as the *Laundry Queen* to wash the clothes of sailors on their shower day. A set would include a pair of dungarees and a change of underwear. That would include the T shirt which was the standard top worn aboard ship. The clothes were hung in the engine room to dry. Socks and handkerchiefs were not washed in the machine since they were too easy to lose. Generally we would just bring about a dozen or so pairs of socks on board and as a pair in use reached the point where it could walk by itself tossed in the trash and a *fresh* pair broken out. Same with the handkerchiefs.

Trash went over the side in weighted bags to insure it went to the bottom and leave no clue to our presence. That might raise some ecological eyebrows, but against sending an entire ship and its contents to the same destination with a torpedo it was a small consideration.

In a war zone we would usually be submerged during daylight and run on the surface at night with the diesel engines in order to re-charge the batteries as much as possible before daylight once again exposed us - as early as 4 AM in some latitudes. Darkness could be as late as 9 PM.

Although allowed to smoke, during long periods submerged the oxygen level would decline to the point that some serious puffing was required to keep a cigarette going. It would become difficult to do manual work. The smallest effort could cause shortness of breath.

If forced to remain for an extended period to avoid detection or elude an enemy already aware of our presence we could use CO_2 absorbent (soda lime) to reduce the built up CO_2 in the air. Oxygen could then be bled into the air from oxygen cylinders to at least partially restore the atmosphere to a breathable - and smoke-able - condition.

We were fortunate in the engine room as we were the first to get the benefit of fresh air on surfacing due to the large volume being pulled in to support the combustion of the diesel engines.

Recreation space on board was severely limited. The mess *hall* was the best place to gather. *Hall* was something it wanted to be when it grew up, and we had to keep our elbows under control. We played cards a lot - poker, cribbage, and acey-deucy were popular.

The sub-tender supplied us with a stock of movies and at least one would be screened in the torpedo compartment on successive watches each day. If the cruise went long, we saw re-runs.

Much of the time between Balboa and Pearl Harbor was spent in further training on board, with daily trim dives and emergency drills, and with occasional merchant shipping contacts, fire control practice.

On 22 August, we rendezvoused with the USS Icefish and PC 575. The group passed through Kaiwi Channel between Oahu and Molokai, and proceeded to the Submarine Base at Pearl Harbor for voyage repairs to both the Sea Dog and the Icefish, and final lading for patrol.

While at the base - for approximately three weeks before our first war patrol - we had the opportunity to go on liberty in Honolulu. Because of the large number of servicemen passing through the island (Oahu) to the Western Pacific, it was not considered a very good liberty port. The Shore Patrol and/or the Military Police would pick men up for any infraction and bring them back to the base and the brig. Even wearing the sailor hat on the back of the head was an infraction.

The houses of prostitution and the reasons for them require a comment. Supposedly at about the beginning of World War II our Military and/or government senior officials became concerned about the large number of servicemen on liberty in Honolulu and the safety of the civilian female population there; so at least three houses of prostitution were made available, run by the US Government and staffed largely by American girls from the States. An honorable profession; working for the war effort. Likely a *war story*, but belief creates its own truth.

Things a sailor might wish to do in Honolulu on liberty:
    1. Go to the beach for a swim in the ocean. Not possible. You could not be seen with your uniform off.
    2. Go to the movies. Possible if you were willing to stand in line waiting for a long period of time.

3. Go to a gin mill for a drink. Stand in line again for a lousy drink, such as Five Island Gin, and be asked to leave after three.

4. To one of the houses of prostitution. Also required standing in line and being asked to leave after a short period of time with one of the working girls.

So where would my friend and shipmate Willie, the lover and drinker, take me? Little doubt as to that.

Follow an old salt for a seasoned liberty.

USS Sea Dog (SS 401) in war zone. Note deck armament: 5" gun aft, 20mm gun center, author's Battle Station as lookout on elevated platform on mast.

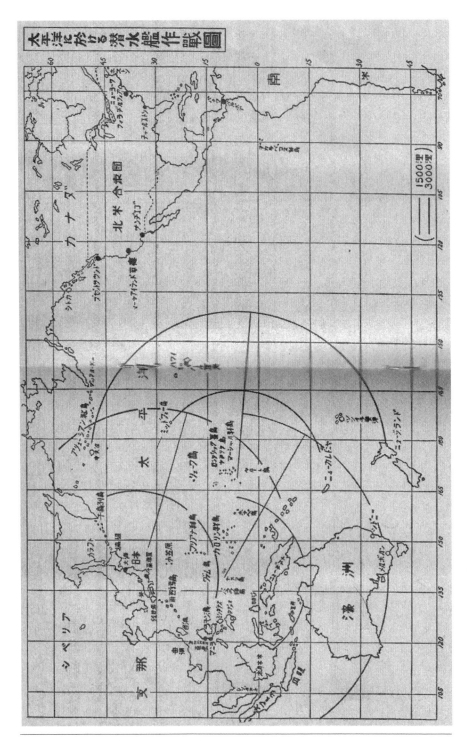

First War Patrol

On 13 September the Sea Dog cast off her lines and left Pearl Harbor on her first War Patrol. Traveling in company with the USS Trepang, we stopped at Midway Island, topped off the fuel tanks, and then on 17 September, set course for the designated patrol area in Empire Waters. Commander V.L. Lowrance, USN, was in command.

Our first patrol covered a period of 54 days of which 31 were spent on station in the waters along Okinawa in the East China Sea. We spent the time on the way with repeated gun and diving drills and arrived in the designated area on 28 September. During the first several days of patrolling we saw little but small fishing vessels, a few planes, and the first of three Hospital ships, all of which were properly marked and not interfered with. Planes would become a problem.

On 10 October the boat took station to the west of Okinawa during the first carrier strike on the Ryukyus with an air raid in progress on the city of Naha. This was the start of the Battle of Okinawa. At about noon, the lookouts sighted a trawler loaded with oil drums, headed for Okinawa and for the first time, the Sea Dog went to "Battle Stations, Gun Action." With our 20mm deck guns blazing she closed on the trawler. The results appeared questionable and the 20mm crew was ordered below with the intention of engaging with our 5" gun but the boat was forced to submerge when five planes, diving out of the sun, made bombing and strafing runs on us. Rapid action was required to clear the topside of the many men in the gun crews, and the boat was fifty feet under water when the last five men came down the gun access trunk ladder. But when last seen, the trawler was dead in the water and burning briskly.

Earlier I mentioned that because of my excellent night vision, my battle station, when we were surfaced on station, was lookout. On the day of the incident I was the port lookout standing on a small platform on the shears of the submarine, about 10 feet above the bridge where our captain was directing our attack on the trawler.

Now, as Paul Harvey, the radio commentator used to say, "The rest of the story."

At the time of the incident we were on life guard duty. Our job was to rescue pilots and/or crews that were shot down during the first carrier strike on the island. The pilots of these planes were informed of the areas where the rescue submarines would be positioned, and if a crash landing was necessary, they would ditch their airplane in one of these areas if possible.

Since we were in a so-called *safe area* from our own planes, our captain must have felt it was safe to put our 5" gun crew on deck for action on the trawler. As the port lookout I had the best view of the gun action. During the battle with the trawler, I spotted a plane in the distance that was heading in our direction. I reported this to the captain who was directly below me on the bridge. He answered, "Aye-Aye," and seemed uninterested. "The plane is closing in on us," I reported again, and received a weak aye-aye again. Checking the plane again, I was sure he was making a run on us from the direction of the bow. Once again I made my report. By now the captain seemed agitated with me and gave me another dismissive aye-aye. He also said, "Friendly I.F.F.," (Information Friend or Foe). With this information from our radar, our captain knew this was one of our planes and assumed he was coming in to ditch. I next looked down at the teak wood main deck below me and saw splinters flying. I thought our old Warrant Officer - who manned the 20 mm behind me on the cigarette deck - was firing into the deck. Not so. I checked back on the plane, and saw the nose of a bomb that looked like a basketball coming directly at us. I didn't wait for orders to clear the bridge. I actually landed on our captain's back in the process of getting below decks.

We were strafed and took five bombs from our own planes. The last bomb broke a lot of light bulbs and knocked large chunks of cork insulation off the pressure hull in the control room. Once safely submerged and out of harm's way, the Captain was heard to say, "I don't care if all the planes get knocked out of the sky. We're staying submerged."

When he first saw me after the incident, his comment was "I don't blame you for being afraid, I was too. But I didn't appreciate you jumping on my back." My reply was, "I reported the plane three times to you". His answer was, "I know you did, but we had friendly I.F.F. on the Radar." However, he took note of his overconfidence in the IFF and from that point on would submerge on detecting *any* aircraft closer than 8 or 9 miles.

I of course had no routine contact with the captain. I was only an 18 year old oiler in the forward engine room. My only communications with him were when we were at battle stations on the surface and I was a battle lookout.

During this patrol only two contacts were made with surface ships worthy of torpedo fire and both were attacked aggressively. The first attack was made submerged on two overlapping freighters in a heavily escorted eleven ship convoy, resulting in two and possibly three timed hits followed by definite and heavy breaking up noises indicating at least one ship sunk and another probably damaged. Following the attack, the Sea Dog was depth charged heavily for about three hours with a total of 109 charges counted during that time. Fortunately the closest they came was about 100 yards away and we had no damage, but that is something only known afterwards.

As I remember the *rest of the story*, during the depth charge attack our Executive Officer approached the captain saying, "Captain, I think we should go up to periscope depth where we can make another attack." The captain responded, "Jimmy, when I look through that periscope I not only see the enemy, I also see my wife and children." We remained at our safe deep depth.

The second attack on 28 October was a fast night attack in the moonlight on two Japanese battleships with a destroyer escort. With a good fire control solution, six torpedoes were fired with six misses, probably due to the extreme range at which it was necessary to fire because of inability to close on these high speed targets and shorten the range. The captain had observed the course pattern of the battleships for about 10 minutes to be sure of his aim but felt later that they had likely made a change in the pattern as they were being fired on. The Sea Dog was forced to dive quickly as soon as the torpedoes were launched to avoid the destroyer that was approaching at full throttle, and observation was broken off.

Results of this patrol:
1 freighter	4000 tons (sunk)
1 trawler	25 tons (damaged)

The submarine combat insignia (pin) was authorized to the crew for the confirmed sinking of the freighter. For his conduct of the patrol, Captain Lowrance received a letter of commendation with ribbon from the Commander in Chief, Pacific Fleet.

In his report of the patrol, Captain Lowrance noted that *all hands had operated to the highest standards of the Navy*. He reserved particular praise for the services of the lookouts. His comments, by way of the report, are widely distributed to those with a "need to know" in the chain of command (such reports are classified *Confidential*) but include five copies to the CNO (Chief of Naval Operations) and seven copies to COMINC (Commander in Chief), both offices under the single hat of Admiral Ernest J. King. Chester Nimitz as CINCPAC (Commander in Chief Pacific) was in for a half dozen copies also. Nice to know.

During this patrol all of us *non-qualified "pukes"* were busy studying for our final examination to earn our coveted dolphins. Once we earned them we would be *Our Brother's Keeper* - a submarine service term that implied the ability to do whatever was required in the interest of the boat and its crew. Enlisted men's dolphins were a cloth patch worn on the lower part of the right sleeve. Officers were issued a gold pin worn on the left chest above any medals and/or campaign ribbons.

At a later date, about 1948, enlisted men were issued silver dolphins to be worn on the left chest which is the practice today.

In preparation for the exam, usually directed by the Executive Officer, we would have to trace out all of the piping systems as well as all the valves and tanks in each system. We also kept a notebook for our drawings of these systems. As we learned each compartment, the Petty Officer in charge of each one would sign our qualification notebook when he was satisfied we knew all of the equipment in that area and could operate it.

For us MOMMs in the engine rooms things were a little different. Our assistant engineering officer, a Warrant Officer (machinist) insisted that he would be the one to test us in the engine rooms. Mr. M, as I will call him, was older and, as the story went, had served on submarines in the Dutch Navy during World War I. The problem was that Mr. M had not served in the engine rooms on such a modern submarine. He didn't, for instance, know the path of sea water through the coolers to keep the fresh water and lubricating oil at the proper temperature. This seemed to be one of his favorite questions. We knew the path of flow in this system, but Mr. M would shoot us down. One day I went to my boss, the First Class Petty Officer in charge of this engine room with the problem. I can still remember what he told me, "Why don't you smarten up, tell the old son of a bitch what he wants to hear and he'll pass you." What an education. I not only used this on Mr. M, I continued using this throughout my Navy career whenever necessary.

Many times in my life I have heard the statement, "there's no such thing as an atheist in the foxholes." It always reminds me of a shipmate on the Sea Dog during the depth charge attack on our first patrol. For the story I'll use his nickname, *Ski*. Ski was a First Class Gunners Mate with about 16 years of service. He always said he didn't believe in God. He believed in the American dollar. He said, "If I was hungry God couldn't feed me, but if I had the American dollar, I could buy food or whatever else in life I wanted." During the attack, a few guys were in the mess hall saying their prayers. Ski came through the mess hall; he told the group that they could pray to God as long as they wanted to, but God couldn't help them. He said they should be praying that the Portsmouth Naval Ship Yard made the hull strong enough to take those depth charges. I don't know if Ski was really an atheist or not, but he certainly was not afraid of the depth charges.

As to my own concerns I can only say I wasn't overly troubled by my first experience - and the second (and last) didn't really amount to much. Old hands delighted in telling their harrowing tales especially when they had a green kid to spook. But I could not fail to see they were still here to tell their stories. We knew, of course, that boats had been lost, but losses were not publicized much to avoid informing the Japanese of any successes, or the folks at home of the price we were paying. And at 18 we're indestructible - until we're not. Trouble will come to the other guy.

From my position in the engine room I had little knowledge of what was going on. There are no windows in submarines. We could however hear quite well. Water is an excellent conductor of sound, and we could tell by the maneuvering of the boat when something was up - and could feel when torpedoes were launched. Submerging to avoid detection was routine and no particular cause for worry.

Naturally any explosion creates apprehension. At some distance it's probably more curiosity; if there are more but diminishing, there's relief; if they approach, concern. At some point fear would come into play, but 100 yards wasn't close enough to trouble me. And I had to carry on with my job. I don't know how I would have reacted if water started shooting in everywhere and light bulbs and electrical panels started shooting fireworks the way they show it in the movies, but we never reached that point so I can't say.

Another story from our first patrol: With a lot of time on my hands, I became interested in reading. I read a couple of non-fiction books on deep-sea diving and became very interested in the subject. One unpopular member of our crew, a First Class Electrician named Kime who was in charge of the Maneuvering Room claimed to have been a diver. If so, he probably was only a Second Class. But with my questions about diving I may have bugged him too much. As a kid, I didn't realize that he felt with his time in the service he should have been a Chief Petty Officer. He only hung out with the Chiefs and probably resented the presence of a teen-aged Fireman. I had spent time - legitimately - in his compartment while studying for my qualification and maybe had overstayed my welcome. One day he told me to, "Get your fucking ass out of my compartment." As only a Fireman, I had to comply. I was too low on the totem pole to give him any guff. Looking back, I don't think he had any right to throw me out of the area, but my questions about diving may have been threatening to expose more brag than fact and he probably wanted to cut it off. Over my Navy career I crossed paths with him a couple of times, and he will re-appear later.

The Sea Dog left the area and proceeded to Midway to refit and on 5 November moored alongside the submarine tender U.S.S. Proteus (AS19). I also received my submarine qualification Dolphins. During this War Patrol, I was no longer a non-qualified "puke." I was now *my brother's keeper* – and I had turned 18.

Submarines at Midway Island

Firing 5 inch gun

Midway

We enjoyed the recreation facilities of the "Gooneyville Lodge" on Midway. Originally Midway, actually three islands, was a coaling station where coal burning ships could stop and top off their coal bunkers as they traveled to the Far East. Later, in the 1930s, Pan American Air Lines built a hotel and a landing strip where travelers could land, spend the night, and refuel to continue their journey.

Early in WWII a submarine tender, I believe it was the Sperry, was stationed there, and a submarine base was created. Midway Island is 1200 miles northwest of Oahu. By having this base in the Central Pacific, the time necessary for our boats to reach their assigned stations was greatly reduced. They could proceed at higher speeds with less concern about conserving fuel, and their on-station periods could be lengthened. And presumably more enemy ships could be sunk.

Some senior medical officer must have concluded that because of the lack of sunshine and battle fatigue on these long patrols we should have the use of a rest camp for a couple of weeks after each patrol. At Midway, barracks and recreation facilities were built. The Officers were housed at the Pan American hotel, now called Gooneyville Lodge, and the enlisted men in the barracks.

The submarine tender that we moored beside was the Proteus. After a welcome home ceremony by the band, a visit by senior officers, receiving accumulated mail from home, and ice cream and fresh fruit, the crew, with their personal belongings was transported to the barracks. The relief crew from the tender took over the Sea Dog to perform repairs and maintenance needed for our next assignment.

Sand Island was the name of the island we were on and was probably given the name because the terrain was almost all pure white sand, with a beautiful beach on the clear waters of the Pacific. It sounds like paradise, but to return to Paul Harvey and the rest of the story, the sun was so bright - combined with the reflected heat off the white sand - that we couldn't spend much time on the beach without getting severely sunburned. This was long before Sunscreen, and there were no pavilions to provide shade.

Before talking further about recreation on Midway, I have to introduce *torpedo alcohol*. On the Sea Dog we carried both electric (battery powered) and steam driven torpedoes. The fuel used in the steam driven torpedoes was 190 proof alcohol. Of this there were two kinds; the pure - good - alcohol was clear and much like an extremely strong vodka. 200 proof is pure alcohol. The other was similar except it had a pinkish color and was known as *Pink Lady*. In addition to the coloring, croton oil was added. Croton oil is a product of the castor bean plant, and a strong laxative. I imagine it was assumed that sailors would consider drinking this 190 proof alcohol and the laxative was added to discourage it.

At the rest camp our Officers could purchase bottled liquor and at times might buy a bottle for the leading Chief. We enlisted men (*Pee-ons*) could only purchase beer - that reportedly was laced with the preservative *formaldehyde*. A few of these beers would cause a severe headache and upset stomach.

Formaldehyde in the beer seems to join Saltpeter in the food in Navy lore. Neither seems to be factual but many men will swear to both as true. How else to explain the headaches? Maybe that a few too many of *any* beers can do it.

Some captains would make sure the *good* alcohol was put on board and would issue a five gallon can as needed to the Chief of the Boat for celebrations. It was also nice to have a torpedo man (such as my friend Willie) as a friend who might be able to *liberate* some of it. Evidently, a couple of old timers in the engine rooms knew we didn't have any of the good stuff but did have plenty of the Pink Lady. A still was necessary to convert it to drinkable alcohol. So a portable still was built in the engine room to be taken to the barracks. It was set up in the shower room and used as necessary for our nightly parties after the sun went down when it became much cooler. This was called a *Gillie* party. I looked up this word in my dictionary and the closest I could find was gill, a unit of liquid measure equal to 1/4 pint (4 oz.). Perhaps this was the maximum amount of Gillie that one should drink at one sitting. Gillie, at 190 proof, was a powerful drink and if not diluted, could cause drunkenness very quickly. We usually mixed it with grapefruit juice. Sometimes at night tame birds know as Moaning Birds because of their odd calls would mix into our drinking sessions and we would feed one a little Gillie and watch it get drunk. Not a whole lot to do on Midway.

Midway was also a nesting-ground for the Albatross, sea birds that hatch their young on the Midway Islands. They are a very graceful bird when flying, but in landing they didn't do so well and were known as *Gooney Birds*, the inspiration for the name Gooneyville Lodge. They were easy to catch on land because they had to run quite a distance to take off. But they had sharp beaks and were quite mean during their nesting time. Many submarine sailors got severe bites from fooling around with them.

The only other activities that I can remember were softball, usually everyday with the crew of any other boat that was in. We also had our movie projector and films that we carried on the Sea Dog that we brought to the barracks for a nightly movie. We could exchange our films with the submarine tender and borrow films from other submarines, so we had a pretty good selection.

After surviving the Gillie parties, the Gooney Birds, and a few fights during our two otherwise restful weeks at the camp, we returned to sea on our 2nd War Patrol.

In writing about our 2nd War Patrol of 69 days, I will use the ship's history of the USS Sea Dog to a great extent to insure I have it right.

Periscope view of torpedoed Japanese patrol boat

2nd War Patrol - Leaving Midway 29 Nov 1944

After a short training period we got underway on 29 November for our second war patrol. Commander Lowrance remained in command. We were joined on 1 December by the USS Guardfish and the USS Sea Robin, forming the wolf-pack *Rebel's Rogues* with the CO of the Sea Dog as Pack Commander. The three boats refueled from the USS Fulton (AS 11) in Tanapag Harbor, Saipan, on 8 December, and the following day proceeded to a sector of the South China Sea bounded loosely by the islands of Luzon, Formosa, and Hainan.

During our brief fuel stop at Saipan we were taken on a short tour of the island in stake body trucks where we saw the B-29s. Although I had seen them fly over us on their bombing runs to the Japanese mainland, I had no idea of their great size.

We also passed a stockade holding Japanese Prisoners of War. They gave us some pretty mean looks. I would have thought they would have been happier now they were out of the war and alive, but from what we understood they didn't see it that way.

Saipan also had a submarine rest camp where crews could stay for two weeks after a patrol. But our stay was only for a single day.

Thirty four days were spent in the area of the South China Sea during which thorough coverage was maintained despite numerous aircraft contacts. These could not be identified as friendly or enemy due to problems with the IFF procedures and either one could be a threat. Based on his earlier experience, Captain Lowrance made it a practice to dive when any incoming contact was made. Ship contacts were scarce due undoubtedly to the activities of our surface ships during this time. Most of our contacts were aircraft, friendly submarines, or vessels too small to be worth a torpedo.

We spent Christmas submerged south of Formosa, and the attitude of the whole crew was aptly summed up by the first entry in the ship's log for 1 January 1945: "Due to circumstances beyond our control,

New Year's Day found us on war patrol; no women, no music, no rum and coke; Just a cold wet bridge and a cup of Ja-moke."

On the night of 5 January Sea Dog and Sea Robin made contact with a small convoy. Despite extremely heavy seas the Sea Dog attempted a surface approach on an anti-submarine vessel. However, the Jap vessel frustrated any possibility of success by radical course changes and, as the Sea Dog reached her firing position, turned toward the Sea Dog and opened fire with a 5" deck gun. The Sea Dog answered with a salvo of four torpedoes from her bow tubes that all missed. A planned follow-up with two from the stern tubes was cancelled because of the estimated shallow draft of the target, and not wishing to risk her gun crews on deck in such heavy weather, retired from the area.

Two days were spent on life guard duty in the middle of the month. We continued patrolling for another week, then headed for Guam to refuel for our return to Pearl Harbor.

One day our oldest Chief Petty Officer, Pappy Gale approached our Chief Pharmacist Mate and asked him if he had anything for his belly. He said it was burning and giving him a fit. The pharmacist asked him how many cups of coffee he drank each day. He replied, "I never really counted them, maybe 25 or 30." The next question: "How do you drink your coffee?" Answer: "Cream and sugar." The recommendation of the Pharmacist Mate (the senior medical man aboard) was: "Quit the use of cream and sugar and reduce the amount of coffee." Pappy followed his first set of instructions and quit the use of cream and sugar. However, he continued with his 25 or 30 cups of coffee every day. Within a couple of days, our Doc asked him how his belly was doing. "No more problems," answered Pappy.

During this patrol I developed a cyst on my tail bone that was very painful. Our Doc gave me drawing salve to apply in addition to hot packs. He told me that I would be transferred to the Submarine Tender Apollo (AS 25) for medical treatment when we stopped at Guam for fuel and supplies before proceeding on to Pearl Harbor. I naturally didn't want to leave my shipmates, so as painful as it was I really worked on the cyst and made it drain. I thought I was in the clear since it did drain, but Doc told me I should still have it taken out as it would probably fill up again. With much begging Doc allowed me stay on the Sea Dog and to this day I have not had any further trouble with it.

Early in the patrol heavy weather was reported. As I remember, that was putting it mildly. One day at Battle Stations on the surface where I was a lookout, we were in a very heavy storm. At one moment we would be on the crest of a giant swell, the next we would be skidding down into the trough. I asked the Officer of the Deck what he thought the height of the wave was from the trough. His answer was 90 feet. I remember the Captain at one time saying "Let's pull the plug (dive the submarine) and get out of here so we can have a decent meal." In diving to a depth of 165 feet we had a slow roll on the submarine because of the wave action on the surface. As I remember, this was the storm that caused two destroyers to capsize and sink with the loss of all hands.

We did take what the Captain later colorfully reported as "a big green one" through the conning tower hatch that knocked out some communications equipment for a while. There were several electronic and mechanical problems during the patrol but all quickly resolved.

During this patrol the crew felt they had found a personal friend in the form of a floating mine, affectionately dubbed "Old Faithful." First sighted while we were changing station on 30 December, the mine was exploded by 20mm gunfire. After witnessing the huge explosion it created the captain noticed - and recorded - an increased level of alertness among the lookouts. A week later, at almost the same spot, another single floating mine was spotted, looking in all respects exactly like the first. Again, the mine was destroyed, but two days later when passing through the area again, there was a mine bobbing on the waves. We destroyed each with our deck gun as we passed by, but even as we transited that area for the last time on 12 January "Old Faithful" seemingly was back on station waiting to be blown up - and she was, for the fourth (and I hope last) time.

Departing the patrol area on 21 January, we stopped over at Guam for mail and provisions, and proceeded to Pearl Harbor for refitting.

While Submarine Division 43 carried out the necessary repair work, the officers and crew enjoyed two weeks of luxury at the Royal Hawaiian Hotel. At the completion of the refit, Commander Earl T. Hydeman, USN, from Piqua, Ohio, relieved Commander Lowrance as CO. Also detached were: Lieutenant F.J. Doerfler, USNR, and Lieutenant (jg) S. Mandekic, USN; while Lieutenant William S. Brown, USN, Fort Benning, Georgia, reported aboard for duty as Communications Officer, and Ensign Edward W. Duckworth, USN, San Francisco, California, as Gunnery Officer.

The boat's history covers the two weeks of luxury at the Royal Hawaiian Hotel only in a brief statement, so back to "Paul Harvey" for the *rest of the story*:

It was great being at the Royal Hawaiian Hotel. The first thing we did was fill up the bathtub with *warm* water and take nice long soaks.

In taking over the hotel the Navy had tried to make it sailor proof. All of the good furniture had been removed and replaced with Navy two tier bunks. About the only things remaining in this concrete building that a sailor could destroy were the louvers in the mahogany doors that let the breeze from the Pacific Ocean come in. Many times when a sailor had too much to drink, he would demonstrate his strength by ripping the louvers from the doors - at a charge of a dollar a slat. This was quite a price to pay in those days.

I don't remember how many of us were in each room. I would say about six. I was lucky to be in the same room with Willie (my sea Daddy) and his torpedo men. The grounds around the Royal Hawaiian were beautiful as you might imagine. The beach looked beautiful, but the part that was under water was all coral and you had to pick your way carefully in order to reach a depth where you could swim.

The dining room was converted to a Navy style mess hall and we were served three meals a day. A Beer Garden on the beach served beer that was not laced with formaldehyde. As I remember, we were limited as to the amount we could consume at one time. But no headaches! We could also go to Honolulu for a couple of drinks. As in Midway, we always had some Gillie in one of the rooms for a real party. This was when the louvers in the doors would take the most abuse.

Willie would take me along on his trips to Hotel St. or one of the other locations that offered indoor sport. I believe they opened at 10:00 am and were closed on Sundays. One might assume that the girls needed this day off so that they could go to church and pray for their sins. Rumor was that Willie would be invited occasionally to the home of one of the girls for a sit down meal, but I never was.

At Pearl, our Chief of the Boat, Lahey, met up with one of his old shipmates who he had served with on the USS Flying Fish (SS229) early in the war. His name was Sheehan and he had been a Second Class Torpedoman. As I remember the story, Sheehan had some disciplinary problems on the Flying Fish and had been reduced in rate to Seaman. He had also been required to serve time at the naval prison at the Navy Yard in Portsmouth, and at present he was still on probation. He was either stationed at the base or on the submarine tender. At this time during the war there was a severe shortage of good seaman, especially men like Sheehan who could splice line and take care of the topside of a submarine. It would take a lot of the load off the back of Chief Lahey if he could enlist him into our crew.

Lahey approached our new Commanding Officer with a request to have Sheehan transferred to the Sea Dog. He approved the request of the Chief of the Boat, but, since Sheehan was still on probation, he told Chief Lahey *he* would be responsible for his conduct and would not hesitate in sending him back to prison should he get into trouble. Sheehan was a great shipmate and an asset to the crew. He had a lot of tattoos, one of which was the faces of twin babies on his back, one crying and the other laughing. There must have been some personal significance to it but if I knew about it at the time I don't remember it now.

The crew was somewhat saddened to lose our first Captain who was loved by everyone in our crew. Commander Lowrance advanced rapidly in his Navy career and retired from the Navy as a Vice Admiral (3 Star). I will have more to say of him later.

Captain Hydeman was a more stern man than Lowrance, but after a couple of patrols with him, we felt the same way about him.

I was promoted to Motor Machinist's Mate Third Class on 7 Feb 1945, two days after our arrival at Pearl Harbor from our second War Patrol and was no longer a Fireman.

Author at Midway June 1945

3rd War Patrol - Leaving Pearl Harbor 11 March 1945

We spent about 20 days in training exercises around Pearl Harbor, then with Barber's Point Light off our starboard beam put out to sea on our third patrol, with Commander Hydeman now as our CO.

This patrol was to the vicinity of Tokyo Bay on the east side of Kyushu, the largest of the Japanese home islands. We were out for 49 days of which 29 were in the assigned area. For part of the time we were part of - and led - another three-vessel attack group, *Earl's Eliminators* that included the Trigger and the Threadfin.

Most of the time was spent on life-guard duty for about 20 bombing missions targeting Tokyo that took place during our time in the area. Our service proved to be of great value to Lt. (jg) Robert Hill when we recovered him after his fighter plane had been forced to ditch due to flak damage. He was a pleasant and enjoyable addition - and I think I can add, grateful to our crew for the month he was on board.

Four contacts with enemy vessels were made, and three developed into attacks.

The first was a submerged attack on a Japanese I-1 Class sub late in the afternoon of 29 March. The Jap sub had been patrolling the same area we were and had surfaced before full darkness, but was able to submerge quickly enough to avoid our torpedo spread.

The next was a submerged approach to a DM-7 Class minelayer, but we think because of her shallow draft our torpedoes missed by passing beneath her.

The third was also submerged, since in daylight, against a freighter being escorted by an AM-13 Class minelayer. Two hits were made and the freighter rolled and sank in less than a minute. An attempt was then made on the escort, but it had closed the distance so quickly in counter-attacking us that it wasn't possible to develop firing control data and at 300 yards with the vessel bearing down and throwing depth charges we opted to *skedaddle*, which translates today as, "Got out of Dodge." An attempt was made to line up a stern shot, but the escort's approach speed was too great to allow it. Fortunately the depth-charging was some distance off and the vessel never got a location on us.

As on the previous patrol we also exploded or sank several floating mines. Several this time failed to explode upon being hit - possibly dummies, cheaper, but requiring the same respect as the real thing.

Nearing the close of the patrol, on the 19th, a ship was sighted that would have been a worthwhile target, but we were never able to close with it. Later in the day the weather deteriorated rapidly and we were forced to submerge to ride out a typhoon.

On 25 April we departed for Guam with our score for the trip One Freighter (engines aft) at 6670 tons, sunk, and one aviator .08 tons rescued.

As a result of being credited for the sinking a star was added to the Submarine Combat Insignia that had been authorized for all hands following our first patrol. The CO, in addition, was awarded the Bronze Star Medal for "meritorious service in the face of the enemy."

We arrived at Apra Harbor, Guam, on 27 April for refitting. The crew and officers, including our guest, spent two weeks at Camp Dealy, the submarine rest camp. Camp Dealy was a much better camp than the one on Midway. It was located in the jungle with access to a nice beach nearby. The Sea Dog was moored alongside the submarine tender Apollo, about four miles from the rest camp. If we needed dental work, haircuts, clothes, etc. a truck would take us to the tender. We were cautioned to stay inside the bounds of the camp. There were still Japanese under arms on the island - in fact the last one to surrender was in 1972.

A few weeks before our arrival the Sea Fox (SS402) had pulled in for a stay at Dealy. Seven of the crewmembers apparently took it in mind to do some Jap-hunting. They armed themselves from the boat, obtained the services of a local guide, and proceeded beyond the safety zone into the jungle in search of un-captured Japanese soldiers. The party was ambushed and five of the crew and the guide killed. The two remaining were badly wounded but managed to escape. As we were told, the group was made up of the Chief MOMM and members of his engine room detail. Seemingly this would have been a serious problem for the Sea Fox on its next patrol with the shortage of engine room personnel.

The official report of the story has it that the group was *souvenir* hunting - although strictly forbidden - at the time, but confirms the ambush and casualties.

Camp Dealy was named after Samuel D. Dealy, who had been the Commanding Officer of the USS Harder (SS257). The Harder was lost with all hands on her seventh War Patrol. Sam Dealy was awarded the Medal of Honor posthumously.

While out on patrol, a lot of gambling went on to pass the idle time off watch. The only other options were sleeping and reading - or letter writing, but there was no urgency for that as the letters weren't going anywhere for some time.

After a few days out a shipmate named Wilson (a 1st Class Petty Officer) had been cleaned out and knowing I always had a few bucks on hand hit me up for a loan of $20. That was a sizable amount in those days, but I *knew* when we came back to shore and collected our back-pay he'd be good for it. And if we didn't make it back, well, it wouldn't matter much anyway.

We received our backed up mail, and chow that included fresh fruit and ice cream. The paymaster from the Apollo came aboard and we received our pay for about two months. Wilson was not in line for his money - supposedly had checked into sick bay.

Later in the day a poker game got under way at the rest camp, and with all the cash available the stakes rose quickly. Wilson, recovered enough to attend but not now to be paid until the next day, put the arm on me again for another loan, this time for $100 so he could get into the game. I didn't see it as a problem - I was young - and thought I would certainly get it all back when he was paid the next morning.

I was at the beach with the rest of the crew the next day when Wilson appeared. He immediately got into the card game still in progress from the night before, and lost his shirt in no time. Fool that I was, I still thought he'd be good for it at the end of our next patrol.

A few days after we left Guam, good old Wilson came down with pneumonia. Apparently at least this sick call visit was on the level.

But I never got paid back the $120. He must have forgotten the name of the boat I was on.

There was in interesting sidelight to the story. On our 4th patrol we had a photographer on board, and as it turned out he filmed the sequence of Wilson being transferred to a destroyer in a whaleboat. Recently a submariner friend of mine came by the house and told me he had found a piece of film on the Internet that he wanted me to see, and I immediately recognized the scene of my former shipmate being ferried away. I could not withhold the comment that, "The sonofabitch still owes me $120.00!"

The day we fished Lieutenant Hill out of the drink, I was once again a battle lookout. I had never seen so many planes in the sky. In reading Laura Hillenbrand's book, *Unbroken*, about Louie Zamperini's ordeal in the Japanese P.O.W. Camp (Omori), Louie mentions some of the raids he saw about this time in that area. He talks about over 200 B29s at a time carrying incendiary bombs to be dropped on the industrial districts, and as many as fifteen hundred American planes - and several hundred Japanese – in the air over their camp on 16 Feb 1945.

According to the members of the rescue party that recovered Hill from his raft, his first comment on placing his feet on deck was, "Another goddam submarine!" They thought we had a very ungrateful survivor, but we later found out this was his second rescue, the first also by a submarine that had received a severe depth charge attack while Lt. Hill was aboard. Hill turned out to be a great guy and was well liked by the crew.

A lot of new special equipment had been installed for our next patrol, and we were not told too much about it or the location of the patrol. It turned out to be newly developed mine detecting equipment. After testing the equipment in dummy mine fields at Guam, we knew we were going to an area that was heavily mined. Some members of our crew requested a transfer, but I don't remember any being approved.

US Naval Base Pearl Harbor c.1941

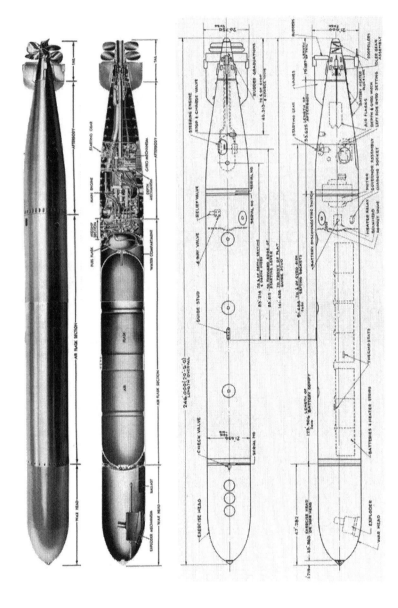

Primary armament: Problematic early Mk 14 Torpedo above, Later Mk 18 below

Sea Dog Crew at midway

Crew departing Midway for Sea of Japan

4th War Patrol - Leaving Guam 27 May 1945

On our fourth patrol the Sea Dog was designated as the flagship of a pack of nine submarines assigned to penetrate the Sea of Japan. The CO of the Sea Dog, Commander Hydeman, was in overall command of the group. The mission was code-named *Operation Barney* after Commander William Bernard "Barney" Sieglaff, who, under the direction of Admiral ("Uncle Charlie") Lockwood had put the operation together.

This was to be an assault on Japan's last relatively secure connection to the Asian mainland through which it was able to continue to receive materials necessary to carry on the war. The Sea of Japan is longer than wide and allowed communication with a large part of coastal China and Korea, and its entrances narrow allowing it to be strongly defended with mines. In the early days of the war England, also an island nation, had nearly been brought to her knees when her supply lines were nearly severed by German U Boats. Now the strategy would be applied to Japan.

Penetration of the minefields to gain entrance and disrupt if not completely halt the flow of materials to the home islands was expected to be a major stroke toward ending the war.

As we would learn in August, there was a *Plan B* that would remain a closely guarded secret until the day of its execution and would quickly end the war with Japan. But until then it was *business as usual* for the fighting forces.

For tactical reasons the nine boats were divided into groups of three. Within the pack - designated as *Hydeman's Hellcats* (we were later also called the "Mighty Mine Dodgers") - were *Hydeman's Hepcats* consisting of the Sea Dog, Spadefish, and Crevalle, *Pierce's Polecats* that included the Tunny, Skate, and Bonefish, and *Bob's Bobcats*: the Flying Fish, Tinosa, and Bowfin.

This nine submarine wolf pack, passing through the minefields into the Sea of Japan at Tsushima Strait, was the most successful wolf pack operation conducted by American submarines, during World

War II. In a period of less than 30 days, 31 ships and 16 small craft were sunk totaling 108,000 tons, and one submarine, the I-122. Additionally a Soviet freighter of 11,000 tons was sunk in a friendly fire incident by the Spadefish on 13 June.

Seadog led in the score column with a total of six ships sunk, five freighters and one tanker for a total of 29,500 tons. One boat, Commander Lawrence Edge's Bonefish, was lost.

As we entered the western channel of Tsushima Strait the current pushing from astern gave us a three-knot speed of advance. It also tended to crab the boat sideways and force it off course so the helmsman had his hands full holding her steady.

At Guam we had been outfitted with a new FM Sonar device that had been installed on the USS Seahorse. The Seahorse had sustained significant damage on her previous patrol and was considered unseaworthy. Her equipment was transferred to the Sea Dog. On detecting a mine the system would display it on a CRT screen and simultaneously trigger an audible alarm with a bell-sound that was referred to as *Hell's Bells*. Hearing that, the boat would be backed off and its course adjusted to evade the mine. But the system proved very temperamental and was out of action on some boats as often as it was in. During the passage of the strait we never heard the signal, which left us wondering if there had been none or if the system had been down the whole time.

As we would learn later, our radar was proving to be equally troublesome at the same time. With our electronics in a state of unreliability, the Sea Dog fell in behind the Crevalle which became our seeing-eye dog for the passage. With our radar systems down we were not only blind but partially deaf. The radar was used in addition to detection for secure communications with other members of the pack using signal pulses in Morse code.

Luck favored both of us and we both passed through with no encounters - and found that the FM Sonar had in fact been operational. There had apparently been no mines along our course.

In the aft engine room on the day we entered the Strait we heard a noise from forward port, and as we proceeded all eyes followed the scraping sound as it tracked down the port side until it cleared the stern and ceased. We took this to have been a mine cable and assumed we were deep enough not to have pulled it down on us. As the official report states there was no contact with mines, the answer to the mystery can never be known. But several of us heard it.

Captain Hydeman ordered the men not on watch to remain in their bunks to conserve oxygen as he expected our submerged run to take at least 16 hours. Not until then could we surface and run our diesel engines to recharge our batteries and draw fresh air into the boat.

The plan was for one group of three boats to enter the Sea of Japan on each of three consecutive days. Our group being the first to enter was required to wait three days before engaging any Japanese shipping so as not to alert the Japanese of the attempted penetration until all the boats were on station and could make concerted attacks on the same day. The planners, Admiral Lockwood and Barney Sieglaff expected the concerted attack to be the most productive in terms of kills due to the surprise while effectively magnifying the apparent size of our force.

At this point I am inserting the following account of Operation Barney as it provides details that are important to the story, but that we of the crew had little knowledge of at the time:

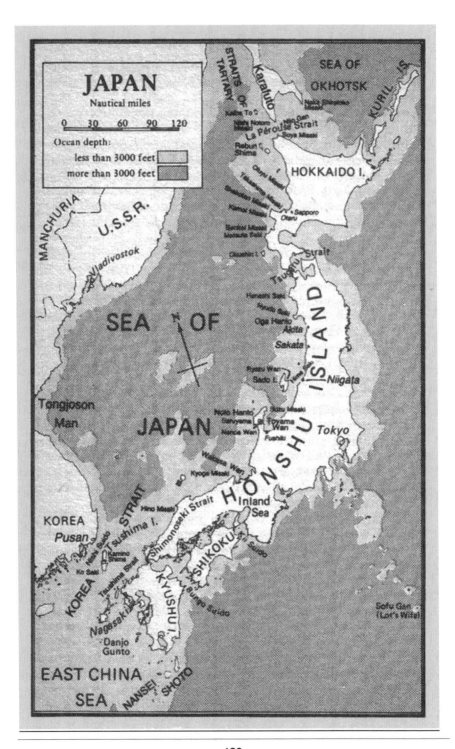

Operation Barney

Months before the Pacific Fleet dropped anchor in Tokyo Bay, US submarines had achieved the goal that had eluded Germany's U-boats in both world wars – the neutralizing of the merchant marine upon which an island enemy depended upon for its very survival.

The submarine force's success appears all the more remarkable in that it began the struggle with a highly flawed weapon, the infamous Mk-14 torpedo. Added to this problem was the fact that the Bureau of Ordinance insisted there was nothing wrong with its torpedoes and blamed the users for the problems. Twenty-one months into the war the problems were finally solved by the submariners themselves.

Two other events contributed to the lethality of the underwater offensive; the cracking of the Japanese Maru Code, and the fleet being supplied with newly developed search radar. While these developments greatly enhanced the US attacks on Japanese shipping, the enemy's provision for the defense of trade remained rudimentary. It was not until November of 1943 when the Japanese developed the Combined Escort Fleet that a serious attempt to protect their merchant ships against attacks by American submarines was begun.

The payoff came in 1944 when nearly 3 million tons of shipping was destroyed, and existing convoy routes cleared of potential targets. Only one potentially productive target area remained – the Sea of Japan. The area had been penetrated as early as the fall of 1943, but it was declared off limits after the Wahoo, commanded by submarine legend "Mush" Morton, was lost trying to exit through the La Perouse Strait in October. Admiral Lockwood was convinced that these early forays into the Sea of Japan had alerted the Japanese Navy and prompted them to heavily mine the entrances. Further operations were precluded until a means of dealing with the minefields was devised. In late 1944 Lockwood thought he had the means at hand in the form of Frequency Modulated Sonar (FMS). Originally designed for use by minesweepers, FMS displayed the mine locations on a screen, and in the event of contact rang an audible warning that submariners named "Hell's Bells."

The first boat to employ FMS was the Tinosa. Following a successful patrol, Lockwood set his staff to planning for a thrust into "Hirohito's Lake." Commander Barney Sieglaff was given operational control. Sieglaff had formerly commanded the boats Tautog and Tench and had collectively sunk 14 ships in the course of seven patrols. The operation would bear his name.

With Hell's Bells pealing on every boat the Hellcats made their way through the minefields blocking the Tsushima Strait, the southernmost of the three entrances, according to the plan for three on 6 June and three on each of the next two days.

Once in the target area they discovered a submariner's dream; unescorted merchantmen steering straight courses with running lights aglow. Skippers were sorely tempted to disregard their instructions to delay attacks until sunset on 9 June (the extra day to insure all boats were on station), but discipline prevailed.

Following the plan, the remaining boats exited under cover of darkness through La Perouse Strait on 24 June. Elated by the overall result, although greatly saddened by the loss of the Bonefish and her crew, Lockwood promptly dispatched seven more boats into the area, and six of those were still on station on VJ Day.

Lockwood saw the operation's real objective as psychological rather than material - to convince the Japanese that having lost control of the Sea of Japan, their last avenue to the resources of the outside world, further resistance would be futile. He would not have been made aware beforehand of the two atomic bombs that would force the surrender before the effects of economic isolation had been realized.

Because of the great contribution the submarines of the Pacific and Southwest Pacific to the victory, Fleet Admiral Nimitz arranged for "Uncle Charlie: Lockwood to be seated in the front row at the surrender ceremony on the deck of the battleship Missouri.

(I have had the above account in my file for many years, but regrettably its source is not indicated.)

The following old clippings were also saved but with identifying information cut away except date of 7 July (1945). Note mention of only eight boats as the loss of Bonefish would have remained classified as of the time of publication.

American U-Boat Flotilla Lay Under Sea Of Japan, Knocked Off Ships Passing By

(EDITOR'S NOTE: The following story was written several weeks ago and just released by the Navy from censorship. It describes the perils and success of one of the many valiant U. S. submarine operations which helped to make V-J Day inevitable.)

By LAURIE JOHNSTON

Eight young submarine commanders just back from invading the "Emperor's backyard"—the Sea of Japan, between the Jap home islands and the continent of Asia—agreed at Pearl Harbor that it will take "a lot of whittling away" to sink the remaining Jap shipping because the days of bagging big enemy vessels were over.

In an unprecedented press conference the eight undersea skippers and Vice Adm. Charles A. Lockwood Jr., "boss" of Pacific submarine operations, described the unique combat mission into the waters behind Japan, aimed at traffic between the home islands and Korea and Manchuria.

The result was 30 ships sunk by American torpedoes and 20 by gunfire. But, as Adm. Lockwood put it, "it was not just a question of knocking off a few ships, but of cutting off the flow of rice, munitions, oil and other war materials—to make it easier for the lads who eventually will be going ashore in landing boats. Saving American lives is the main thing we're thinking of."

It was the first American penetration of the Sea of Japan since about two years ago, when a volunteer submarine patrol went in mainly for "nuisance" and observation purposes.

That the present mission wasn't easy was indicated by Adm. Lockwood when he described it as "one of the most daring deeds of the war" and commented, "Playing in enemy waters is not recommended for retaining your health."

The skippers themselves were unanimous in their warm praise for

Adm. Lockwood's part in the special training and plans which preceded the mission. He was turned down six times on his request to go with it himself. But the men said their own lurking doubts about whether they would come back were quieted by the admiral's confidence.

Commenting on the secrecy and the lack of public acclaim which has surrounded submarine activities until recently, Cmdr. Everett H. Steinmetz, USN, said, "We felt kind of lonely up there under the Japan sea, and we wondered how the hell we were going to get out of there. Those personal dispatches that kept coming through from the admiral were just like a shot in the arm."

Most of the ships sunk by the patrol were freighters.

One Jap submarine was included in the haul. "We got him when he came across our bow," said Cmdr. Richard B. Lynch, USN, of Citronella, Ala. "He was a set up."

Japs' Ships Small

Most of the vessels sunk were small freighters, ranging from 500 to 2,500 tons, and most of them were also old and frequently coal-burning, the skippers reported. On the other hand, they said, they also encountered a lot of new steel-construction small freighters, sometimes armed and built to the same design in varying sizes from 800 to 2,300 tons.

"The Japs appear to be concentrating on small ships," said Cmdr. Richard C. Latham, USN, 34, of New London, Conn., "so that when a ship is sunk its loss is not so serious. Small ships are also suited to the short-haul traffic to Korea and Manchuria, as compared with the long-haul traffic to the Dutch East Indies and such places early in the war."

The latest official figure on the remaining Jap shipping was 1,-500,000 tons, Adm. Lockwood said, "and we figured a large percentage of it must be running in that area."

Shipping Bottled Up

Actually, there was less shipping encountered than had been expected, and the men said they assumed it had been "bottled up" after they sank their first ships. The result was that some of the submarines went into harbors and close to shorelines looking for quarry.

Cmdr. Robert D. Risser, USN, 35, of Charlton, Ia., said he was submerged near a breakwater when a tug with two barges in tow was sighted through the periscope, coming straight for his sub-

marine. "We didn't want to be detected there, so we let him alone, but we took a look and found the barges were loaded with boulders.

"Apparently they were going to build a new breakwater, and it looked for awhile as if they were going to build it on top of me."

Backed Off Beach

Probably closest of all to the Jap mainland was Cmdr. Earl T. Hydeman, USN, 34, of Piqua, O. "We had just sunk a good-sized ship when we had to submerge in a hurry. It turned out to be such shallow water and so close to shore that we had to back off the beach while on the bottom."

"It was foggy about 75 per cent of the time," reported Cmdr. Alexander K. Tyree, USN, 29, of Danville, Va., "and it would lift at the most unpredictable and inopportune moments."

Trailed by Destroyers

One such experience was described by Cmdr. Latham, who said his submarine started a submerged action against a Jap ship and then lost track of it in the fog. Since visibility was so bad, it seemed safe to surface—but just as the guns were manned to continue the attack, the fog suddenly lifted. "The rest of the action, a seven-mile chase which lasted a half hour, was completed in clear sunlight. We expected to be discovered any minute."

Cmdr. Steinmetz said that, while operating near a "fair-sized" Jap naval base, his submarine met considerable opposition from destroyers, destroyer escorts and frigates, which caused him and dropped depth charges.

Almost no aerial opposition was met, the commanders said, and most of the planes which were seen were old. "We had only two plane contacts during the whole operation," said Cmdr. Pierce. "One was something like a Piper Cub. It waved at us, and we waved at it, and then it went away."

..., July 7. (Delayed).—The Sea of Japan no longer has a "private property" sign on it. It is now part of the extensive hunting grounds of United States submarines.

Commanders of eight U. S. submarines related today how they took their vessels into more than a dozen ports of Japan and Korea, sank at least 50 vessels and roamed the Japan sea almost without opposition.

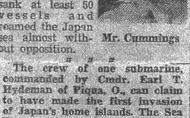

Mr. Cummings

# # #

The crew of one submarine, commanded by Cmdr. Earl T. Hydeman of Piqua, O., can claim to have made the first invasion of Japan's home islands. The Sea Dog went aground on the Honshu coast while submerged and had to back off the beach.

# # #

The eight submarine commanders besides Cmdr. Hydeman, all of whose ships have returned into the Japan sea, were Cmdr. Alexander K. Tyree of Danville, Va., in charge of the Bowfin; Cmdr. Everett H. Steinmetz of Rockville Center, N. Y., in the Crevalle; Cmdr. William Germershausen of Groton, Conn., in the Spadefish; Cmdr. Robert D. Risser of Chariton, Ia., in the Flying

Wreak Havoc In ...my's Front Yard

Fish; Cmdr. George E. Pierce of Kansas City, Mo., in the Tunny; Cmdr. Richard B. Lynch of Citronella, Ala., in the Skate, and Cmdr. Richard C. Latham of New London, Conn., in the Tinosa.

All of the sub skippers agreed that Japan is apparently in desperate straits for shipping. Only one or two of the submarines found any new type merchantmen. Most of the ships were old and battered and none of them was over 5,000 tons.

# # #

Vice Admiral Charles A. Lockwood Jr., commander of submarines Pacific, told correspondents that although our subs first went into the Sea of Japan two years ago on reconnaissance, the eight commanders were among the first to seek combat in Japan's hitherto closed sea.

I heard the Bonefish being depth-charged. The commanding officer, Lawrence Edge, had observed some ships in his area entering a harbor. He requested permission from Captain Hydeman - who was in overall command - to pursue them. That afternoon we were watching a movie in the aft torpedo room and heard sounds of an apparent depth charge attack and assumed from the direction that it was against the Bonefish. Some joking remarks were made - gallows humor - but it wasn't taken too seriously. We had no way of knowing that it caused the loss of the boat.

As noted, the Sea Dog sunk six Japanese ships on this patrol. A couple of attacks remain as vivid recollections:

The first - and our first sinking on this patrol - was on 9 June at 2000 hours (8:00 PM). On surfacing among the life boats only three minutes later we made contact with a second ship, a heavily loaded tanker of about 10,500 tons. On the surface, my battle station was that of lookout and I had a front row set to what followed. It was a thrill to mark the hit of our first torpedo on the tanker. A second pass was made with another hit just forward of amidships. A tremendous explosion showed the foremast toppling and the bow breaking away. Both sections quickly sank leaving only the light of burning oil slick and the lights of the city of Niigata that could be seen in the background. In the silence following the disappearance of the ship beneath the surface I suddenly became aware of my knees violently shaking.

On 19 June at 0559 we were patrolling submerged about four miles south of Kamui Misaki on the west coast of Hokkaido. Three freighters were spotted in the haze at 4000 yards, heading toward us. We fired our bow tubes when the range had closed to 600 yards but only hit the first vessel which began sinking by the stern. The crew quickly abandoned ship. While observing the sinking a low flying plane was spotted diving toward us. We quickly went to greater depth to avoid bombs but due to the relatively short distance from shore hit bottom at 116 feet. Sitting there with the beach to starboard, ahead of, and beneath us, and a sinking ship to port, the only choice was to back out to gain sufficient room to turn.

Backing for a considerable distance while submerged is a very difficult maneuver, but it was skillfully accomplished by the Diving Officer (who was also the Engineering Officer) Lt. E.M. Hindert. We cleared the area with damage only to one of our sound heads.

While Hindert is fully deserving of the credit granted to him, the two men operating the bow and stern diving planes should have been cited as well for their part in the operation.

When this incident was released to the press, they reported us - unofficially - as making the first landing in the invasion of the home islands of Japan.

Captain Hydeman had the responsibility for selecting our exit route for the planned return to Pearl Harbor on the 24th. Tsushima Strait, to the south and where we had entered, was not a good choice as we would be running against the three knot current. La Perouse Strait to the north was the other option, but also mined, and with a depth of only 160 feet, too shallow to run below the mines. But surface ships (we believed neutral Russian) had been passing through, so Hydeman decided to form up in two columns and on 22 June and prepared to make a surface dash from the Sea of Japan into the Sea of Okhotsk. Since the strait was mined, all the watertight doors between compartments were dogged shut so that damage from an exploding mine to one section of the hull would be isolated and men elsewhere would have a chance of survival.

The strong eastward current increased the speed of our escape, and we think also tended to pull the mines deeper by drawing them away from their anchors and causing them to arc downward.

As we reached the time for departure radio messages were sent out to the Bonefish, but with no replies. The feeling was growing that she was gone. Hydeman waited until 0300 - as long as he dared so not to lose the cover of night - and ordered the remaining eight boats to get under way.

On the way through we encountered a large surface ship that signaled to us. We flashed something unintelligible back and continued on our way. As I remember the fog was so thick that evening I couldn't see the bow from my watch station.

Captain Pierce, Edge's group commander, requested permission to remain behind in the Sea of Okhotsk to render assistance if needed, and he was authorized to remain for no longer than two days before starting back to Pearl Harbor.

We stopped at Midway on 30 June and stayed one night to refuel and have some repair work done, then continued on our way.

The Submarine Combat Badge was authorized for all crewmembers on the patrol. For those of us on the Sea Dog since the first War Patrol this would mean a second star added to the badge we had previously earned. For "extraordinary heroism in action," Commander E.T. Hydeman, USN, was awarded the Navy Cross. For "gallantry and intrepidity in action against the enemy," Lt. K.B. Reed, USNR, Lt. J.R. Lynch, USN, Lt. (jg) W.B. Argo, USNR, A.P. Dell, Chief Torpedoman's Mate, USN, and G.A. Grossman, Motorman's Machinist Mate 1st Class, USN, were awarded the Bronze Star.

We arrived back at Pearl Harbor in two separate groups on 4 and 5 July to a tumultuous welcome. Admiral Nimitz, a submariner himself, was there to shake hands with the members of the Hellcat crews - officer hands maybe; somehow he missed mine. Lockwood and the COMSUBPAC staff turned out as a group to meet us at the piers. Lockwood had even managed to round up a group of good looking nurses - well, maybe not all *good looking*, but they sure were looking good - to join in the homecoming festivities that included a Navy band playing "Anchors Aweigh," and several popular numbers.

Lockwood held a meeting in the sub base auditorium that he filled with officers of the sub force. Barney Sieglaff introduced Hellcat skippers. Each told his story of the patrol, and repeated it at a press conference that followed.

After the formal meeting, Lockwood hosted a dinner dance for the skippers (and saw to it that each had a female companion). We enlisted men from the Hellcat boats made do with the beer and booze available on Hotel Street. As for female companionship, we probably had the most fun. I never got any closer to the nurses than I did to Nimitz's handshake, but to be fair, it would have been over 600 handshakes, and there was no chance of coming up with 600 nurses.

It was great to be back safely from a successful War Patrol, but the most important thing was the mail from home, especially now that the war was over in Europe, and to learn that my brother, in General Patton's Third Army, had survived the war. I also looked forward to the letters I received from a couple of girls I knew.

However I also received the sad news that my grandmother - who had lived with us prior to my enlisting - had passed away. I had been looking forward to a visit with her when I came home. My mother always said it was her prayers that had brought Jack and me home safely.

With the festivities at the base over, we could enjoy a two week rest at the Royal Hawaiian Hotel. As I scratch my brain about what occurred during our second stay there, I can only remember it as a repetition of our earlier stay.

We returned to the Sea Dog for ten days of training in and out of port. This refresher was very important, especially for the new members of our crew that had come on board between patrols. Before leaving on our 5th patrol we loaded our torpedoes and ammunition for our deck guns, topped off our fuel tanks, and loaded our food stores. Every nook and cranny was filled; 5 gallon cans of ground coffee would be stored outboard of the main engines in the engine rooms. Occasionally a can would be punctured and allow a small amount of diesel oil to get in. What a flavor! No wonder our old Chief who drank 25-30 cups of coffee each day (or so it seemed - he was never without a cup in his hand) had a problem with his insides. Cases of canned goods would be stored in our store rooms and on the walking deck of the sleeping quarters until we ate enough to recover the space. Bags of potatoes were stored in our two shower stalls, and, yep, no showers until we had room to move them elsewhere.

Rear Admiral Lockwood above left; right, Spadefish returns. Below, Lockwood greets returning Hellcat officers at Pearl Harbor on 4 July 1945 below, Barney Sieglaff center with sunglasses.

On August 13 we departed Pearl Harbor accompanied by the USS Flying Fish. The next day we received orders to not to fire, and at 0215 on the morning of August 15 to reverse course and return to Pearl Harbor. Making full speed on all 4 main engines, on the afternoon of 16 August, the Sea Dog once again was moored at the Submarine Base, Pearl Harbor, and our war had ended.

If what we were told is correct there was quite a drunken party at the base on the night of the 14th, "VJ Day." We heard that the Commanding Officer's jeep had been found in the swimming pool. Presumably because of that security was tightened and we weren't able to celebrate VJ (Victory over Japan) day as we might have liked. However, the beer garden on the base opened at about 1600 hrs. (4 PM) and if we were not in the duty section could drink beer until the effects began to show and we were cut off. Later in the evening - in darkness - there was a little party on deck near the after engine room hatch *fueled* by a little torpedo alcohol. I had to say it.

Even though the war was over we continued light training operations for the remainder of the month of August. This perhaps "just in case," but I think more just to keep us occupied. "The devil finds work for idle *hands!*" Many submarines and surface ships were ordered back to stateside ports for big celebrations and we felt we were left out - which we were.

At the end of the month we were ordered to the Philippines to be part of a holding force there. We departed for Subic Bay on 6 September in company with the USS Redfish, USS Scabardfish, and USS Sea Fox as a group referred to as *Hydeman's What-The-Hellcats.* Many of the veteran crewmembers had been transferred back to the States at the end of the war so the long trip to the PI - that included a stop at Guam on 18 September for fuel, supplies, and mail - was used extensively for training new personnel

One of the crew members heading back to the States before we got underway told me a story that I think is worth retelling here.

Lamar Wright came from Arkansas was known as *Traveler* (naturally). He was a Motor Machinist Mate 1st class in the forward engine room and I was his oiler. I enjoyed standing watch with him.

He let me do everything in the engine room. I learned a lot working for him and he treated me very well. To some it might appear it may have been from laziness on his part, but in reality it is the best way to educate a trainee - a lesson that would serve me well in the future. Although Traveler never gave the impression of being a *bullshit artist*, he once told me this sea story that I had difficulty believing. But, after the war I came across the same story in a military magazine, so will share it:

Early in WWII Traveler had served on the submarine USS Thresher, (SS200). On their 10th War Patrol they were submerged outside the Japanese naval base on the island of Truk. The water is so clear there that an airplane can sometimes see a submerged submarine at a depth of 150 ft. The Thresher apparently was spotted and a ship of some kind equipped with a large grapnel hook was sent from the base to drag the area in an attempt to snag the boat. At this time submarines had screw (propeller) guards installed to protect the screws when docking but could be snagged by the hook.

Traveler said they could hear the noise from the cable or chain as it was dragged over the Thresher, and the grapnel caught in one of the guards. With the use of its winch, the Japanese ship slowly pulled the boat toward the surface. The crew members on watch in the control room could watch the depth gauge and see that the Thresher was going up.

The Captain ordered maxim power to the screws and shifted his rudder from full left to full right and back, with the hope of breaking the chain or cable attached to the Thresher.

Traveler told me men were saying their prayers, afraid the Japs would be sending a depth charge down the cable. As a last resort, the Thresher took the maximum amount of sea water into her trim tanks to make the boat as heavy as possible and in doing so finally broke the cable. But now with a down angle, full speed on the screws, and in a heavy condition, they were in a perilous situation and heading rapidly for the bottom. Before they regained control they had far exceeded their test depth. On returning to their base, the screw guards were removed from the Thresher - and all of our other submarines.

Ed. Note: The Thresher mentioned above was not the vessel of the famous sinking many years later. This boat was the SS-200, and had a long career in the war having sailed on 14 War Patrols. She was decommissioned at the end of 1945, re-commissioned briefly but found to be no longer seaworthy, and scrapped in 1948. The Thresher of the later disaster was the SSN (Nuclear)-563 commissioned in Portsmouth on August 3, 1961 and lost with all aboard during deep-diving trials off Cape Cod in April of 1963.

On the way to Subic Bay in the Philippines we continued to operate as in wartime conditions. It remained a possibility that we could make contact with enemy forces that might not know the war was over - or might be unwilling to accept the fact. For most of the trip we traveled on the surface. We had to keep a sharp eye out for floating mines that had parted from their anchors during recent typhoons in the Western Pacific.

At the time I don't think I realized what a great experience visiting the Philippines would be. While at Subic Bay I was advanced to M.O.M.M. 2nd Class. My basic pay went to $96.00 per month plus 50% submarine pay and 20% sea pay for a total of $172.80 per month. I am sure this was more money than my father made at this time. Some of the old timers in the Navy would say Second Class Petty Officer is the best rate in the Navy. Not too much responsibility, but senior enough to avoid the *shit* jobs.

Life was good during the months we spent in the Philippines. Our routine was as follows:

Week one, (Monday-Friday, weekend off) in daily operations we would get underway at 0800 hours for our operating area where we would dive and surface the submarine and conduct drills both on the surface and submerged. We would usually be back to the base at 1600 hours (4 P.M.) Providing we were not in the duty section, we were free to drink beer at the beer garden or participate in whatever sport activities were in progress at the time.

Our second week was a week of upkeep when we did our routine maintenance on the Sea Dog. Although this was a work week we were on *tropical* working hours, 7 am to 12 am. The Navy at some point realized because of the extreme heat of the Tropics, it was better for the crew and more could be accomplished by working only in the morning hours with the hot afternoons off. So with tropical working hours established, more time to drink beer and enjoy life in the tropics.

Week three was strictly recreational. After a quick cleanup of the submarine, a truck would take us up the mountain about a mile away, where there was a river. This was our recreation area. We had a softball field and the river had a small dam built into it so it was great for swimming. There were also grills in place that our cooks barbequed our meals on. All of the food was from Sea Dog stores.

After a few beers, a softball game, barbecue, a few more beers, and - should we have enough strength to participate - another *sport* could follow. We could hike down the mountain to where the river emptied into Subic Bay. Tents were set up there by some of the local working girls from Pom-Pom Island and Subic City for *indoor activities.*

I can't remember at this time how many submarines were in the "holding force" at Subic Bay. I do recall that each submarine was using an LCVP (landing craft vehicle personnel) boat. These landing craft were 36' long with a ramp on the bow that would be opened when landing on the beach to discharge troops or vehicles. Many of these landing craft had been used by the American forces liberating Luzon.

Olongapo was the name of the naval base at Subic Bay. Before WWII it was the command center for submarines in the Asiatic Fleet, and a destroyer base. At the time we were stationed there a number of the LCVPs were tied up in a nest nearby - possibly over 100. This was where we procured (liberated: stole) our own LCVP in the middle of the night. No one seemed upset about it. I am quite sure our Captain knew the boat was unauthorized, however he thought it could be put to good use during our recreation week for fishing parties. Yes, we did use it for fishing parties, but the greatest use of the boat came after dark making trips to Pom-Pom Island and

Subic City where we could drink *tuba* (the local drink of fermented coconut milk) and engage in - indoor sports.

At this point I return briefly to my shipmate Sheehan who you may remember we picked up in Pearl Harbor after our second War Patrol. Sheehan had been on probation from the Naval Prison at Portsmouth. He had been informed by our Captain that should he foul up he would send him back to prison at the drop of hat. Sheehan was a great shipmate at sea and well-liked by the crew, but he had a few problems at Subic Bay. The Captain was going to hold a "Captain's Mast" on him, and Sheehan felt quite sure he would be heading back to prison. So he jumped ship (went over the hill) and was now missing.

Stay tuned.

As we entered Manila Bay which is a very big area, I was lucky enough to be topside on deck and to see the masts of so many sunken ships. I overheard one of our old Chiefs say, "There's going to be a lot of money made here." I asked the Chief what he meant. He said all of these ships would have to be cleared out of the harbor and if it was not done by a salvage company, the Navy would do it and the divers would make a bundle. Having read a few books on deep sea diving, I listened to the Chief with great interest and filed the information in the back of my mind. Little did I know then that I would become a Deep Sea Diver later in my Navy career. For the short period of time we were in the Philippines we only visited the city of Manila about three times during which the following events occurred but I'd be hard pressed to separate them after all these years.

Manila welcomed us with open arms. The local ladies enjoyed being wined and dined by American sailors. Many of these *ladies* were prostitutes, and many of them in the profession to earn money to feed their families. Other women were just out to dance with the servicemen and have a good time. I met a lady and enjoyed her company on my first visit. She used an oily type dressing for her hair that was in short supply and asked me if we would have anything suitable on the submarine. Our Pharmacist's Mate provided me with a bottle of mineral oil and I added some of my Mennen's after shave lotion for aroma. She was thrilled with it. But after an evening of dancing with her on my next visit my cheek was well oiled - and I had no need to apply my after shave.

There was a shortage of drinking glasses in the bars. Any suitable empty bottle would have a string soaked in alcohol or gasoline tied around its lower half. After being ignited and allowed to burn briefly, the bottle would be immersed in cold water. The resulting crack would usually produce a clean cut of the bottle, and after some filing of the sharp edges, a perfect drinking glass. Food was also in short supply. About the only thing we dared to eat in Manila was chicken. We usually tried to return to the boat for our meals.

On one of our stops at the Royal Bar, a popular Navy hang-out, we ran into our missing shipmate, Sheehan. He was dressed in a nice tropical suit and had a beautiful lady on his arm. In talking with him, he told us his lady friend was a madam and had a bevy of nice girls working for her. He also showed us his Merchant Marine I.D. card. Probably because of Sheehan's status as AWOL, someone in our group realized that we shouldn't be in his company we should relocate.

This is not the end. Sheehan will return.

The bar that we moved on to when we left Sheehan was a well-known place called the "Yankee Dollar." The song "Rum and Coca Cola" was a big hit at the time and included the line, "Working for the Yankee Dollar," that provided its name. The bar and dance area were located on the first floor and a wide set of open stairs rose to a balcony where rooms were available for *indoor sports*. Many years after my time in the Pacific, I was reading either a *Life* or *Look* magazine and came on a section of drawings of places in Manila. One that took my eye was of sailors dancing with the girls of Manila and showed the stairs going up to the balcony where the rooms were. When I read the caption, "Working for the Yankee Dollar," I had to smile; it brought back great memories.

On the outskirts of the city there was a huge dance hall called the "Santa Ana Cabaret." It was known as the *marathon dance hall of the Pacific*. There were always plenty of ladies to dance with, some likely were prostitutes. One evening there with my friend Willie and several other shipmates from the Sea Dog, Willie linked up with a not-too-attractive prostitute. A couple of young sailors who worked for him in the torpedo room suggested that he should come over to their table where they had some nicer looking girls. They suggested that his companion looked like she could have a venereal disease. Willie answered, "A venereal disease once saved my life - I'm not worried about a venereal disease."

One of the new sailors to come aboard the Sea Dog before we left for Subic Bay was well enough liked but his (un-pressed) military appearance left something to be desired. Within a short period of time he had received a nickname - as many sailors do. His became "Foreskin." He received so much attention from the crew that he was probably proud of the name. He developed an attachment to one of the girls at the "Yankee Dollar" where his nickname quickly followed him. On one evening when he had the duty a group of us from the Sea Dog showed up there. His girlfriend, disturbed at seeing us without him, greeted us with the question, "Where Foreskin, where Foreskin?"

Early one morning at Subic Bay - prior to our 7:00 AM muster - Sheehan was spotted hiding under the pier where the Sea Dog was moored. He was in a very disheveled condition and said he needed money. We made a fast trip through the boat and collected as much money as we could for him. And to head off the question of why - why would we go to any trouble to help him out? - I can only say that he was a shipmate, and that's what we did. But it had to be done before he was spotted by one of the officers. That was the last time we saw him. Years later - at the 25th year anniversary of the Sea Dog's commissioning - in talking with Captain Hydeman I asked him if he had ever heard anything about Sheehan, but he never did. He had a good laugh when I told him of the money collection.

One day Commander Barney Sieglaff, who at that time was our Division Commander, went to sea with us for the day. While submerged I was the helmsman in the Conning Tower. I overheard him asking our Captain if the *goddamned* Walton brothers were aboard the Sea Dog. Captain Hydeman told Barney that Jen Walton had been in the crew but had been transferred back at Pearl Harbor.

U.S.S. SEA DOG

Top: At Pearl Harbor, engine rooms gang with Chief Whitey Kahn front center. Below: Letter mailed home from the Philippines

Getting ideas!

On 26 August, Ensign D.C. Tipps, U.S.N.R., was detached.

Ordered to Philippine waters as part of the holding force there, the SEA DOG got underway on 6 September enroute to Subic Bay, P.I., in company with the U.S.S. REDFISH, the U.S.S. SCABBARDFISH, and the U.S.S. SEA FOX (unofficially comprising Hydeman's HAT-THE-HELLCATS. Many of the ship's veterans crew had been transferred at the conclusion of the war for transportation back to the United States, and full advantage was taken of the long cruise westward for intensive training of new personnel. The SEA DOG stopped overnight in Guam for fuel and mail on 18 Septemb. At this time Lieutenant K... Price, U.S.N.R., was detached.

On 26 September, 1945, the SEA DOG moored at the Submarine Base, Subic Bay, P.I.

Following is a summary of the results of the SEA DOG ....

PATROL NUMBER	SHIPS SUNK	TOTAL TONNAGE SUNK	SHIPS DAMAGED	TOTAL TONNAGE DAMAGED	AVIATORS RESCUED
1	1 Freighter	4,000 tons	1 Trawler	25 tons	-
2	-	-	-	-	-
3	1 Freighter	6,670 tons	-	-	1
4	5 Freighters	19,000 tons	-	-	-
	1 Tanker	10,500 tons			
		29,500 tons			
Total for war	7 Freighters 1 Tanker	40,170 tons	1 Trawler	25 tons	1

As a matter of additional interest, during her participation of one year in th war, the SEA DOG earned the following decorations for her personnel:

Commander V.L. Lowrance, U.S.N.; Letter of Commendation with rib on.
Commander Earl T. Hydeman, U.S.N.; Navy Cross, Bronze Star Medal.
Lieutenant James P. Lynch, U.S.N.; Silver Star Medal. Letter of Commendati with ribbon.
Lieutenant K.B. Reed, U.S.N.R.; Silver Star Medal.
Lieutenant (j.) J.E. Blashew, U.S.N.R.; Silver Star Medal.
Lieutenant E.H. Hindert, U.S.N.R.; Bronze Star Medal.
Lieutenant (jg) V.B. Argo, U.S.N.R.; Bronze Star Medal.
Chief Torpedoman's Mate A.F. De.1, U.S.N.; Bronze Star Medal.
Motor Machinist's Mate first class G.A. Gressman, U.S.N.; Bronze Star Medal.
Letters of Commendation with ribbons to:
Lieutenant V.S. Brown, U.S. Navy.
Chief Quartermaster N.G. Heebner, U.S. Navy.
Chief Electrician's Mate W.G.E. Holden, U.S. Navy.
Chief Torpedoman's Mate L.B. Lewis, U.S. Navy.
Radioman first class J.A. Sims, U.S. Navy.
Yeoman third class, T.S. McKenzie, Jr., U.S. Navy.
Motor Machinist's Mate first class E.V. Parder, U.S. Navy.

-8-

Awards USS Sea Dog (SS401) and decorations to personnel

Barney said, "I had those two bastards with me on the Tautog. They were great sailors at sea but they sure gave me a fit in port. I'd split them up with Ed going to the Sea Devil and Jen going to the Sea Dog, but I always thought they would get back together again."

After a shorter stay in the Philippines than expected, the Captain informed us at quarters one morning that we would be leaving Subic on 12 January 1946 and hopefully would arrive in San Francisco early in February. He also told us we would be going to the town of Legaspi for the coming weekend. Legaspi was located on the southern tip of Luzon near San Bernardino Strait between Luzon and Samar. The idea was to plot a course through the Islands for our trip back to the States. By doing so we saved many sea miles going north around Luzon.

I have no idea if the Captain realized what a great time his crew would have in Legaspi. We were the first American sailors to come to this port since the Japs left. We were treated like kings, and the girls were especially nice to us. The pier at Legaspi was not large enough to accommodate the Sea Dog so we were required to anchor in the harbor. The army had a small radar station close by and they provided small boat transportation from the boat to the pier for our visits ashore. After spending the weekend there we were scheduled to get underway for Subic Bay at about 0800. But there was a problem. Sometime during the night a couple of *working girls* had visited the Sea Dog. They were discovered in Willie's compartment, the after torpedo room, at about 5:00 AM. After much discussion on how to get the girls back to the pier, someone realized that the Duty Officer (who was asleep) would have to be called since only he could make arrangements with the Army radar station to transport the girls ashore before the Captain discovered he had women aboard his ship. The Duty Officer, Ensign Brand, was a good guy and never informed the Captain. He did make one comment to us, "Why didn't you call me a little earlier? I could have used some loving too."

Shortly after 0800, with the two stowaways safely ashore, we raised our anchor and got underway for Subic Bay and arrived there in the afternoon. A couple of days later we set course for Guam to top off our fuel tanks and pick up food supplies and the next day headed for Pearl Harbor for a stay of a couple of days. Next port: San Francisco. There was no fanfare for the departure of the Sea Dog. The war was over now. Before going ashore on liberty in San

Francisco, we received a talk from our Executive Officer about our conduct and language now that we were back in *civilization*. He specifically advised us the nickname *Foreskin* would no longer be tolerated.

San Francisco, 1946: Trucelli, Bryant, Swain, and Lupe.

San Francisco: Doug, Willie, Trucelli, McLarty, and resident atheist, Barkowski (aka Ski).

We were berthed at Hunters Point Shipyard where some work was done on the boat. Sometime later we went to the Mare Island Naval Shipyard in Vallejo for our regular overhaul.

I had the chance to go home to see my parents while on leave. What a mistake! I should have realized I would be discharged from the Navy within a few months, and five days in each direction across country in a railway coach was a tough trip. When I got home my uniform was not much protection for the below zero weather they were having in Madison, and coming from the South Pacific didn't help. I bought myself a not-so-good used car, a 1941 Chevrolet, for transportation. Most of my friends were married or had steady girlfriends. So it was not a very enjoyable leave, and I was wishing I had stayed in California.

San Francisco: Author left, Bill McAuliffe right, obliging waitress center.

In Vallejo, Georgia Street was the hang out for us sailors. This was a short street with bars on both sides. On occasion a sailor, or a group of, usually with a wager involved, would try to have a drink in each bar on the street before returning to their ship. I don't think anyone ever succeeded.

By the time I returned from leave, our crew was well established at a bar in Sacramento. Being a follower, I soon joined the group. This was where we hung out on weekends. I had my eye on one of the bar maids who was a little older than myself. With a couple of stripes on my arm, a couple of years in the Navy, and visits to a lot of foreign ports, I must have thought I was a lover. On approaching this lady for a date, she told me she enjoyed her loving (I am not so sure this was the word she used) but she didn't have time to train me. I believed I picked up my hat from the bar and took my red face to another drinking establishment.

Being in the Navy Reserve we were to be discharged on the point system. A married man and with children would receive more points than a single sailor like myself. It looked as if I would be getting out in early April. I had never thought about re-enlisting in the regular Navy, nor was I asked. Maybe my talents were not in too great demand.

On 2 April 1946 I was transferred to the receiving station San Francisco, California for further assignment to Shoemaker, California for discharge from the USNR on 6 April 1946. I received my mustering out pay, money to pay for my meals for five days, and with the cash I had in my billfold I felt rich. A few of us who were traveling across country together pooled some of our money to buy a supply of liquor for the trip. A problem. At that time Navy Shore Patrol units were riding the trains. When approaching the train at Oakland, the Shore Patrol informed us that we couldn't bring the booze aboard. Before a fight broke out, the Chief Petty Officer of the Shore Patrol arrived. He informed us that we could take our booze on the train. However, if the seal on the bottle was broken, it would be confiscated by the Shore Patrol.

After a few hours traveling east, we had re-arranged a lot of the seats and joined with some young ladies. Within a short period of time, a member of the Shore Patrol was heading toward us. We were sure we were in *deep shit*. Very much to our surprise, he was very pleasant. He asked if he could have a couple of drinks for their own lady friends. Our answer; definitely yes. Now we owned the Shore Patrol. Within a short time, they joined us.

As the booze flowed, the girls were doing a lot of country and western singing. One very popular song at that time was "Sioux City Sue." (Number one on the *Hit Parade* for several weeks running.) The girl I had my eye on - a little older than I - also apparently had her eye on me. She was going to Sioux City and invited me to the farm to meet her parents. I was sorely tempted to change trains and go with her. What probably saved me was my experience of growing up on a farm. I did not want to be a farmer. To this day whenever I hear the song "Sioux City Sue" I have to smile.

Our cross country train made only a few stops. However, if time permitted we would replenish our stock of booze. We eventually made friends with the cooks in the dining car who would join us for drinks in the late evening. They would also bring us food from the dining car. This was my third trip across country and certainly the best. I believe we changed trains in Chicago, then on to Boston where I spent the night with my Aunt and Uncle, and the following day returned to Madison.

USS Sea Dog 401at San Francisco 1946; battle flag above.

Returning to Madison and Spinax

My first priority after coming home was my car. Without a set of wheels, I was *dead in the water*. My father had been using my car and I expected it to be dirty, and it was. However it also had a leaking head gasket. With the benefit of his training as a kid and what I learned in the Navy, that was easily dealt with.

I visited to my two favorite school teachers, one of whom tried to talk me into coming back to finish high school in the fall. I may have told her that I probably would be more interested in the lady teachers than my studies.

With the car in good working order, and a few bucks in the bank, I wanted to see my brother Jack whom I had not seen for a couple of years. He was still in the Army and stationed at Fort Monroe, Virginia. I spent a few days with him and visited a friend from the Sea Dog who also lived in Virginia.

After returning once again to Madison I had a visit from my former Boy Scout Leader, Bob Chick, who offered me a job in his family business. I really wanted to work as a mechanic, but was unable to find a position. My father, who was probably not terribly pleased with my lifestyle of loafing and drinking (too much) with my buddies, asked me if I would help him with a well job he was working on. At that time I still did not have complete faith in the divining rod and I asked him again to drive wooden stakes where we would see the veins of water come into the well when we reached the required depth. Once again he was proved correct. Working with him on that job was a pleasure. He would ask me about my work in the Navy. It was amazing how much he thought I had learned during my short time there.

After a few weeks at home, I began to feel like a ship without a rudder. I had no direction and no idea of what I wanted to do. One morning when I rose from my bed, probably with a hangover, and lit up my first Camel cigarette of the day, I realized I had to get out of Madison.

I drove to the Navy recruiting station in Manchester - about a sixty mile drive - to see what they might offer me. Because I had been out of the Navy for less than ninety days, I could enlist in the regular Navy with the rate I held when I was discharged - Second Class Motor Machinist Mate. They also could offer me a two year enlistment. This sounded good to me. Perhaps in a couple of years I would know better what I wanted to do in life. I signed on the dotted line and they gave me a date to report back to Manchester to be sworn into the regular Navy. I would no longer be a *dumb ass* reservist.

Within a week I was back to Manchester for my physical and swearing in. I was then bussed to the Naval receiving station - the Fargo Building in Boston - as before for further assignment to a ship or station.

Because I was a qualified submarine sailor, I was supposed to be transferred to the submarine base at New London for submarine duty. I received instead a set of orders to a destroyer berthed at the Boston Navy Yard. After a special request "chit" was submitted to see the Executive Officer of the station, my orders were changed to Submarine Base New London.

I reported to the base receiving barracks, to what had been known as "Spritz's Navy" a couple of years earlier. Spritz was long gone. We no longer had two thousand men to deal with; more like a hundred or so to muster each morning at quarters. The Chief in charge of the receiving barracks was Chief Mac, our old Chief from the Submarine Diesel School. He still had the short cigar tucked in the corner of his mouth. I did not attempt conversation with him as I doubted he would remember me.

One Thursday morning at quarters Chief Mac called out my name. Stepping forward he asked me if I had any *fucking* mechanical ability. Not knowing whether I should answer with a yes or no, I probably stood with my mouth open. Chief Mac said he needed hasps put on some lockers. He also said he had a *fucking dumb ass* torpedoman working on them who had *fucked* them up. Within a couple of hours I informed Chief Mac that I had completed the job. He asked me if I had a place to go for the weekend. This was on a Thursday morning. I told him I could go to see my parents. He said I could have the long weekend off, but I better not get *my fucking ass* in trouble. My kind of Chief.

While at the receiving barracks, before being assigned to a boat, we had a few classes to attend as well as a session at the submarine escape training tank for a refresher.

At the receiving barracks I made a great friend, Lee Eldridge. Lee was a First Class Electrician who had served on the Tautog during the war. He was also coming back into the Navy. One afternoon, returning to my barracks after my daily assignment, I found a note on my locker from Lee. He told me he had been assigned to the U.S.S. Spinax (SS 489), a brand new submarine being built at the Portsmouth Naval Shipyard. He also gave me the name of the Detail Officer to see if I should be interested. Portsmouth sounded good to me; my second new submarine. When I requested the Spinax from the Detail Officer, I believe he asked "Are you sure you want the Spinax?" I answered in the affirmative and he said, "You will receive your orders for the Spinax."

Checking in at the main gate with my orders, I was directed to the Spinax barge. Since it was late in the evening, a proper bunk was not available for me. However a pile of dirty mattresses was located at one end of the barge. With a few beers in my belly, this was good enough for me. Shortly after waking in the morning and doing a lot of scratching between my legs, and after a close inspection, I realized I had acquired a case of the *crabs*. Although I had not been with any lady friends in quite some time, the Spinax sailors would not accept my story that I caught them from either a toilet seat or the dirty mattress I had spent the night on. Our Chief Pharmacist Mate, with his can of DDT spray quickly solved my problem. However word spreads fast on a submarine. I became known as a lover and was quite popular, although at times they would call me "Scratch." Now I knew how my shipmate "Foreskin" on the Sea Dog felt about *his* nickname.

The Spinax had a fine crew, the majority of whom were already qualified in submarines, wore the dolphins, and had made war patrols during WWII.

In looking back on my Navy career and the submarines I served on, I would not rate the officers on the Spinax too highly among those I had known, perhaps because a Chief Radioman I had served with on the Sea Dog was busted for an infraction that did not deserve such severe punishment.

I wondered then if the above incident was behind the reason the Detail Officer questioned me about being sure I wanted the Spinax?

For access to the shipyard at that time, we were issued a special I.D. card. This card was made up by our Chief Yeoman, Red Maguire. The picture I.D. carried your name, rate, height, weight, date of birth, and the ship you were attached to. Although I had served in WWII and was on my second submarine, I was only nineteen - almost twenty - and could not yet be served in bars. Red informed me that any sailor who served in WWII should be allowed to drink. So he *adjusted* my birth date to show that I was 21. Thanks, Red.

This would not be the only time in my career that Red helped me out.

I should have been a throttle man in one of the engine rooms, but because we were so rate heavy at that time, I was an oiler standing watch with a throttle man. I had no complaints and was treated well. Our Chief Motor Machinist Mate was a good guy and a great Chief. I never happened to cross paths with the welder I stood fire watch for on the Sea Dog a couple of years earlier who had wanted me to meet his daughter. I might have enjoyed meeting her.

Towards the end of WWII we had captured two of Germany's most advanced submarines, the U3008 and the U2513. Both had been equipped with a snorkel that could be used to provide air to the main engines so that they could be operated while the submarine was submerged. This was something we didn't have on our submarines. The U3008, with an American crew aboard, operated out of Portsmouth. My former Chief of the Boat from the Sea Dog was the COB on the U3008. I thought his was a cool submarine and asked Chief Dell if he could get me aboard. His answer was, "What the fuck is wrong with you? Do you have rocks in your head?" At that time I probably didn't realize that he was doing me a favor steering me away from a boat plagued with mechanical problems.

I don't remember having a party when we were commissioned a US Ship of the Fleet. The important thing about being on a commissioned submarine was that we would now receive our submarine and sea pay.

Several years ago I wrote the following article "The City of Lynn's Ship" for the Lynn Item. After the article had passed through a couple of hands, this is how it appeared in the paper. I include it here to best describe our shakedown cruise after leaving the Portsmouth Naval Shipyard.

The City of Lynn's ship

The following is information submitted to me by Ray Comeau of Saugus, who is the present commander of the Marblehead Submarine Veterans Base, Inc., and was written by Doug Bryant of Danvers who has actually served on; "The City of Lynn's Ship." That is the title.

The City of Lynn's Ship
By Doug Bryant

Yes, the City of Lynn did have a so called ship. During World War II bond drives were held in various cities and Defense Plants around the country. This was thought to give the citizens who purchased these bonds a personal interest. The money from the sale of these bonds would be used to pay for a plane or a ship needed to fight the war. The money from the bonds sold in Lynn was used to pay for a Submarine being built at the Navy Yard in Portsmouth New Hampshire.

That submarine which had the distinction of being called, "The City of Lynn,s Ship" was actually the USS Spinax SS489. She was the first "Radar Picket" submarine. She was designed to operate with the fleet and direct air craft to their targets. The keel of the submarine Spinax was laid on 5/14/45 and launched on 11/20/45. She was commissioned a United States Naval Ship on 9/20/46.

Previous to "Armed Forces Day" each of the armed forces had their own day to celebrate, Navy Day was in October, so where does the USS Spinax go to celebrate Navy Day? You guessed it! Lynn Massachusetts but first there is a small problem to solve. The Spinax needs a crew member form Lynn. Enter Robert Mac Donald a submarine veteran, serving on another submarine. Understanding that he was a Lynn boy he was transferred to the USS Spinax.

The Spinax arrived in Lynn and tied up at Lampers Wharf in October and planned to spend a few days and celebrate "Navy Day." The Lynn City officials rolled out the red

ROBERT LARAMIE
VETERANS' AFFAIRS

carpet for the crew of Lynn's ship. Many parties followed and there was never a shortage of beautiful young ladies who provided companionship for the officers and crew of Lynn's fine ship.

The Spinax reciprocated by opening their ship to visitors each day. Thousands of people from the area had a chance to visit the Navy's newest submarine. Many articles and pictures appeared in the newspaper, "The Daily Evening Item," and local boy Robert MacDonald was in the lime-light.

The Spinax left Lynn and traveled to the Submarine Base at New London (Groton) Connecticut. The crew underwent submarine escape training at the Submarine Escape Training Tank.

After a few days of local operations the Spinax was off on a shake down cruise. Because the Spinax was the newest and the best, her first stop was Washington, D.C. on the Potomac River. The next stop was in St. Thomas in the Virgin Islands where daily operations and training were carried out.

The next port of call was Havana, Cuba. Liberty and recreation. Training was not a top priority in a submarine sailors mind in a liberty port such as Havana. Goodby Cuba, the Spinax was off to Panama where she traveled through the canal to the Pacific Ocean for a short stay in Balboa, in the Canal Zone. The

Spinax returned through the locks of the Canal to the Atlantic Ocean.

After all the traveling and all the ports of call the Spinax made the American dollar was in short supply. However, King Neptune, must have felt that the good crew of the Spinax deserved more rest and recreation so it was off to New Orleans for the Christmas Holidays. After the holidays The Spinax returned to New London (Groton) Submarine Base for a short stay before joining the fleet at Norfolk Virginia to operate with Air Craft Carriers.

The crew of the Spinax that put her in Commission at the end of World War II was an outstanding crew. Nearly 90% of her crew were veterans of combat submarines in the Pacific during World War II. The City of Lynn can truly be proud of her ship.

While conversing with Mr. Bryant, who is a wealth of information, I learned first hand about the Spinax. All the years that I lived in Lynn I never knew about "The City of Lynn's ship." I know now and it makes me wonder how many other great stories are out there just waiting to be told.

Mr. Bryant is a true Navy man and completed over twenty years of dedicated faithful service to this country. Life after the Spinax included Deep Sea Diving School and a three year stint aboard the submarine Sea Dog that was berthed in Salem and was used to teach the Naval Reserve.

As I have stated on many occasions, you don't have to travel far to find a true hero. Most times you only need to look around and who knows, you may have one standing right beside you.

It could be your next door neighbor, the person you see on television who is receiving a great big retirement party or it could be the guy on the corner selling newspapers. You never know!

ROBERT LARAMIE writes on veterans' affairs for the The Item.

I was quite happy serving as a crew member on the Spinax at Norfolk, VA. However, I still wanted to become a Navy deep sea diver. One day I approached our Chief Yeoman - my friend Red Maguire - on the subject. Early in Red's career he had served on a submarine rescue vessel. This ship carried Navy divers in her crew, including a Master Diver. Red explained the 'pecking order' of divers in the Navy:

Master Diver (sits at the right hand of God)
First Class Diver
Salvage Diver
Second Class Diver

Red told me that the Navy's deep sea diving school at the Gun Factory in Washington, D.C. was a six month course and upon graduating I would be a First Class Diver. As a First Class Diver I would be assigned to a ship or station that had a diving billet, thus would receive diving pay every month. Should I go to Salvage School and become a Salvage Diver, I would not get diving pay unless I was assigned to a ship or station that had a diving billet. The same limitation would also apply to a Second Class Diver. So with Red's advice I applied for the First Class Diving School.

Souvenir of Cuba 1946

U.S.S. "SPINAX" -489-
Entering Havana, Cuba.

MERRY CHRISTMAS and MAY EVERY DAY OF THE New Year BRING YOU HAPPINESS

PHOTO ILLA

Deep Sea Diving School

In June of 1947 I received my orders to report to the Navy's Deep Sea Diving School at Washington D.C. One might wonder why this school would be located here. Actually it was located at the Gun Factory, also known as the Navy Yard, on the Anacostia River. Most of our dive training was conducted from floats on the river located in front of the school. For deeper diving, our diving boat would take the class to Chesapeake Bay via the Anacostia and Potomac Rivers.

Within the school were offices, class rooms, and tanks filled with water with glass portholes that allowed the instructors to observe the tasks we were working on. To achieve the deep depths that we were to be qualified for (300 ft. breathing compressed air and 320 ft. breathing a mixture of compressed helium and oxygen) we were placed in a large water filled pressure tank where, using compressed air, pressure could be applied to the inside of the tank to achieve the equivalent pressure that we would experience at sea at that depth. This pressure tank also had glass portholes in the side, where the instructor could observe how we tolerated the pressure.

After our physical by a Diving Medical Officer, we were placed in a re-compression chamber for a 50 psi pressure test. This would be the equivalent pressure a diver would experience at 112 ft. in the ocean. Also, each student was required to be able to equalize the pressure on his ears by *popping* his ears.

In our classroom studies, I didn't realize how much math we would have to learn and with my limited education I was concerned about it. Our classroom instructor, a Chief Boatswain Mate and also a Master Diver, put about five formulas on the blackboard. He then asked for a show of hands of those who could understand the formulas. He then said, "You smart asses sit in the back of the room and you dumb asses move to the front and I will show you how I do the formulas." He was a lifesaver for me and also a great Chief. We were also taught the medical and physical aspects of deep sea diving.

Although I was a Second Class Petty Officer (Motor Machinist Mate Second Class) and knew all about submarines, my knowledge of surface craft was very limited, especially the seamanship knowledge required to be part of a dive team on a Navy salvage ship. I would have to learn that on the job.

Our class consisted of twelve men, with various specialties that would make them assets to a diving crew. Of the twelve, we had a section leader who was in charge of the group. We also had two officers from the Brazilian navy training with us. Even though they were officers they were expected to work with us as a team in such duties as dressing and tending divers. One of the officers was a great guy and pulled his share of the load; the other felt he was too good for that and wouldn't.

One day while diving from the floats on the bank of the Anacostia River, the less popular officer was dressed and about to descend into the water. Before his face plate was closed, we inserted a few grasshoppers into his helmet. By the time he reached the bottom of the river, the grasshoppers had become quite active. The officer, by now in panic mode, had to be brought to the surface and undressed. We thought he was going to quit the class. Our Instructor read the riot act to us. I am sure he was worried about an international incident because of the treatment of a foreign officer.

In dressing a diver for his dive, if the tenders do it in a sloppy way the suit will sometimes leak. That seemed to be a recurring problem for this same officer who frequently had wet suits. A wet suit from a leak would not justify bringing a diver to the surface for a dry one. The dive would continue, and the diver had the job of drying his suit at the completion of his dive. Also, in most cases, should a diver request the use of a rest room, it would be denied. This was good training at the school because if a diver was at a great depth it would be impossible to bring him to the surface without a decompression stop. Otherwise he could develop the *bends*.

Many of the training jobs we performed in the river required communications between two or more divers. We pre-arranged signals to get the other diver's attention. It could be two loud strikes with a hammer on the tank that we might be working on. At that time both divers would shut their air supply valves off (for silence) and place their helmets against the tank. In doing so a clear conversation could take place. Should the divers be close, the helmets might be placed together directly to converse.

The Anacostia River had a lot of yachts moored along the river. Occasionally one of these vessels would sink due to a leak or a collision with another vessel. Usually the school would get a call asking for assistance in raising the vessel. The school was happy to become involved since it was good training for the students. We had a well-equipped diving boat to operate from. Usually the owner of the vessel would provide us with food and drink on the job. On one such job our Instructor, a Chief Gunner's Mate and Master Diver, was given a case of beer and a bottle of whiskey, and sandwiches for us at lunch time.

In the process of raising that particular vessel, our instructor utilized all the equipment we had on our work boat. Two divers were put in the water, one on the port side amidships and the other on the starboard side amidships. With the use of our high pressure water pump a tunnel was created under the keel by the divers. Two salvage balloons, one on each side, were placed in the water. The two balloons were connected together by the divers in the tunnel. After the balloons were properly secured, air from our compressor inflated them enough to raise the vessel to the surface. Once on the surface, our high pressure water pump was then used to pump the remaining water from the inside of the yacht. The operation went very well and we learned a lot. Our class of twelve consumed the case of beer; the instructor took charge of the whiskey. At the end of the day, on our return to the school, our Instructor was feeling no pain. A small amount of the whiskey remained in the bottle. His comment to us in *sharing* the bottle, "O.K. you guys can kill the bottle but I don't want to see you staggering around drunk at the school."

One class member was Second Class Boatswain's Mate. A Boatswain's Mate should know all about rigging, rope (line), knots, and splices. But ours had earned his stripes as a caretaker of a small landing strip in a jungle in South America during the war, not in the usual way of *this man's Navy*. One day working on the floats on the Anacostia River, our instructor, himself a proud Chief Boatswain's Mate, sent our classmate to the storeroom for a *hank of marline*. Not knowing what a hank of marline was, he simply requested *some* marline (a light rope used for whipping the ends of line) and brought the chief only a few turns wrapped around his arm. On presenting these few turns to the chief, he was ordered to turn around and face the river. When he had done so, the chief kicked him in the behind with enough force to knock him into the river. This was in December. Our classmate was forced to continue his duties for the day in wet clothes. A harsh lesson that I'm sure had him reading his Bluejacket's Manual as soon as he was off watch - and dry.

One morning at quarters I spotted my former nemesis from the Sea Dog, Kime, (now a Chief Petty Officer) in the ranks of a new starting class. He was the First Class Electrician who had tossed me out of his compartment. Although he was a CPO, I had no reason to fear him since he was only a student in the new junior class. For a few days I simply avoided him, but one day we came face to face. He asked if we had been on the Sea Dog together during the war. He extended his hand to me and we became friends. Ten years later, I would once again cross paths with my former shipmate.

With our class close to graduation, we were given a chance to fill out a *dream sheet* once again to note our preferred assignments. In filling out this form emphasis should be placed on the word *dream*.

My request was for any salvage ship in the Far East, such as an ARS (auxiliary rescue and salvage ship). I was already counting the big bucks I would make clearing Manila Bay. And maybe I could locate the lady I supplied with mineral oil and Mennen's after shave.

A few days before graduation, and for planning purposes, we received a copy of our transfer orders. With a quick look I saw Solomon's Island. I thought I was going to *the Solomon Islands* in the South Pacific. Upon a closer inspection I read the complete address: United States Naval Ordnance Test Facilities, Solomon's Island, Maryland. Little did I realize I was going to a torpedo and mine testing range in Maryland less than forty miles away. So much for my dream of amassing a fortune in the PI.

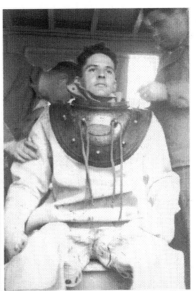

Solomon's Island, Maryland

On 3/2/1948 I received my orders to report to the Naval Ordnance Facility at Solomon's, MD. This base was located on the Patuxent River and its purpose was to test torpedoes and mines in the river. It was the test facility for the Naval Ordnance Laboratory at White Oak, Maryland.

After receiving my diploma as a First Class Deep Sea Diver, I set out for my new station. It was a very small station with only 15 enlisted men and a Warrant Officer as Officer in Charge. Of the 15, only 6 of us were divers. One of the divers was a Chief Motor Machinist Mate with a questionable reputation. Behind his back he was known as "Rat Fink". He thought he had a new *whipping boy* when I reported aboard. Luckily, as a first class diver, I worked for the master diver, Warren Thomas, who was a great boss. The WO running the station told me that as long as the engine, generator, and air compressor worked on the diving boat when we were involved in a diving operation we would get along just fine.

On my first Liberty in Solomon's I was introduced to the night life. Solomon's had about 4 bars. The furthest from town was Gravy's Bar, also called the Black and White. At that time, 1948, segregation was still very much in effect in that area. Gravy's Bar had two entrance doors. One was marked white and the other marked colored. A partition ran down the center of the building to the bar where blacks and whites were served by the same bartender. A juke box was installed in an opening in the partition so that both colored and white could play the music of their choice. Occasionally someone might have to ask a patron on the other side to punch selections that couldn't be reached from his or her side.

After a couple of drinks there, we moved down the highway to the Highway Tavern. This was the most popular bar. Every Friday and Saturday evening a band would play country and western music for dancing. Local beer sold for 15 cents a bottle and top shelf for 25 cents. No cover, no minimum.

I am sure my new shipmates plan was to get me drunk and they succeeded.

The next day I had a memorable hangover. We also had a diving job that day to recover some mines from the river. Our Master Diver, seeing the condition I was in, decided he would test me out. He told me to suit up - I was to be the diver for the recovery. I don't know how I made it through the morning without throwing up in the helmet. That was the worst dive I ever made. I don't think I ever overindulged again when I had a dive scheduled for the next day.

I suppose my reporting for work with a raging hangover on the first day was somewhat like my first day on the Spinax with the crabs. Young and foolish, but I was learning.

We lived on a work barge tied up to a large pier on the river. The first deck had a large work area and the second our galley, mess hall, and sleeping area.

In addition to the Navy personnel on the base, we had a nearly equal number of civilian employees who worked on the mines and torpedoes that were being tested there, and we interacted with several tradesmen who provided services to the base.

I had several additional duties aside from diving. At the station we had about 12 small craft to maintain when we were not diving. My priority was the diving boat. It was rewarding to work for a good Chief, who put faith in me and let me work on my own without supervision. We also had two locator boats used to find lost sunken mines or torpedoes, and a yard freighter that had a torpedo tube mounted in its bow to fire torpedoes for testing. It was my responsibility to make sure the engines ran on these boats when they were needed. The remaining boats were maintained by a civilian worker who was very helpful to me when I was in over my head.

One day the torpedo shop on the base needed some torpedoes picked up at the base at Indian Head, Maryland. Our yard freighter (well over 100 feet in length) was to be used for the pickup. Our Chief Boatswain's Mate, who knew navigation, was on the bridge and was responsible for the safe operation of this vessel. Rat Fink was also on the bridge acting like the Executive Officer on a large vessel. I was in the engine room operating the main engine with my fireman helper. On deck we had several line handlers. We backed safely away from the pier and headed down the river for Indian Head.

The main engine on this freighter was a direct drive reversible engine that used a lot of compressed air every time it was started in the forward position or restarted in the reverse position. This would need to be done repeatedly when coming alongside the pier at Indian Head. Because of this we always put the air compressor starting switch in manual mode rather than automatic when coming into port. By doing that we always had the maximum amount of starting air for the engine. Unbeknownst to me and my fireman in the engine room Rat Fink had heard the relief valve lift on the starting air compressor and at that time placed the switch in the off position. After we answered a couple of reverse bells on the engine, we were out of air and made quite a crash landing on the pier.

A friend of mine, Harrington, a First Class Petty Officer, had seen him turn the air compressor switch off. He also heard him tell the Chief Boatswain Mate that we should be restricted to the ship that evening because of improper watch standing. Harrington told Rat Fink that if he had he kept his *dick scratchers* off the compressor switch we would have had plenty of air.

In explaining our living arrangements on the barge, I have to mention our meals. Because we did not have a mess hall on the base, we were on partial subsistence. The Navy paid us each about $45.00 a month to purchase our food from the local stores. We also had a First Class Cook in our crew who prepared the meals, and a Mess Treasurer who would collect the money from the crew and keep records as to how it was spent by the cook. For some reason I was elected Mess Treasurer. With good planning by the cook only about $30.00 per man was needed each month. The crew was happy to have the extra $15 in their wallets. I ran a *slush fund* where members of the crew could borrow money between pay days if needed. However, the interest rate was high. Ten dollars would cost eleven even if only for a day. I was required to submit my books to our Commanding Officer for his signature every month. The profits from the operation - all very much above board - would be applied to our food fund to supplement our normal fare with *good stuff.*

Our CO, who I will refer to as Mr. F, was a horse player who at times would run short on money. He knew I was very conservative about money and usually had plenty in my wallet and from time to time he would borrow from me to avoid borrowing from the fund because of his status as an officer. This was not too smart on his part, but it paid off for me when I met my wife to be, Virginia, and needed a long weekend to visit her.

I was quite happy at Solomon's and my brother Jack was in Virginia in the Army about 70 miles away so we could visit each other frequently. Jack was stationed near Front Royal where they had a large dance hall and they played country western music. I always wore my uniform and I was quite popular with the girls as the only sailor.

In the spring of 1948 I was nearing the end of my 2 year enlistment and not sure if I wanted to stay in the Navy. I really wanted to get a diving job and make some big money. A large bridge was being built about 40 miles from our base. I thought I would take a ride to the site and see if they were hiring divers. But first I went to see my friend Hank in the machine shop. I had a lot of respect for him - he was a lot older than I and was a *savvy* man. I told Hank my story and asked him if he would go with me to see if I could get a job. Hank said he would be happy to go with me on the coming Saturday. As it turned out they were not working on this particular Saturday, but we found a time keeper working in one of the offices. I told him I was looking for a job as a diver. He told me that they were not ready for divers on the job yet but that I could probably get a job as a watchman that would pay me more money than my Navy pay and that I could very likely get a job as a diver when they were being hired. He took us outside and showed us some monstrous steel pilings and asked, "Who do you think is on the bottom to make sure they are driven in the right place?" He went on to tell me he had a son who was a First Class Storekeeper in the Navy and if he thought this construction business was a piece of cake, he would have his son with him. He also said, "My advice to you son is - stay in the Navy". After listening to comments from Hank on the way home, I found myself re-enlisting in the Navy for yet another two years.

Across the Patuxent River from us was the Patuxent Naval Air Station. This was a high level test facility for modern Navy air craft. If a plane was to crash in the ocean, in most cases the pilot would bail out and survive. The air station had a crew of divers and a recovery boat used to recover the aircraft. On occasion divers were sent back to the deep sea diving school for a short requalification course. Whenever the air station divers were sent back to Washington for this course, we would cover for them, in case of an emergency. One day we got a call for our services. It was an inconvenient day because our Master Diver was on leave. We had plenty of talent but because Chief Rat Fink was the senior man he tried to take charge. He wanted to be taken up in a helicopter thinking he might be able to spot the plane underwater. He must have thought that his eyes were much better than those of the pilots looking for the crashed plane. At the end of the first day without any luck, the old Salvage Officer asked my friend Harrington if we would be back the next day. Harrington answered in the affirmative. The Salvage Officer said he needed a favor - to pick up a swab (Navy term for a mop), put a white hat on it, and bring it with us tomorrow - but leave that *fucking* Chief back at your base!

When it came time for Chief Rat Fink to receive his orders back to sea duty, the base joke was that his going away party would be held in the phone booth at the main gate.

One type of mine that we tested at Solomon's was dropped by planes from the air station. This mine was equipped with a parachute. The purpose of the parachute was to slow down the rate of fall to protect the instrumentation in the mine when it hit the water. One day on a drop, the pilot via voice radio asked our Officer in Charge, Mr. F, where he wanted the mine dropped. Our OC told him, as close as possible to the can buoy. The pilot's drop was so close to the can buoy that he actually hung the mine on the buoy by its parachute. The pilot's comment to Mr. F, "Is that close enough for you, sir?" That mine was more difficult to recover from the can buoy than it would have been in 300 ft. of water.

My favorite time of the year to go on leave was always over the 4th of July. With July of 1948 fast approaching, I put in my request, planning on going home to Madison to visit my mother and father, and a few friends in the area I wanted to see. I had no idea how important July 1948 would become in my life.

Top: Master Diver, Thomas, Corpsman MacDonald, Divers, Author and Harrington, 1949. Below, Solomons Island crew, Author 4th from right, standing.

Top, shortly after marriage in 1950. Below, Virginia at 17 (1948), Effingham NH. Inset, 1970 at San Juan, Puerto Rico.

Virginia

The drive to Madison from Solomon's was about ten or twelve hours, so other than a visit with my parents, I didn't have time for any other recreation that day. Over the next couple of days I visited friends and checked out the old hangouts in the evening. Things were pretty quiet. Most of the girls I knew were now married. I was ready to jump in my car and finish up my leave in Washington D.C. where I had friends I had met in diving school there. Luckily as it turned out I bumped into a high school friend and we decided to go to a popular dance that was held every Thursday evening in the summer at the Midway in Freedom N.H. After nearly seventy years, I still remember the date: Thursday July 2, 1948. We went in my friend's car, and probably had beer in the trunk. However when I went to a dance like this I usually didn't drink. I was hoping to meet a nice girl to dance with. If that didn't happen, I would start on the beer.

We saw a couple of nice looking young ladies but thought they seemed a little young. We asked them to dance anyway and they were quite happy for the invitation. I enjoyed dancing with the girl I had for a partner, but my eye kept wandering to the other one. When it came time to ask them for another dance, I told my friend I wanted to dance with the girl he had been with. This worked out quite well and we spent the remainder of the evening with them. The girls were cousins. Virginia was from Lynn and Corrine from Malden, Massachusetts. They were staying at the family's summer place in Effingham, N.H., not too far from the dance hall. They were both seventeen. Corrine was going to college in the fall and Virginia had a job in the office of Hood's Milk Company in Boston. They had been brought to the dance by Corrine's mother and father who were waiting for them in their car outside. I really enjoyed my short time with Virginia and wanted to see her again. I asked her if she would like to go to another dance with me on Saturday evening at "Weed's Barn Dance" which was near her family's summer place. This Saturday night happened to be on the Fourth of July and would be a great night for the dance with the holiday celebration. Virginia said I would have to go outside with her to meet her aunt and uncle and ask their permission. I was a little nervous but very happy I had not been drinking that evening. I was not in my Navy uniform, nor had I even told Virginia that I was in the Navy. My civilian clothes were neat and I passed the test. We were allowed to drive the girls home so I would know where to pick up my date on Saturday. I don't remember my friend making any arrangement with Virginia's cousin - I know he didn't go to the dance with Virginia and me.

I found I was quite excited about my date and no longer had any thoughts of heading back to the D.C. area. I had a 1940 Buick Super that I always kept nice and clean, much nicer than my friend's car. I decided to wear my Navy uniform. I had a nice starched white uniform to wear.

On arriving at the summer place to pick up Virginia, I felt like I was on display. I had to meet the whole family but they were very nice to me. In Lynn Virginia lived with her grandparents. Her grandfather always gave Virginia's boyfriends a bad time which always embarrassed her. I'm sure she was worried about how he would respond to me. As it turned out, her grandfather had put a lot of time at sea in his younger days and because of my Navy uniform we hit it off from the start. After learning I had been a submarine sailor during the war, they had a lot of questions for me. I was afraid they would think I was too old for Virginia; at that time I was twenty-one, almost twenty-two, and Virginia only seventeen. I guess they trusted me.

I had a great time with her at the dance that evening. I can't remember how many times I saw her during my short leave. On my last visit before my trip back to Maryland I asked for her address and phone number. The only thing I had for her to write on was my deep sea diving card from school. I still have that card today. At that time in the Navy, we always were addressed by our last name. Because of that I was in the habit of telling people my name was Bryant. This was the name I had given Virginia. When I gave her my Navy address, she couldn't understand why I went by my last name.

All too soon it was time to drive back to Solomon's. In less than a week I wrote a letter to her. In my letter I said I would be up to see her in the fall when I could get a long week end off. This would be when my Commanding Officer (the horse player who borrowed money from me) would let me off for a long week end. This continued with my being able to see her about every three months.

Virginia, like many girls, wanted to *go steady*. I told her I didn't think she should stay at home and only see me four times a year. I felt she should be going out with other guys. I also wanted my freedom, and *fair's fair*. I felt I was in love with her, but was not ready to get married at that time. And I also had no idea where - in the world - my next duty station would be.

Back at Solomon's, we were all happy to have Rat Fink gone. I don't recall where he went, but was quite glad to be shut of him. In a short time we had a new Chief Engineman called Swede report for duty. He drove a new 1949 Buick Super. He was somewhat drunk and had been following too closely behind a truck that was applying hot liquid tar on the highway and his new car was covered with tar and sand. We all pitched in and with the use of fuel oil managed to clean it up. Swede was a single guy and a submarine sailor and had been sent to Solomon's for a tour of shore duty. He was a great guy and everyone liked him. He was certainly a much better Chief than Rat Fink. I enjoyed working with him when we were not on a diving operation. He was neither a diver nor part of our crew on the diving boat. However, we would take him out on occasion, dress him up and put him on the bottom, especially if we were in an area where the mud was very deep; and you could sink into it up to your waist to show him what we had to deal with.

On the subject of mud, one type of mine we tested was dropped by a plane from 30,000 ft. This mine was not equipped with a parachute to slow it down and resulted in the mine being buried about six feet deep in the soft mud on the bottom of the river. This resulted in a lot of time being spent locating it. Once we found it, we used our high pressure water pump to wash away the mud so that we could reach it and connect our recovery cable.

This effort proved too time-consuming and it was decided to conduct these tests from Eglin Air Force Base in Florida, on the Gulf of Mexico. The plan was to send our divers to Florida to retrieve the mines. Our Master Diver drove his car equipped with a trailer to haul our diving gear. The rest of us were flown from Patuxent Naval Air Station to Eglin. We were treated well by the Air Force. We even had a Master Sergeant as our host. At times he would have to fly to other bases for a few days. When that happened his wife would provide hostess service for our Master Diver. One week end when the Sergeant was going to be out of town for the week end, our Master Diver was also scheduled to be away on a trip with one of the pilots. He gave me the keys to his car and told me to go and see the hostess. He said that she had told him to send over one of his men to see her, since he was going to be out of town. This lady was older than I and I didn't feel too comfortable going to ring the doorbell of a married woman. Then again maybe my conscience was kicking in. On his return and a subsequent visit, she told my boss, "The next time you go away, send me a man, don't tell some dumb ass kid to come and see me." Over the years, I have often wondered what I missed out on.
The mine recovery was quite easy in the Gulf of Mexico where the water was crystal clear with a nice hard white sandy bottom.

At this time in the Navy - now1949 - we were not trained as Scuba Divers, however we had shallow water diving equipment known as the Jack Brown outfit. With the water being so warm, we used only the mask and air hose connected to our air compressor for these dives. This saved us a lot of time, rather than dressing up in our deep sea equipment. Within a few weeks we had trained the Air Force personnel for the job and were sent back to Solomon's.

At Christmas when I was going home on leave to see Virginia - and also my parents - I wanted to bring home some oysters for my mother and father. The best oysters were located under our pier. This was an area the local oyster fishermen couldn't reach with their boats and oyster tongs. The day before going on leave my boss had me suited up for a dive under the pier to go oystering. My father said they were the best he ever had. I suppose he told everyone in Madison that his son the Navy Diver picked them on the bottom of Chesapeake Bay.

On this trip home I asked some of my friends if any of the automobile dealers in the area had any new cars. New cars were still very scarce in 1948. I was told a Chevrolet dealer in Conway had one, but he wouldn't sell it. My car was in great condition. I went to see the dealer and arranged to trade my Buick in on the new Chevrolet. I don't think I could have made the deal with him without having a *creampuff* to trade.

I had planned my leave so I could spend the week end with Virginia before returning to Solomon's on Monday. When I arrived at Virginia's with a new car she was thrilled. The family must have thought that Navy divers made a lot of money. On Monday morning on my return to Solomon's I drove Virginia to work. Her office was in the North Station area of Boston. I believe she was hoping some of the girls in the office would see her being dropped off.
Back at Solomon's I resumed my old routine. I was able to get a long week end every few months so that I could see Virginia.

Sometime during the summer of 1949 Mr. F. had received orders for sea duty. He was into me for about $40.00 at the time - a lot of money in 1949 (about a week's pay for a civilian). I started putting the pressure on him for what he owed me. I was afraid he would be gone without paying me – like Wilson. He promised to pay me in a couple of days when he got his travel money for the transfer. I told him I would go and see his wife if I didn't get it as promised. I guess that got his attention. He said, "Oh God, please don't go to my wife!" And I received the money as promised.

In the short time I had known Virginia, my brother Jack had met her and had been in her company a few times. He asked me if I ever had any intensions of getting married while I was in the service. I don't remember my reply, it may not have been a flat out, no, but it wasn't a yes either. He continued on, "If you do, you should marry Virginia." This must have been in the late fall of 1949, and shortly afterwards I purchased a small diamond engagement ring from the ship's service jewelry store at the Patuxent Naval Air Station. Over the Christmas holidays we became engaged. She was very happy with the ring. Years later we often talked about how small the diamond was. Eventually, after I had retired from the Navy and had a good civilian job, Virginia got the diamond of her choosing.

Our plans for marriage had to wait until I received my orders to my next duty station. I expected that to happen in a couple of months. After waiting out that time, and with no orders in sight, we decided to get married on 2 July 1950 to mark the day we had met. We had a nice wedding followed by a honeymoon in Canada. Returning to Solomon's, I received my orders to the USS Sunbird (ASR 15) stationed at the submarine base at Groton. The Sunbird was a submarine rescue vessel.

As I said good-by to my friends at Solomon's, I didn't realize that I would cross paths later in my career with my Master Diver Warren

Thomas and also with my good friend Hank, the machinist on the base who had gone with me when I was looking for a diving job on the bridge. I've always been glad that didn't work out.

USS Sunbird ASR 15 (Submarine Rescue Vessel) 1950

USS Sunbird

On 26 July 1950 I received my orders to Submarine Squadron Two at New London for further assignment to the U.S.S. Sunbird as of 2 August 1950. This gave me a few days to be with Virginia before reporting aboard. Our plans at that time were that as soon as I could find a suitable apartment, she would join me in the New London area.

Virginia was very happy to have me home with her for a few days and we enjoyed being together even though her house was quite crowded.

When I reported in at New London I met my old friend Red Maguire, the Chief Yeoman from the Spinax, little realizing how this chance meeting with Red would affect my Navy career in the near future.

The Sunbird was tied up in port only a few piers from the Squadron Offices, and I was directed to report aboard. After stowing my gear and being assigned a bunk, I was given a tour of the ship, and was told I would be in charge of the air compressor room for maintenance, repair, and housekeeping. This was a very large compartment with eight air compressors that produced compressed air at 200 pounds per square inch, 400 PPSI and 3,000 PPSI to meet the varying requirements of salvage operations.

The Sunbird had been built during WWII but was decommissioned after the war and placed in the Reserve Fleet. A couple of months before I came aboard it had been re-commissioned. A lot of work was needed, such as cleaning and painting, to bring the ship up to par. We were scheduled for an inspection on Saturday morning, only a few days away. The Chief Engineman wanted me in the engine room to stand watch on the main engines when we were underway.

Every time I tried to work in my compartment, a Chief in air storage would grab me to help him. The only way I could get my compartment ready for inspection was to stay aboard in the evening to do my work. The Master Diver, who should have been my boss, ignored me. After a couple of weeks I couldn't see any future on this ship for myself. I went to the Squadron offices to see my friend Red and told him my problem. I had to get off the Sunbird or get out of the Navy. Red's answer, "You don't have a problem. Didn't you serve on the Sea Dog during the war?" My answer, "Of course, you know that." Red then asked, "Don't you know who the Commodore is?" By then he had me by the elbow and was pushing me toward the Commodore's office. On entering he said to the Commodore, "Sir, I have one of your old shipmates here." My old skipper, Rebel Lowrance, stood up and shook my hand. He said, "I remember your face but I don't remember your name". He also said "You've grown up a lot." He had been my captain back when we were bombed and strafed by our own planes and I had jumped on his back in clearing the bridge for a dive to escape them.

I told him that I wanted to go back to submarines. He told me they were short of divers at this time, but within a couple of weeks we would have our divers back from the Bluebird that had been given to Turkey. They had been members of the crew delivering the vessel. In the meantime, the Sunbird was going to the Naval Shipyard in Philadelphia for some minor repairs. He told me to go back aboard the Sunbird, keep my nose clean and my mouth shut, and if I did not receive a set of transfer orders in 30 days to call him directly. I walked back aboard the Sunbird with a smile on my face. I now had a connection with more clout than either the Captain or Executive Officer of the Sunbird. I might add that I never heard any member of the crew say anything positive about either of the ship's officers.

We were a couple of days at sea and a few days at the Navy Yard. On one of my trips to pick up my mail from the ship's Post Office, near *Officer's Country*, I was spotted by our unpopular Executive Officer. He confronted me saying, "What's this shit about your going back to submarines?" Not being smart enough to follow the Commodore's advice to keep my mouth shut, I replied, "Guess they need submarine sailors more than deep sea divers." I could clearly see I had *pissed him off*. He told me to get my ass out of there. I don't remember if I had picked up my mail or not but I left.

I remember once saying that the Spinax had been a *horseshit* ship. I can now say that the Spinax could have learned a lot from a really horseshit ship!

In a couple of days the Yeoman presented me with my orders. I packed my sea bag and signed off the ship at the Quarter Deck. There certainly was no fanfare on my departure.

Although I speak badly about the ship, I made a lot of friends there. One - another diver - wanted me to stay on the Sunbird. He would say that as bad as this ship was it could only get better - it couldn't get any worse. The Captain had been wounded during the war and it was rumored he had a steel plate in his head. When we went to sea my friend would always say, "I hope the old man doesn't get too much sun on his head and expand the plate or we'll all be in deep shit." In my short period of time on the Sunbird, I did learn a lot about surface ships that would be useful to me later. If the quality of the Officers and Chiefs had been better, it would have been a good ship to serve on. It proved to be a good example of what can be learned from bad leadership.

On reporting back to the squadron, Red went through the roster of submarines in Squadron Eight and the Sea Owl looked to me like a good choice. I asked the Commodore if I could be assigned the Sea Owl, and he said, "It's yours." How many Second Class Enginemen can sit down with a Commodore and have their pick of assignments in the Squadron? Several years later when Rebel Lowrance was a retired Vice Admiral I had the opportunity to thank him for getting me on the Owl.

I told him I was on it for five years. (I didn't want him to think that I was a boat jumper and never happy). He said if I'd stayed on it for 5 years, no thanks were necessary.

Returning to the Submarine Base was like coming back to your old home town. You always meet some old shipmates. While serving on the Sunbird, I met one on the base who I had served with in Solomon's, MD. MacDonald was a Chief Pharmacist Mate who had been stationed on the base for a tour of shore duty. I had told him I was looking for an apartment for Virginia and me to rent once I was settled down. He was very helpful in our finding a place at a time when they were very hard to find.

USS Sea Owl (SS405)

I reported aboard the Sea Owl on 31 August 1950. I was happy with my assignment as this was the same type of submarine as the two I had previously served on.

I doubt the Captain or Executive Officer knew of the political pull that got me there. I do know that all of the submarines were rate heavy and I am sure they would rather have had a seaman or fireman report aboard than a Second Class Petty Officer. A seaman or fireman could be used for the lower level jobs like mess cooks or lookouts at sea.

I was assigned to the forward engine room as an oiler which was fine with me. Because we were so rate heavy I could not have expected to be a throttle man at the time.

The Sea Owl was beginning a two-week upkeep period when I reported aboard. (*Upkeep* is a period of time that the submarine remains in port for repairs and painting.) During upkeep the Chief Engineman or the leading Petty Officers of the engine room were called upon to send a couple of firemen to the topside gang to assist in wire brushing and painting the submarine. I was sent to the deck gang while a couple of (lower rated) firemen remained working in the engine rooms. This created a situation for me: what kind of Chief would do that? But I was so happy to be off the Sunbird, I decided not to make any waves. Reporting to John, the Second Class Petty Officer (the same rate as mine) in charge of topside gang, he couldn't understand why they would send me there. But John said, "You're a Navy diver, you know all about the marker buoys." (These are the two buoys that can be released from a sunken submarine. They have telephones in them so that the rescue ship can communicate with the sub.) "Why don't you release them from their compartments, check them out, clean and grease the cable reel bearings, and get them ready for painting, but make sure the job lasts for the duration of the upkeep period."

By keeping my mouth shut I had landed a good job in the sun for a couple of weeks. Most of all I had made a good friend in John. Who knows, maybe they were testing me to see if I would ask for a transfer.

Our Chief Engineman, Big John, was from Texas and known as a "good old boy." Big John couldn't pass a dumpster without checking its contents, and in most cases he would find some piece of junk that he would bring back to the submarine "that might be useful." Might have worked out back on the farm but not very effective on a submarine. At times during upkeep, Big John would get some vinegar from the mess hall and would go down to the lower flats of the engine room to wire brush the diamond deck plates. I don't think he ever understood his job was to get things done not do them. Shining up deck plates was a bit below his pay grade.

The captain, Cmdr. George C. Cook, was a *hard-charger*; defined as: one who does his job well and has the respect of others - similar to a *hard-ass* but with better motives. There was no doubt as to who was in command of the Sea Owl. I believe he had earned a commendation for his actions while serving on the USS Tusk in a submarine disaster involving the sinking of the USS Cochino (SS345) following a battery explosion in August 1949. Commander Cook had taken command of the Owl in April of 1950 and would remain at the helm until July, 1952.

After I was settled in I contacted my friend Chief MacDonald from Solomon's. Mac and his wife were living in Mystic, only about eight miles from the base. They put me in touch with the owner of a nice furnished apartment. With a list of items from Virginia that we needed to set up the apartment, I made the place ready for her. On my first weekend off from the Sea Owl, I picked her up along with our wedding presents and we moved in.

When the Sea Owl was in port I was free to go home every evening, except when I had the duty - every third day. On those days, and every third weekend, I would have to remain on board for 24 hours. Our operations on the Sea Owl were varied. If we had school boat duty - taking out students from the submarine school - we would be back in port every evening. At other times we could be out for a week or two. In winter (January and February) we operated out of the Virgin Islands during my 5 years aboard. We also made a couple of Mediterranean trips that took about three months. While we lived in Mystic, any time I was away for an extended period, Virginia would take the bus to Boston and from there to Lynn to spend time with her family until I came back.

As an oiler in the forward engine room I operated the trim manifold in the control room when the submarine was submerged - the same job I had six years earlier on the Sea Dog. But we were rate heavy, so I couldn't and didn't complain.

The rates had been closed since the war ended. Rated men with better jobs - and making better money - were more inclined to remain in the service after the war whereas the lower paid hands left for better opportunities in civilian life, and many just to get clear of the service life, thus the *rate heavy* situation. This created an awkward imbalance in which necessary but menial jobs would often have to be held by rated men who considered the work beneath them. To return to an earlier analogy, the command structure now had too many chiefs and far too few Indians, and in this case more literally true. But, after five years, slots were starting to open up. We had seven Second Class Enginemen on board all preparing for the examination for First Class. Naturally everyone was guessing who - if any - might make it. The thinking of many in the crew was that whoever had served on the Sea Owl the longest should be selected. However, this was fleet competition and not limited to a single boat. Many factors were involved in arriving at a candidate's final score. He must first pass the written test, then his performance record, time in rate, and time in the Navy would be combined with the written test mark to determine a final score. Even then promotion would only follow if there were open slots to be filled.

I don't know how many Second Class Enginemen were promoted throughout the Navy from that examination, but I was the only one out of the seven applicants on the Sea Owl who made First Class. Several of my shipmates asked, "How the hell did you do it"? Did they think that I cheated?

But now I was a throttle man in the forward engine room and with another fifty some dollars a month in my pay, Virginia and I were doing pretty well. Virginia had made friends with some of the wives of my friends on the boat. We could now afford to go to New London on pay day for a couple of drinks. One evening a sailor that I only knew slightly was looking at my wife. He came over to our table and asked me if that was my *old lady*. I knew this sailor liked to fight and he also was much bigger than me. I answered with a guarded, "Yes," and he replied, "You have a goddamn good looking old lady." I just said, "Thank you."

Sometime in the spring of 1951, we were ordered to the Philadelphia Naval Shipyard for a routine overhaul, and an upgrade that was to include the addition of a snorkel. A snorkel was a device that permitted operation of our diesel engines while the submarine was submerged.

Our close friends, Betty and Larry Yessak, from the Seal Owl family, decided they would move to Philadelphia for this six month period, and talked Virginia into making the move. I found a second-rate apartment in North Philadelphia, not too far from our friends.

The apartment had two rooms, a kitchen and combination living room and bedroom with a shared bath in the hall. Virginia was nervous about staying alone there on the nights I had the duty. Luckily, Larry and I were in the same section and had the duty on the same nights. This worked out good for Virginia and Betty and on those nights, they could spend the night with each other.

We had a *hang-out* downtown where we spent some time around pay day when we had a few bucks in our pockets. The girls had it made. They could stay in bed until noon while Larry and I went to work, and on arriving home they were ready for a night on the town.

Our "good old boy," Big John, had been transferred and we had a new Chief, Pappy Powers. I had worked for Pappy on the Spinax and he treated us well. We also had a new Captain, Commander Lamar S. Taylor. His nickname among the crew was "Ace," but I'm sure no one would have dared to call him that directly. He came from Georgia and retained his strong southern feelings about blacks. There are many stories that he told while I was in his presence, especially in the Navy Yard where many black men worked, but repeating them here would be an embarrassment. President Truman had ordered that segregation in the military was to be ended, but old ideas die hard. Other than that, he was a good guy. However, he came up short as the Commanding Officer of a Naval Ship - as will be seen.

Also at this time we received a new Chief of the Boat (COB). He too was a good guy, and within a short time the crew was referring to him as either "Uncle Eddie," or "Steady Eddie" - both meant as compliments, and taken as such. (Unlike "Ace.")

Most of the overhaul work performed on the Sea Owl at the shipyard was done by civilian workers from the various shops. Because of the addition of the snorkel, all four main engines had to be overhauled. The machinists from Shop 38 handled the two main engines in the forward engine room, and the two in the after engine room were done by *ships company* - enginemen from the Sea Owl. Everything went smoothly, but the yard workers were unable to get fuel pressure to their engines, and they could not be started. My Chief asked me to check out the fuel system. After making sure that all the valves in the system were open, I started the fuel pump and was in the process of venting the system. Meanwhile a rather arrogant boss from the pipefitters shop had been called in. He was a very large man, and crowded his way next to me in the confined space I was in. He said, "Kid, you have to vent the fucking pump." I told him I was venting the pump. He gave me the strong arm and said, "Out of my way kid." From where he pushed me I could clearly see the end of the electric motor that was connected to the fuel pump and the arrow on the motor that showed the direction of rotation. And I had the answer. All of the electric motors had been removed from the boat and taken to the shop for any necessary repairs. When this motor was reinstalled, two wires were reversed and the fuel pump was being turned in the wrong direction. At that time I only weighed about 145 pounds, but I didn't appreciate this loudmouth and the way he talked to me. I had no reason to fear him; he wasn't my boss. So I decided to stall as long as possible to increase his blood pressure before I told him what the problem was. I said to him, "You may be a lead pipefitter, but until you get that motor cranking in the right direction, you won't get any fuel to the engines!" I sure didn't make any points with him, but his men loved seeing him put in his place.

Philadelphia was not far from Solomon's Island. One Saturday morning Virginia and I got up early and drove down there. I showed her the base and all of the diving equipment. I looked up my old friend Hank, the machinist and we were invited to dinner. Hank was happy to see me and to hear that I made First Class. Another friend of mine who had recently married invited us to stay with them for the night. I had met his wife-to-be when I was stationed there. It was a great week end.

Now that we were nearing the end of our overhaul, it was time to move Virginia back to the New London area. We were lucky to find a furnished apartment near our friends Larry and Betty. I left our car with Virginia and rode the train back to Philadelphia, and within a few days we got underway.

Once at sea, and at a safe depth, we had a lot of drills with the new snorkel. At times, if we didn't follow the procedure correctly, our engine could shut down and exhaust gas would fill the boat. Captain Taylor would go out of his mind. On one occasion when it happened, a sharp young seaman put the record "Smoke Gets In Your Eyes" on our record player. The captain didn't see the humor. On another occasion he came through the forward engine room while I was on watch. He said to me, "Don't put too much oil in that engine." He must have been on a submarine where that had been done.

Our First Class Engineman in charge of the aft engine room was being transferred to another command. He recommended his buddy for the job to the Engineering Officer. This decision should have been made by the Chief Engineman, but the Chief was not much of a leader and usually allowed the First Class to bypass him and go directly to the EO. So the word was out as to who was going to be put in charge of the engine room. By now I was the senior First Class. Normally I would have gone to the Chief with my problem. However, since he could be expected to let the First Class bypass him, I was afraid the Engineer would listen to the FC and I decided to go directly to him. Luckily, I saw him up on deck, which was a better place to talk to him privately. I said, "Mr. B, I understand that Larry will be in charge of the after engine room?" His answer to me, "So?" I reminded him that I was the senior First Class and if not considered qualified for the position I would request a transfer to another submarine where I would be. He replied to the effect that he didn't know that a final decision has been made.

A few weeks prior to that conversation, it was found that the wrong oil rings had been installed on the pistons of the engines in the aft engine room. Correcting the problem was a big job if we followed the normal procedure, and would have required at least two weeks to complete. I was one of the workers on the job, not any smarter than anyone else, but I could see that by using a small band cut from our regular ring compressor, we could do the job without a complete disassembly of the two engines. I passed the suggestion to the First Class, Nick who told me it wouldn't work. Meanwhile that evening while he had the duty, he cut a narrow band from the ring compressor as I had proposed. In the morning he followed my original suggestion without as much as a thank you to me. It gets better. After a few days our Engineering Officer came through the engine room and expressed amazement at the progress we were making. Shortly he noticed us using the cut down ring compressor. He said to the Petty Officer in charge, "What an idea, who thought of that?" He replied, "Well boss, when the chips are down we have to get our heads together." The Engineer said "I know whose idea it was." Nick, with a big smile on his face, took all of the credit.

The day that Nick was transferred I was told by our Chief that I would be put in charge of the after engine room. I did feel badly for my shipmate, Larry Yessak, who Nick had recommended, but I felt I was in the right. We were friends, and I'm sure he realized I was senior.

Our Engineer, Mr. B. was a good officer and well liked on the boat, but after our conversation about who would be in charge, I had the feeling that he resented me. It's too bad he never learned whose idea the ring compressor really was.

Being put in charge of an engine room was a big step forward, but I was concerned that my early marks in my enlisted performance record were not higher to improve my chance of making Chief Petty Officer when it came time to take the examination.

Both engine rooms on the Sea Owl were in good shape. We took a lot of pride in them and kept them extra clean. When we had an inspection by Commodore Lowrance, or our captain, we installed special blue light bulbs that made the rooms look outstanding.

Occasionally the Commodore would ride with us on a daily operation. He always made a courtesy walk through the submarine. On one of these trips I was on watch in the after engine room with both engines running. He came to my ear and he asked me how I liked the Sea Owl? I answered, "Outstanding." He said I picked a good boat.

Things were looking up for me. A new Engineer reported aboard and about the same time we received a new Chief Engineman, both of whom I liked.

The new engineer, Mr. Harkness, was very pleased to be the engineer on a submarine that had Fairbanks Morse diesel engines because his father was an executive in the company. He said, "If you guys ever have a technical problem, my father can put you in direct contact with the technical support group." Fortunately, we never had any problems so serious that we couldn't handle them, but it was nice to have an *ace* in the hole.

Mr. Harkness liked to verbally lock horns with me. I also liked to batter him with words. I had more time in the Navy than he did, but he was my boss and I knew how far I could go. He was an officer, but as young as I was he was younger by a year or so.

One day he came into my engine room with a serious look on his face. I knew he was going to pull something on me. He asked me why the engines were painted gray. I told him it was a standard Navy color, although some submarines had them painted white and others beige. He asked why he couldn't have them painted red. My answer, "Mr. Harkness, you're the engineering officer on this submarine and you can have them painted any color that you want. We can even candy stripe them for you. The problem is, you're only a short-timer on this submarine." He interrupted me saying "What the hell do you mean by that remark." My answer, "You will only be on this boat for a couple of years, and hopefully you will move on to another submarine as the Executive Officer. We have men here who have been on board for up to ten years. Would it be right for them to bust their asses to paint these engines red, and when you move up the ladder, have a new engineer say, "Who the hell painted these engines red? I want them gray." Mr. Harkness looked at me and said, "Bryant you have a good point." I don't believe Mr. Harkness wanted them painted. I think he was just wished to raise my blood pressure.

Our new chief, Chief Coover, was well liked by the men. I don't believe he had served on a submarine with Fairbanks Morse engines but he had confidence in his men and did not micro manage the engine rooms. He believed in taking care of his men. He was loud and was soon nicknamed "The Senator." No chief or officer messed with his men; any complaints were to go through him - or someone was going to get an earful.

The dress code on a submarine while at sea was pretty relaxed. Shorts were permitted but an undershirt was required when eating meals in the mess hall. Sleeping in the nude was not allowed. One day at meal time, a young sailor was required to set up the battery ventilation for a battery charge. This required that he stand on one of the seating benches at the chief's table while they were eating. This was not a problem. He only needed to place the toe of one shoe on the bench so that he could stand up to reach the lever on the battery ventilation system. But at an inopportune moment our COB, "Steady Eddie," turned his head to see what was going on and was faced with the family jewels of the young sailor in his short shorts. Steady Eddie was not too steady in giving the young sailor an *ass chewing*. In the future, underwear would be required when wearing shorts! When the other Chiefs decided to have some fun with him they would ask how the kid measured up.

Bringing in a ship by the Officer of the Deck (OOD) and tying it up to the pier was known as "making a landing." This could be quite difficult at some ports where the current was very strong. Our captain was arguably the world's worst ship handler. At times when we were returning from a long trip our wives might be waiting at the pier when we came in. Several squadron officers would also usually be on the pier to greet a returning vessel. On one of the days after "Ace" had made a landing Virginia asked me what had been so funny when we came in, and why were all the officers on the pier laughing? I then explained to her that "Ace" was not known as an *outstanding* ship handler.

Every Commanding Officer is responsible for his ship. He is also responsible for the training of his officers in ship handling. In most cases when another officer was making a landing "Ace" would get nervous and step in to relieve him before the landing was completed. One day I heard "Ace" talking to Mr. Harkness about his landings. Mr. Harkness was quick witted. He reminded the captain that he had never made a landing since the captain always relieved him before he was able to make one.

While we were in port, and especially when we had school boat operations, we had the use of a barracks to sleep in on the nights that we didn't have the duty aboard. Occasionally our COB would have to furnish a man to the barracks for a week as a compartment cleaner. This was a great job; clean up the barracks for a couple of hours and have the rest of the day off. The Chief of the Boat always sent a non-rated man for the job. One day I asked him if I could be assigned as a compartment cleaner for a week. He said, "Oh no, this is a job for a seaman or fireman." I explained to him what an easy job it was and the fact that I could be at home by noon. I also told him that the most of my work was cleaning anyway. He said, "You want the job?" I said, "Yes!" What a great week. I was at home for most of it.

This was about the time that we went to the Mediterranean Sea for three months to operate with the Sixth Fleet. Virginia went home to Lynn for the time I was gone.

My brother Jack was married now, and stationed in Frankfort, Germany. I put in for a week's leave and rode the train through France to Germany to see him and his wife Olga, and their baby - my nephew - Carl. Olga was a friend of Virginia's whom I had met before she married Jack. What a beautiful clean country Germany was. I didn't see any evidence of World War II in the area I visited. When it came time for me to return to the Sea Owl, Jack and his wife drove me back to the Mediterranean via the Alps, Switzerland, and France to Nice on the French Riviera where the Sea Owl was anchored off shore.

Shortly before Virginia and I were married, Jack had been transferred to Korea where he had been shot and left for dead, and eventually taken prisoner by the North Koreans. When he was later at the Army's Murphy Hospital in Waltham, Massachusetts for recuperation, he was introduced to Olga, his wife to be, by Virginia.

Going through the Alps was quite an experience. Although we spent one night in a hotel, part of our driving through the Alps was at night. At times with the fog so thick, I sometimes had to walk alongside the car to make sure we stayed on the narrow road.

During my time on the Sea Owl, five years, from 1950 to 1955, I made two trips to the Mediterranean and another in 1959 on the Entemedor. It's difficult to remember now what happened on which trip of what boat. I do recall that Lucky Luciano, the noted mobster, had been deported from our country and was living in Italy. Some of our crew members met him as a restaurant in Naples. He was very cordial with them and bought them a round of drinks.

While I was on this trip, Virginia was pregnant and her delivery date expected to be in November when I would have been back at home from our trip to the Mediterranean. But things did not work out as planned. My daughter Susan was born prematurely on Sept 10, 1952, at the Chelsea Naval Hospital. Virginia's health records were not available as they were at the submarine base in Groton. An R/H factor was involved in the delivery. We always wondered if her records had been on hand and her blood had been changed, Susan might have been a normal child.

At first we had no cause for concern but as time passed her development problems became more evident. We had thought her progress was the result of her premature birth, but after a year or so her doctor made the diagnosis of Cerebral Palsy. At the age of two she was able to walk with crutches. She was being seen then by doctors at the Crippled Children's Hospital in Newington, Connecticut. They recommended stretching exercises for her legs that Virginia performed faithfully and I was involved when at home.

One Friday afternoon at the end of upkeep - at about 3 PM - we were sitting around the after engine room hatch on deck waiting for liberty to start. Our engineer, Mr. Harkness, came walking on the deck toward us and motioned to me that he wanted to talk to me. When I approached him he said "Don't your men have anything to do?" I explained that all of the upkeep work was completed. He then asked if the men couldn't be holding "field day" (clean up ship). I told him we had the cleanest engine rooms of any submarine on the river, and if he could show me a cleaner engine room, we would stay aboard until ours was the cleanest. I could see that I had pissed him off, but I wasn't sure why. He said, "God damn it Bryant don't you know if the Captain sees your men sitting around the hatch and not working, he will be all over *my* ass. Now goddam it, send them up on the base or anyplace, but get them away from that *fucking* hatch." Mr. Harkness was absolutely right. My answer, the only one possible: "Yes Sir, Mr. Harkness."

On one of our operations at sea we spent one of our weekends at Norfolk, Virginia, tied up to the submarine tender Orion. My old friend Warren Thomas, our Master Diver from Solomon's, was a Warrant Officer on the Orion. He was the Diving Officer in charge of the tender's divers. I had the duty Friday when we pulled into Norfolk. On Saturday morning I went aboard the tender and was able to get his address. This was before the telephone was available for most Navy people. I took a cab out to his house. He and his wife Betty were happy to see me and glad to learn that I had made First Class. Warren was also happy to see me because he was painting a couple of rooms in his house. He had a paint brush for me!

That evening, he and his wife Betty were going to the Officer's Club with another couple for dinner and they invited me to go along. I felt a little out of place at the O Club; however, he always introduced me as his diver from Solomon's. He was a great guy to work for and I spent a very pleasant weekend with them.

About this time the Reader's Digest published a story about a *man without a country*. His name was O'Brien. He had served some time in prison prior to World War II and wound up in China during the war. He wanted to come back to the States, but the States would not accept him. He claimed that he had helped American fliers that had been shot down over China during the war. Eventually he ended up on a ferry boat that ran from Hong Kong to Taiwan and spent 18 months on board. The English in Hong Kong wouldn't accept him either, nor would Taiwan. His friends and/or family would bring him food at the boat. Finally, after the 18 months, he was accepted by the Dominican Republic. He opened up a bar in Santo Domingo, appropriately named, "O'Brien's Bar."

As luck would have it, the next winter, operating out of St. Thomas, our winter submarine base, we visited Santo Domingo for a weekend. And where does a Sea Owl sailor go for his first drink but "O'Brien's Bar." We had no problem finding the place, with a big white sign shouting, the name in Kelly green paint, with green shamrocks of course.

Mr. O'Brien was a disreputable looking guy with tattoos over most of his exposed body. He had a couple of ladies of the night that were available for a price. Not terribly appealing. His stock of booze was so low that it was necessary for him to collect money from us in advance to stock the bar before we could start drinking. But it was a good investment. Mr. O'Brien had some great stories. As I remember the ladies of the night didn't look any better as we continued to get drunk.

As I have mentioned, our captain was not the best of ship handlers. One day we were out in the Gulf Stream where the sea water temperature is quite warm; up in the 80 degree range. Often, if time permits, a captain will stop a submarine for a swim call for the crew. A couple of the mooring lines would be draped over the side to help the swimmers climb back on deck. At times if a swimmer should drift too far from the boat, the captain might engage power to the screws and maneuver the boat to pick him up. On one occasion a swimmer was some distance from the Sea Owl. Our captain called out to the swimmer, "Don't get nervous, I'll come and getcha." The swimmer, who was a line handler on deck, knew the captain was, to tell it plainly, a *lousy* ship handler, replied, "No, Sir. No. Park that sonofabitch and I'll come along side!"

About 1954 the Sea Owl got a new Executive Officer. I will call him Mr. N. He soon concluded that the Sea Owl had a lot of *personnel problems* and thought her Captain was one of them. He was a good officer and wanted to make the Sea Owl a better ship. He decided to interview all of the First Class Petty Officers individually as he felt the First Class Petty Officers were closer to the problems than the Chief Petty Officers who lived in their own world. This was to be done without informing the Captain and we were all sworn to secrecy when each of us met with him. Should the Captain get wind of it, Mr. N would have been *in the crapper*. When my turn came to talk with him, he explained the purpose of the meeting and asked me what I thought was wrong with the Sea Owl. I answered him by saying, "I want a transfer to another submarine." Mr. N. said to me, "Goddam it Bryant, I didn't call you up here to talk about your personal problems. I want to know what is wrong with the Sea Owl!" I replied saying, "Everywhere we go we are outstanding. We always have the cleanest submarine in the squadron. But the crew never receives any reward for it. For example, we are on 3 section liberty - every third day or weekend we have the duty aboard the submarine while in port. Most of the other boats are in 4 section liberty. I want a transfer to one of the submarines that are on 4 section liberty. Also, when submarines come into port after an extended trip, wives and families will usually be waiting on the pier. On most submarines the Chief of the Boat is authorized to start liberty. Not on the Sea Owl. We have to wait until the captain returns to the ship after briefing the Squadron Commander. Many times sailors on other boats have said, "You must love your ship, why don't you go ashore?" "

Things did get better thanks to Mr. N. And we went to four section liberty.

Our Chief of the Boat, Uncle Eddie, was transferred to shore duty. However, we lucked out when our Chief Pharmacist was made the COB as we thought as highly of him.

At that time most of the officers had second cars that they drove to the base. Our captain had a 1936 Ford. My buddy Maguire in the engine room suggested that we put a car bomb on his car. This bomb was a joke-shop device that would whistle and make a lot of smoke but wouldn't cause any real damage. With our lookouts in place, Mac and I put the bomb on the engine of his car. For some reason it failed to ignite when he started it and we thought it was a dud. We found out the next morning that the bomb worked quite well, later, and the New London Fire Department was called. We accused Mr. Harkness of the prank.

One of these!

One of the ports that we visited when we were operating out of the Virgin Islands was Havana, (BC - Before Castro). The people there were very friendly. Top shelf rum and Coca Cola was 10 cents. If more rum was wanted in a drink it was free. If more Coca Cola, it would add 5 cents. At St. Thomas good rum sold for only $8.00 a case.

The time had come for another overhaul. This time we were sent to the Navy Yard at Charleston, South Carolina. This was a good yard with dedicated workers.

In a few days I located an apartment in downtown Charleston. On my first long week end off I hitchhiked to New London to pick up Virginia and our baby, Susan. Hitchhiking was a good way to travel in those days for a serviceman in uniform. Our apartment turned out to be loaded with cockroaches. We didn't even bother to unpack, and within a couple of days rented a mobile home. With spraying we could control the cockroaches. Bugs of one sort or another are a way of life down there.

When a submarine enters a Navy yard for overhaul, the only jobs done are the jobs there are work orders for. If the crew wants something extra, like a locker made and installed, or to have some parts chrome plated, then *cumshaw* becomes involved. Cumshaw is a term that has its origins in the early trading days in the Far East and is something that is used as a present, gratuity, bribe, or payoff to get something done. What does the Sea Owl use for cumshaw? 190 proof torpedo alcohol, ground coffee in 20 pound cans, or maybe a canned ham from the galley? The Sea Owl brought about 40 gallons (in 5 gallon cans) of alcohol to the yard to be used as cumshaw. Someone has to guard the chicken coop and the best qualified was the "Senator," Chief Coover. As mentioned earlier, Chief Coover took care of his men. Occasionally we would have private house party. Money was tight. We could always go to the chief for some alcohol; it was like vodka, but at 190 proof had to be diluted with something to make it drinkable.

Every day at the end of the yard worker's shift, our duty section would go through the Sea Owl and pick up all the trash left behind by the workers. One day when I had the duty as the section leader, the Duty Officer approached me at clean up time. He said, "You know, when we do our cleaning up the Captain will be here to supervise." (He did not have his wife with him and was always around the boat.) "Could you do me a favor and pile a bunch of crap at the bottom of the ladder to the forward torpedo room (the entrance to submarine). He'll see it, blow his top, and leave the boat, then we can leisurely finish up.

But this is the way it worked out:

Prior to the cleanup, I was sitting down on a cleat on deck, waiting for the yard workers to leave the ship when the yard whistle was blown. At this time the Captain came aboard. I stood up to salute him and he motioned for me to sit down again. He sat down with me on the other end of the cleat and started to vent his feelings about blacks in a way that would be embarrassing to repeat today. But this was still a time when such views were common - before the Civil Rights movement of the 1960s and long before the invention of Political Correctness. During his one-sided conversation with me, he began focusing on a particular black worker nearby, and kept looking in his direction. The man realized he was being talked about, so he disappeared below. The captain said to me, "Go down below and see what that .... is doing." I went down and returned some minutes later to report that I couldn't find him (I didn't look) being fairly certain - rightly - that the subject would have left his mind.

Work on the Sea Owl was nearly complete and we began preparing for going to sea. Taking advantage of a long weekend, I drove Virginia and Susan back to New London. We had sub-let our apartment to friends, another Navy couple so were lucky that we had a place waiting for us when we arrived home.

Returning to the shipyard late on Sunday, I was told that one of the main generators had been replaced in (my) aft engine room. That had required removing a large section of the main deck and cutting a large piece out of the pressure hull over the engine room to provide enough room to remove the generator and get the new one into place.

So Monday morning was a horror show in the engine room. The new generator was installed, the yard welders were welding the section of the pressure hull back into place, and mechanics and electricians were working on the new generator. I was in the engine room with my crew of five plus Chief Coover, our Engineer Mr. Harkness, and our Captain, Commander Taylor. "Ace" was ranting as usual and trying to run the show. Chief Coover asked the captain when the engine room needed to be ready for going to sea. The captain told him we were scheduled to leave the Navy Yard on Thursday. Chief Coover said, "Captain, at 0800 on Wednesday morning I will knock on the door of your stateroom. I will take you aft to inspect the engine room. We will be ready to go to sea in all respects. However, in the meantime, I don't want to see you in this engine room. The captain's answer was, "Yes, Chief," and he quietly departed. That was something no officer of lesser rank would usually dare to say to a ship's captain but Coover had a forceful personality and such complete confidence in his abilities that he could put it over.

We had a lot of work to do to clean up and paint the engine room, in addition to our regular duties. This required us to work late in the evenings. About 8 PM Chief Coover came in, not to check on us - he had faith in his men. He came with a gift of appreciation in a brown paper bag. From the bag he removed a bottle of whiskey, removed the stopper which he threw away, and passed the bottle around. We all had a drink; he left the remainder of the bottle with us, and was on his way.

What a great Chief. I learned a lot from him that would help me out in later years when I made Chief myself, and more so when I became an instructor in Leadership. Quite a difference from the Chief at Deep Sea Diving School who *shared* a bottle with us when we raised the sunken yacht. Well, yes, he did leave us the beer; there is that.

It need not be said that we completed our work in the engine room on time and left the Navy Yard on schedule to return to the base at Groton (New London, but on the opposite side of the river).

I am somewhat embarrassed about some of my stories about our captain on the Sea Owl. He did have his good qualities. He was older than most captains at the base. I do not know his path to becoming a submarine officer in the Navy on submarines, but he was not a graduate of the Naval Academy - did not "wear the ring." He came from a different background from most officers of the Navy. He was good to his crew and would talk to the lowest seaman as well as his officers although he did not treat blacks the same as whites. But I'm sure he thought more of his black steward than any man in his crew.

In later years, crew members of the Sea Owl had an annual reunion - as they still do. "Ace" made every one of these until he became ill. He loved his crew and said the command was the pinnacle of his career.

The command of a ship of the US Navy is a pinnacle not reached by many men. Commander Cook, who preceded "Ace" in command of the Sea Owl, took equal pride in the same accomplishment as will be seen in his letter below.

One other thing I accomplished during my time with the Sea Owl - a decade late, but better late than never - was to obtain my GED through the base educational office. I never regretted having left school when I did since my life would have been completely different if I had stayed at home to finish and missed my wartime experience. As a lot of men will tell it, they wouldn't give a nickel to do it again, but wouldn't take a million dollars for it. But that "piece of paper" was becoming more important in daily life and I still had some miles to go. How many I wouldn't have guessed at the time. So I became a high school graduate - and felt pretty good about it.

Shortly after returning to the base, my friend George at the Submarine Escape Training Tank told me that the tank had to fill a quota and send an instructor to underwater swimmers school at Key West, Florida to become a scuba diver. The CO of the tank preferred not to send one of his trained instructors at the tank to fill the slot as he would be short an instructor for 6 weeks. George knew

I was a first class diver and suggested that I talk to the CO if I had any interest in becoming an instructor. I got in touch with him right away. I told him I understood he had a quota to fill at Underwater Swimmers School, that I was a first class diver, and would like to fill the quota if I could be assigned to the tank after completing the school in Florida. He said he would contact the personnel officer to see if he could arrange to get me orders to the Training Tank, and within a couple of weeks they came through.

*USS Sea Owl
at sea*

*USS Sea Owl
launching*

September 4, 1958

Dear Bryant,

When the NAUTILUS was out here, I ran into James PRATER (TM1) who was one of her crew. Naturally, we talked over the old days on the SEA OWL when I had command. PRATER is one of the few of the old gang which I have had the pleasure of meeting during the past six years, so I was very anxious to know what had become of you and how you were making out. I was more than pleased that he knew the where-abouts of about forty ex-SEA OWL personnel. One of the things which pleased me the most was the fact that so many had stayed in the Navy (I guess it proved that, if you could stand me, you could stand anything). The other thing which made me happy was that everybody on the list was either an officer, a chief, or first class (I am attaching a copy of the list in case you desire to get in touch with one another).

After reveiwing the list, maybe you will accept my apologies for making this a form letter. I realize each one of you deserves a personal letter, but what I have to say applies to all of you.

My one and only command was the SEA OWL. I look back on it as the highlight of my naval career. I was proud of the SEA OWL and I was proud of her crew. Although we weren't any great "ball of Fire" and we didn't win any "Es", it was a great source of personal satisfaction for me to know we were ready and able to fight effectively as a team in the event we had to go to war. It was your spirit and cooperation which made this possible. As it turned out we didn't get a chance to prove our potential, though there were times during the Korean War when I though we might. However, the fact that we were ready was not overlooked by our seniors. In my last fitness report upon leaving the SEA OWL, the DIVCOM stated that the SEA OWL was the boat he would prefer most to go to war with. This was a great compliment and one which you should all rightfully share. Your cooperation during my tour with you also played a large part in my personal career. This is minor compared to the job we had to do, but I want you to know I appreciate it. The fact that I was recently selected to Captain is another honor which you should rightfully share for if the SEA OWL wasn't successful, then I wouldn't be either.

Thanks again for all the fine support you gave me many years ago on the SEA OWL. I look forward to the time when our courses will cross and we can discuss old times.

Best personal regards,

George C. Cook

GEORGE C. COOK
COMMANDER, U. S. NAVY
PCO INSTRUCTOR

Training School/Underwater Swimmers School

The training tank was only a short distance from where the Sea Owl was tied up to the pier - about 5 piers away. I thought that I would be going directly to the tank, but was directed to the Submarine School on the upper base. The plan was for me to remain at the school for a few weeks until the next scheduled instructor's course started. They apparently were unaware that I was scheduled to report to Underwater Swimmers School in less than two weeks.

When things got sorted out I was sent to the tank to keep me occupied while awaiting my start date at Underwater Swimmers School.

Scuba (self-contained underwater breathing apparatus) diving was relatively new to Navy diving except in the UDTs (underwater demolition teams), now evolved into Navy Seals. Most of the hard hat deep sea divers were not scuba trained.

While waiting for my orders, I was assigned to an instructor at the tank for training. He taught me about the medical and physical aspects of diving, much of which I already knew from deep sea diving school. He also taught me about the air systems, the water systems, and the art of free diving - diving without an air supply (holding your breath), the type of diving done by most instructors at the tank.

My orders read that my class was to begin on 22 Aug 1955, and stated that I was to be returned to the tank upon completion of school. The course would be for about 6 weeks and my scheduled return for 7 Oct 1955; a long wait for Virginia. However, I would then have three years of shore duty.

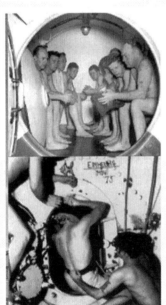

Views of Escape Tank at Groton with interior air locks

My transportation to Key West was by air from Hartford to Miami, and bus to Key West.

The class consisted of about 30 men, some of whom were officers. Our instructors were well trained in swimming and scuba diving. Some had been former UDT personnel.

A large part of our class was being trained preliminary to their next assignment at the EOD (explosive ordnance disposal) School at Dam Neck, VA. Some of us were qualified deep sea divers not trained in scuba. A few students were from various ships in the fleet. In my case, I was to become one of the instructors at the submarine escape training tank's scuba class that was given about 4 times a year.

At that time most ships in the Navy wanted a trained scuba diver aboard. They could be used for various jobs; perhaps the most frequent and important would be checking the screws and other submerged parts of a ship's hull.

In addition to the instructors, we had a First Class Boatswain mate in our class who was our section leader. He was in charge of us when we were not with the instructors. We also had a self-appointed *assistant section leader*. He was a real *suck ass*. He was a First Class Engineman, the same rate as mine, but acted like he was the Senior First Class in our class. Our air tanks were charged to 2,000 psi (pounds per square inch). He thought he was the only one who knew how to charge them, so he charged all of our tanks. Great, less work for the rest of us.

From the time we arrived at the school until graduation, our uniform of the day was olive drab ball cap, light jacket, shorts, (used to swim in), and canvas swim shoes.

We began in the class room where we covered the medical and physical aspects of diving, followed by swimming in the pool. Next we wore swim-fins and spent a lot of time holding on to the side of the pool learning the proper leg action for an underwater swimmer. The next phase was using the scuba gear underwater in the swimming pool. In addition to swimming, we learned to ditch our scuba gear in the deep end of the pool and make a safe ascent to the surface - the easy part. The hard part was swimming to the bottom of the pool to don the gear, and return to the surface. After we became proficient at that, we would have to do it without face masks.

Back in the classroom we were taught about the different types of explosives we might encounter as an underwater swimmer. We were also taught how to effectively search a specified area underwater, and searching for a drowned person.

We had a lot of physical training to get us in shape for our long swims. One instructor liked to take us on a long double time run through the streets of Key West. I think it did something for his ego, but I have to admit, it got us in shape.

At this point we were ready for our first ocean swim. We used the buddy system for safety, always swimming with a partner. My partner was a big First Class Gunners Mate - a much better swimmer than I was. I am sure I held him back on most of our swims. Our first swim was with face mask and swim fins only. We were taken about a quarter of a mile from the shore in a small boat, an LCVP (landing craft vehicle personnel). We then teamed up with our *buddy* and were told to swim to a designated spot on the beach. We continued these swims over a period of several days until we worked our distance up to a mile. Being dumped in the ocean one mile out, the beach looked a lot further away than that, and maybe it was.

We then moved on to the underwater ocean swims with our scuba gear. The same routine was used, working our distance up to one mile. On these swims we were tethered together with a piece of line about 6 ft. long, an enhancement to the buddy system. Also attached to us was a flotation bladder that floated to the surface. We were provided with a compass on our wrist to aid in maintaining our bearing to the landing spot on the beach. Being tethered together and with the bladder attached, we had to be careful to both enter the water at the same time. Once in the water, the designated navigator would take a compass bearing to the beach. After descending to swim depth, usually 10-15 ft., we were not allowed to come to the surface. Should a pair of swimmers get completely lost and be swimming in the wrong direction one of the instructors would spot the bladder as being off course. They would then pull the pair to the surface and get them re-oriented. The navigator would be the lead swimmer, keeping his eyes on the compass at all times. His buddy would swim to the rear and slightly above him. From that position he could control the depth and also act as lookout.

After swimming for about a month with the use of fins, the instructors took us to sea for a good mile, took our fins away from us, and made us swim to the beach without them. Thus we learned the value of the fins!

In our last few days we had a chance to use some explosives to blow up a few things underwater.

I did quite well on my final examination however I was not a strong swimmer so was not in the top of the class.

At graduation time the class *suck ass* noticed that I had three hash marks on my jumper signifying that I had at least 12 years of service to his two stripes. He asked me *where the hell* I got all the hash marks. I told him, "Cracker Jacks." He asked what the hell I meant. I told him they came in Cracker Jack Boxes as a prize and maybe if he bought enough boxes, he might get three hash marks like I did. I was wishing I had my First Class Deep Sea Divers patch on my uniform at that time but I had not updated my qualification so was not entitled to wear it. He would have been really envious.

Returning to the submarine base was really easy. A friend in the class gave me a ride to the airport in Miami and Virginia picked me up at Hartford.

Postcard view of Submarine Base Groton CT

Returning to the Training Tank as Instructor

My tour of duty as an instructor at the escape training tank ran from 1955-1958.

In many conversations with fellow submarine sailors we have disagreed about the methods of escape taught at the tank. But I have to remind them that the training and equipment over the years has changed, and my knowledge of it was what I learned - and taught - in an earlier time.

Another problem that I sometimes have in discussing submarine escape training is explaining what the students are expected to do on the escape versus what the instructors working in the water do. As will be seen, the two are quite different.

During the early 1900's there was no effective means of escape for the crew of a submarine that went down. A submarine escape training tank was built in 1930 at the submarine base at New London, and a second at the submarine base at Pearl Harbor, to develop and teach escape procedures. In the tank, an escape could be simulated by duplicating conditions that would apply to a sunken submarine. This cylindrical steel tank measured 18 ft. in diameter and was approximately 120 feet high. On top of the tank was a cupola that added another 20 feet for a total height about 140 feet. When filled it held a little over a quarter million gallons of fresh water that was heated and maintained at 92 degrees.

The cupola on top was the area where training was conducted and supervised by the Officer in Charge. This is also where the students surfaced after making their ascents.

The tank was equipped with an elevator that carried students and instructors to the top or to the two escape locks located on the side of the tank, one at 18 ft. and the other at 50 ft.

Above: Interior view of escape training tank with instructors and a student making a free ascent from the 110ft compartment, roving bell at right. Below Right: Line ascent with Momsen Lung. Below Left: Compartment for tank entry

Submarine sailors from boats in port were required to undergo retraining at intervals to keep their skills updated. I will describe the routine for students from the submarine school versus crews from submarines with previous training since that is more comprehensive.

At the start of the program students enter a *recompression chamber* for a pressure test in which they are exposed to a pressure of 50 pounds per square inch (psi). This is the equivalent of the pressure the human body experiences at a depth of 112 ft. in sea water.

The requirement of the students during this test is to learn to equalize the pressure on their ears and sinuses while the pressure is increasing in the chamber. This is done by closing the nostril passages with a pinch of the thumb and forefinger and a forced blow to the nose when pressure is felt on the eardrums. This will cause the ears to pop. This procedure is necessary whenever pressure is felt on the ear drum to prevent the eardrum from bursting - not a fatal condition, but painful.

This chamber has a lock out section, and should a student have ear problems he can exit the chamber and allow the remaining students to continue without interruption.

Once at 50 psi, returning to the surface pressure (atmospheric pressure) is no problem; the ears will pop automatically.

The primary type of escape device used at that time was the Momsen Lung. This was developed by Lt. Charles Momsen in the 1920's and accepted by the Navy in 1929 as the preferred submarine escape device from among several being proposed. In operation it would remove CO_2 from exhaled air by passing it through a canister of soda lime and by adding oxygen from an integral supply to provide breathable air to a swimmer although eventually it was found that the process, while reassuring, was unnecessary. It was attached to the chest and had a mouthpiece at the top, and a nose clip to keep water out of the nose during the ascent. At the bottom of the bag there was a rubber flutter (relief) valve. This valve would allow the compressed air inhaled by the student in the escape lock to be released as he made his ascent to the surface and prevent him from developing an air embolism. With proper instruction students make their escape ascents from the 18 ft. then the 50 ft. locks on the side of the tank. Instructors cover each student in the water at all times. Should one make a mistake, or have a problem, an instructor would return him to the lock where he could breathe normally. Usually with minimal instruction, a student could complete his ascent to the surface successfully.

Demonstration of early Momsen Lung in use (USN photo)

During training the Officer in Charge, with the use of a hand held microphone connected to speakers in the tank and the escape locks, directed training activities. A glass bottomed floating box was located at his feet. With this box to calm the surface waves of the water he could clearly see everything going on, even to the depth of the 110 ft. compartment. The tank was well lighted and the water was treated and as clear as a bell. The reason the water was heated to 92 degrees, as noted above, was for the benefit of the instructors. This was the ideal temperature for breath holding (necessary for the instructors) and to permit working in the water for periods of several hours. At temperatures substantially below body temperature, even if relatively comfortable, hypothermia can develop with prolonged immersion.

At that time the majority of the instructors were neither deep sea divers nor scuba divers. This may sound strange, but the tank required a different type of diving; skin diving, or, *breath holding*. Because of this, it was as easy to train a submarine sailor such as myself for the job as it would be to train a certified diver. In my case, I was a First Class Deep Sea Diver *lapsed qualification*. This didn't affect my getting assigned to the tank. I got the job as I noted earlier because I had been willing to fill the quota required at the underwater swimmer's school.

Many people - including submarine sailors - often ask why the instructors, once trained, didn't use scuba gear instead of the breath holding method since they had to remain in and under the water. Seemingly that would be great except that within a short period of time the tank would be so full of bubbles that the instructors would be unable to judge whether the students were properly expelling the expanding compressed air in their lungs that they had inhaled in the escape locks. Similarly, the officer in charge could no longer see if the students were ascending safely.

Instructors were able to hold their breath for periods of up to three or four minutes, and in some cases longer. If students were making their escapes from the 50 ft. lock, one of a pair of instructors would leave the surface and drop down to the lock to cover them when they emerged from the lock. When the first needed to come up for air he would raise his arm to signal his partner who would drop down to relieve him. The out-of-breath instructor would use a line attached to the side of the tank to pull himself to the surface.

I have purposely used the word *drop* rather than *swim* in describing this process. We didn't swim or use fins in the tank since by doing so we would use up the oxygen in our lungs too quickly. We also didn't want our face masks being kicked off our faces by a swimmer. But how does one *drop* down to 50 ft. without swimming?

The average human body, with lungs filled with air will float in fresh water. This is referred to as positive buoyancy. This same body, at a depth of about 15 ft. becomes somewhat smaller in volume due to the compression of the lungs and can no longer float. It becomes negatively buoyant at that point and will sink. The instructor, using this principle, can walk his way down the 10 ft. underwater ladder on the side of the tank, and with a strong push can reach his depth of negative buoyancy. He will then continue to drop to 50 ft. (or more) without swimming which would burn up his oxygen. To return to the surface he would use the rope - as stated before - to pull himself to the surface. This would require less energy than swimming back.

While I was at Underwater Swimmers School, I had missed attending Instructor's School which was a requirement of the Submarine School for teaching a class. A special class was convened for me and one other student to remedy the situation. At times I have mentioned to people that I graduated second in my class in Instructors School, but my conscience requires me to tell "the rest of the story." Vinnie would probably say I was at the bottom of my class.

During training sessions, in addition to our officer in charge, we also had a Diving Medical Officer on duty. We all wore bathing trunks. The officer's trunks were blue and the enlisted men's were yellow. This has an importance as follows:
 Even though over the years a few students have actually died during training yet the most important thing we had to tell our students was, "When you reach the surface and climb out of the water our Officer in Charge (blue bathing trunks) will ask you, how you feel. You had better answer, "Fine, *sir.*" Should the answer be simply, "Fine," he will point the stub of his index finger at you and scream, "*Sir* when you speak to me and don't you ever forget it!""

I would be very unhappy to have reported to a duty station only to find he was to be my Commanding Officer.

We had two great diving medical officers at the tank during my tour of duty there. Captain George Bond, was later involved in the Sealab I and II projects that involved living in a habitat under water. The purpose of the project was to develop decompression tables for divers who spent long periods of time underwater experiencing the pressure of the depths.

The other doctor, who later became a Captain, James Stark, made the trip around the world (submerged) on the USS Triton, the first submarine to do so.

Both of these men liked to play in the water at the tank and make bottom drops before training started. I would often join them. They always called me by my first name which would make our Officer in Charge cringe.

With two qualified scuba diving instructors at the tank, George Zipp and myself, we were now able to teach scuba diving to at least one member of the crew of each submarine at the base, as well as the submarines tied up to the sub tender USS Fulton at State Pier in New London.

Our course was not as involved as that of the Underwater Swimmers School in Key West, and only lasted for 2 or 3 weeks. We only ran it 3 or 4 times a year, and had to coordinate it with the escape training because a lot of the scuba training required the use of the tank.

The class started with plenty of physical exercise, class room work on the medical and physical aspects of diving, and, should we need him, Dr. Stark for assistance for any of the above. He was always pleased to help us out. A lot of time was spent at the base swimming pool learning to swim properly with fins and a face mask. At the tank we had the use of the re-compression chamber for the 50 pound pressure test. Our biggest asset was the tank itself. We taught all of the escape methods from a sunken submarine and how to make a safe free ascent to the surface should their scuba gear malfunction. I believe what the class enjoyed most, was when we taught them how to make a free dive while holding their breath. With a lung-full of air we would take them down the rope on the side of the tank to a depth where they would achieve negative buoyancy and could sink without any effort as we instructors did.

One member of our class was a civilian who was employed at the Navy's Underwater Sound Laboratory. He was involved in the construction of a two man free-flooding submarine that would require both the pilot and the co-pilot to be equipped with scuba gear while operating it. In order to test the submarine - that was to be used as a mine hunter - the civilian was required to attend a Navy approved scuba class. The man was well into his forties (that I thought was old at that time!). When I took him down the rope on the side of the tank for his first try at free diving he reached a depth of 40 feet. I have no idea as to the depth he might have gone had I not signaled him to return to the surface. At a later date, when the submarine was ready for its first test dive, I was invited to ride as his co-pilot. After the test I thanked him for the ride. He said "Don't thank me. I felt safe with you as my co-pilot."

We next spent more time at the swimming pool where the students learned how to ditch their scuba gear while swimming at the deep end of the pool and make a free ascent to the surface. This was the easy part. Next, they were required to swim to the bottom of the pool, put on the scuba gear, and continue with their underwater swimming.

The last phase of the class was open water swimming with the scuba gear. This could not be accomplished in the Thames River because the current was too strong. We had a small lake (Rock Lake) on the base - and a larger lake in Old Lyme - that we used for these swims. We received many great compliments from the students at the end of the classes.

Now for the end of the story as promised some time back on Chief Kime.

A duty section of two men was required to spend the night at the tank to maintain the water at the proper 92 degree temperature and treat the water with chemicals as necessary. We also would have to treat any diver in the recompression chamber if one had developed the bends or had some other diving accident. My partner at the tank was a First Class Diver, a Chief Ship-fitter. He was not a submarine sailor but he had served on submarine rescue vessels. During our time in standing watches together, I found out that he knew Kime and I had related my feelings about him. One evening after working hours, my partner (Swede) and I were in our lounge watching TV. Kime entered the building and came up the stairs to see Swede. He must have known Swede had the duty. This was the first time I had seen Kime since deep sea diving school about 13 years before. I spoke to him and shook hands with him. Swede was my friend but he also liked to put me under the hammer. His greeting remark to Kime was, "What's this shit about you? Bryant tells me you were a big prick on the Sea Dog during the war." Kime looked at me. My only choice was to take the high ground and answer, "You were." Swede looked at him and laughed. It took some time but I finally got to him with the Swede's help and I think we parted as friends.

One day our Officer in Charge received a phone call from the captain of the submarine school. The captain had a long-time friend, his name was Bill Maguire, who was looking for some divers for a salvage operation. Many instructors, including our Chief were planning to meet with Bill at the Mohegan Hotel at New London, but at the meeting only George Zipp and I showed up. Bill told us that he had salvage rights to a sunken submarine, the G2, commissioned on 2/6/1915. The G2 had been sunk in Long Island Sound in 1919 in a depth charge test, with three men lost.

Bill showed us the construction plans of the G2. He said his idea was to first locate the sub and should we be lucky and find it, we would inspect it and decide how to salvage it. George and I told Bill we would need a sturdy boat to work from, and also could only work on weekends. Bill found an old timer who knew Long Island Sound like the back of his hand. Bill had the location of where the sub went down, but the visibility in those waters was only about 15 ft. and the current so strong it would be impossible to swim against it in our attempt to locate the sub. George and I decided to use a method we had learned at Underwater Swimmers School, the Use of a *Planeing Board*. This simple piece of plywood measured 3 ft. long and 2 ft. wide. This board would be towed (with about 200 ft. of line) by the old timer's oyster boat at a slow speed. George or I would ride the board wearing our scuba gear. We could control our depth by the angle we put on the board. By doing so we could travel along the bottom and look for the G2. The depth of the water was about 65 ft. Our plan was, should one of us spot the sub, he would release the board and surface. At that time the oyster boat would return to the diver and drop his anchor. In doing so we knew we would be close to the wreck. The first day of searching turned up nothing. I don't think either of us had any hope of finding the G2. However, the pay was good at that time (in 1956). We were each getting $50.00 a day. We could only work a couple of hours a day when the tide was slack. At other times, the current would rip the face mask off our faces. On our second day we found the G2 and everything fell into place. We attached a strong cable to her with a marker buoy at the surface.

The G2 was in remarkable shape considering how long it had been on the bottom. I guess the strong current had kept the hull clean of sea growth. We worked on this project for a couple of summers. But without pontoons and heavy equipment to attach the pontoons, George and I realized the project was a failure. Bill did not have the money for this kind of equipment. He did find some divers the next summer who agreed to work for free and share in the profits.

About 4 years later, 1962, in an article in *Skin Diver's* magazine, a diver claimed he had salvaged the G2. I contacted him and he told me they had used explosives to salvage the lead and propellers.

But it was a great job while it lasted.

At the bottom of the outside of the training tank we had a gasket leak on an oval shaped removable plate that seated on the inside of the tank. This plate could be removed from the outside of the tank. The opening was used during repair work in the tank to remove rust and accumulated dirt. But with the tank full of water, the plate could not be removed and it appeared the only solution was to drain the tank of its one quarter million gallons of treated fresh water just to replace this gasket.

My buddy George and I came up with an idea. We thought we could do it without draining the tank. We took our idea to our Chief in Charge, who was a nice guy. He in turn took it to our Officer in

Charge. He said to go ahead and try it, but it won't work. What a great leader. With our connection at the ship fitter's shop, we had a steel box made up. This box, with one open side, was designed to fit the curvature of the tank and cover the plate, with a split-hose gasket fitted around the edge of the open side to create a seal against the side of the tank. A hydraulic jack was used to force the box against the inside of the tank. On top of the box we installed two valves connected to two hoses. The hoses ran to the top of the tank, one was connected to our air supply, the other vented to the atmosphere. Our plan was to blow the water out of the box with our air supply valve. We would then quickly vent the box. When this happened the pressure of the water at 120 ft. would force the box against the tank creating a watertight seal. Our plan worked perfectly. Now we could remove our access plate from the outside of the tank and replace the faulty gasket. With a shot of air to the box, the seal was broken and our job was done. After saving one quarter of a million gallons of treated water and the loss of the use of the tank for several days, we never received a well done of a thank you from our Officer in Charge.

If I am suspected of suggesting the OIC was something less than a credit to the Navy in taking care of his men, I am.

At about this time we began using the *buoyant ascent* method of escape. This device was nothing more than a life jacket worn by the student that was filled with air. The student when released from his escape station was instructed to blow out all of his air and to continue blowing on his ascent as his residual air continued to expand on his way to the surface. The rate of ascent to the surface is approximately 225 feet per minute - much faster than with the Momsen Lung.

In a free ascent it was necessary for a swimmer to remain behind his exhalation bubbles to insure that he was getting rid of enough of his expanding air. This was easy enough to do in the controlled conditions of the tank, but in a real situation would be a problem as the water would not necessarily be clear enough to see the bubbles, and in some cases it would not be possible to know the way to the surface. In *buoyant ascent* the vest would automatically raise the swimmer to the surface and he needed only to blow air out continuously as he rose to compensate for the expansion of the air.

Author demonstrating Buoyant Ascent.

In the few cases of the men who died at the tank during training, it was probably caused by failing to release the expanding air in their lungs during free ascent, resulting in an embolism.

This is the part of the training that is sometimes difficult to convey. What amounts to throwing away perfectly good (and seemingly needed) air seems to go against common sense. But when the air increases in volume as the pressure is reduced it occupies more space than the lungs can provide and is forced to go elsewhere.

To treat an embolism, the victim needs to be placed in a recompression chamber as quickly as possible and taken to the equivalent depth of 165 feet. In doing so, the air bubble in his blood stream will be reduced to one eighth of its original size and will be absorbed into his body after a proper time in the chamber.

While I was at the tank, a small recompression chamber was installed in the cupola at the top of the tank where a victim could receive immediate treatment instead of making the long elevator ride down to the main floor where our chamber was located. Had this chamber been installed when the tank was originally built, some of those lost lives might have been saved. Previously anyone showing symptoms would have to be brought down to a chamber at ground level and critical time lost.

We eventually had a new Officer in Charge assigned to the tank. I found him more down to earth than his predecessor.

During my time there, the local fire and police departments had no personnel trained in scuba diving. In the event of a drowning accident in the surrounding towns, we would usually be called to assist. We were always glad to do this sort of thing as it was an opportunity to build on our training in other situations.

One evening our C in C called me at my house. He told me that a car had gone off the highway and into Long Cove. The driver of the car was believed to be trapped in the submerged car. My chief told me that he was at the base on duty as the assistant Officer of the Day. He said he would pick up the scuba gear at the tank and for me to meet him at the scene of the accident. Arriving at the site I was told that a couple of men had plunged into the cold water and saved the driver from drowning. My job would be to further check the car for a possible passenger. I found no one in the vehicle but my trip was not wasted. I was needed to attach a chain to the car so a derrick could lift the car from the cove.

On another occasion, my Chief and I were called to Groton, to search for the body of a young black kid who had drowned. This one was like a wild west show with too many Chiefs trying to take charge: my Chief from the tank, the Chief of the sub base fire department, and both the Chief of Police and the Fire Chief of Groton. I was the diver and the only Indian. They were figuring tides and currents. They had me making 300 foot circles with my circling line trying to locate the body of this poor kid. Another kid

Salvage Crew Pulls Car Out of Water

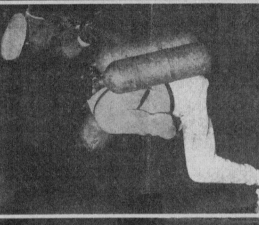

SURFACING . . . Late model car, which was driven by sailor Larry Isenbarger, is pulled from Long Cove by a derrick. Another sailor, Charles Wilson, escaped drowning when he was rescued by a Navy man and an E. B. guard.

Dramatic Rescue as Car Plunges into Cove

HELPING HAND . . . River Douglas Bryant is aided by Chief J. K. Peterson as he straps on his oxygen tank. Earlier, two sailors narrowly missed death when their car plunged off the highway into Long Cove, trapping one of them inside.

OXYGEN . . . Preparing to dive into Long Cove to help salvage the submerged automobile, a diver gets his gear checked. Car left Military Highway at Ledyard, trapping a 25-year-old sailor underwater.

on the scene had been trying to speak to one of - any of! - the Chiefs. Finally someone in the crowd asked, "Why don't you ask the kid where he was when he last saw him?" The kid told them they were on the railroad bridge when the other one fell in the water. My Chief decided that would be a likely place to be looking. I made one circle with my line on the bottom and found him. Great leadership from the *Combined Chiefs*.

The hardest part of the recovery was bringing the kid's body to the shore where I was sure his parents would be waiting.

During my tour at the tank, my daughter Maureen was born on October 25th, 1957. This time there were no problems. We were blessed with a normal child and she with a happy and healthy life.

Earlier I wrote about free diving to 100 ft. in the tank. A full understanding of what that involves requires some explanation about what happens to the lungs of a diver in a descent to 100 ft. The average human has a total lung capacity of 6 quarts with a full deep inhalation. Of this approximately 1/4, or 1 1/2 quarts is *residual air*, the air left in the lungs after exhaling as completely as possible. This is the air that prevents the lungs from collapsing and cannot be expelled.

I have to insert a bit of science here. The above is the normal condition at sea level at what is considered to be one *atmosphere* of pressure – the pressure of gravity. In making a descent in water the pressure increases at the rate of one atmosphere for each 33 feet of depth. There are decimal points involved in this, not needed for our purposes here, but at 100 feet the body is subjected to four atmospheres of pressure. The body itself, since being mostly water anyway, is relatively unaffected by the increase in pressure, but the air in the lungs is a gas and highly compressible.

As a diver descends to 100 ft. his lungs will be compressed to his residual capacity of 1 1/2 quarts. When he returns to the surface the air will expand back to his original 6 quarts, minus the small amount of oxygen used by his body during the dive.

This is applicable to free diving only and explains why relatively deep dives are possible without external air supplies. The depth is limited by the ratio of total lung capacity to the residual capacity of an individual diver. Free diving is not subject to the various problems that can occur with supplemental air sources, particularly those involving rapid returns to the surface. These will be discussed as they appear.

Many free divers have achieved depths far greater 100 ft. The reason they are able to do so is because they have a greater than average lung capacity and possibly a slightly smaller residual capacity.

Whenever dignitaries were invited to the base, their tours would always include demonstrations at the tank. These demonstrations would generally be held after our working hours - in the evening and the two or three man duty section would become a part of the demonstration. Our chief in charge would call in extra instructors if necessary. Glass bottom boxes would be placed at the edge of the tank in the cupola where the visitors could watch the show in the water below. These boxes were the same as that used by our officer in charge during training sessions.

The demonstrations routinely consisted of the following: escapes from the 50 ft. lock with both the Momsen Lung and the buoyant ascent. One of the instructors would then make a free ascent from the 110 ft. compartment to the surface. This, as explained before, is when the instructor with his positive buoyancy would slowly float to the surface. He would also be blowing a small stream of bubbles from his mouth to get rid of the expanding air in his lungs. This was a slow ascent to the surface lasting well over a minute.

For effect the next escape would be the buoyant ascent from the same (110 ft.) compartment. With his life jacket the instructor would travel at a rate of about 225 ft. per minute to the surface. When he reached the surface in about 30 seconds, he would be propelled out of the water to well below his waist.

For the *grand finale* two instructors, dressed in our yellow EM bathing trunks, wearing sneakers and equipped with face masks, would push off from the ladders on the side of the tank and drop to the bottom 100ft. They would both sit on the deck and slowly remove and exchange their sneakers, then slowly lace and retie them. To return to the surface, they would use the line (rope) on the side of the tank to reach the surface. To the spectators observing the performance it would seem like a very long time, but actually would be completed in about three minutes.

Nearly all the instructors at the tank were married. We didn't eat our meals in the mess hall. By not eating in the mess hall we received commuted ration money. For lunch and food for overnight duty we brought food from home. We were known as the *Brown Baggers.*

In our living quarters we had a stove and refrigerator. At times we had a problem with leftover food remaining in the refrigerator so established a rule: after 4 pm (when liberty would commence) the leftovers could be used by the duty section, or discarded with the trash. This worked quite well in keeping the refrigerator clean. However, there was another problem. Should a member of the crew bring in chocolate milk or some other desirable beverage for his lunch, at times someone would help themselves to it. With a little detective work my buddy George Zipp - who taught the scuba course with me - and I figured out what duty section was the culprit. George said, "We have to get those bastards -the next time they have the duty, and a demonstration is scheduled." Within a few weeks a demonstration coincided with the night they were on duty. My friend George brought in the chocolate milk, Ex-lax, and the blender. George said, "We're going to get those bastards tonight." We were hoping the Ex-lax would produce a brown stain in the clear water of the tank that evening, but as luck would have it, the demonstration was canceled. The next morning George asked me if I had heard anything. My answer was no. Several weeks later, I overheard one of our suspects talking to his friend. He said, "I don't know what the fuck happened to us the night of the demonstration. We just about shit ourselves to death." My message to George: "It worked."

With a lot of studying over two years, I was advanced to Chief Petty Officer, effective 16 Jan. 1958. This was the rank that I had hoped to achieve before my retirement from the Navy. My job at the tank would not change now that I was a Chief Petty Officer. All of our instructors were either Chief or First Class Petty Officers.

I now realized, with all of my negative comments about the few bad chiefs I had worked for, I would have to start thinking about what kind of a chief *I* would be when I was transferred to my next submarine. I hoped I would be more like Chief Coover than Rat Fink.

Becoming a Chief Petty Officer in the US Navy is a notable milestone and cannot pass without recognition. Traditionally the older Chiefs within shouting range will gather to accompany the new Chief to the Chief's Club for his or her initiation. All quite mild aside from getting the new CPO blind drunk.

Virginia also arranged a party of our closest Sea Owl friends to celebrate the occasion.

In the pre-WWII days when the submarine fleet operated out of China in the summer and the Philippines in the winter the ceremony was a bit more rowdy. After the new chief was sufficiently inebriated his hosts would all urinate in his hat before crowning him with it. If ladies of the night were present, they would be invited to contribute some maiden water to the festivities.

In the photo (below) of the house party, held at my house to celebrate my promotion, my Sea Owl shipmate Weaver is mimicking the peeing-in-the-hat ritual while my wife Virginia is hiding at the right rear behind Simonson (right front) -not at all convinced it was a gag. I am at the left front with similar thoughts of my own about then.

Equally appalled wives in rear: photographer Maguire's wife, left, Mrs. Weaver and Mrs. Simonson.

It was a great evening, and all the better on finding my cap perfectly dry the following morning

One extremely cold night in the middle of winter, we received a call that a girl had gone through the ice on a dam in the river in Danielson. They wanted us to attempt to retrieve the body. Our rescue group consisted of Dr. Bond, our Chief in Charge, my diving partner (Tuckfield), and me. Arriving at the site, we were shown the open water where the girl had gone through the ice. On the bank of the river there was a club. I believe it was a French Club. The ice near the shore was loaded with onlookers. However, the ice was very thin where she broke through. Someone came up with a ladder that we could lay flat on the ice out to the open water. By staying on the ladder we could safely work our way out to the open hole. We were both dressed for the dive and we were equipped with a battery powered water proof battle lantern and a grapnel hook with several feet of rope attached to it. Tuckfield was selected to make the dive. I lay on the ladder as his *tender* (partner). Tuck entered the water with his light. Within 10 seconds he was back to the surface. His eyes were very big. He said, "I seen her. She is beautiful with her blond hair lying on the black bottom." I said, "Bring her up and pass her to me." Tuck said, "I don't think I can." I then told him, take the grapnel and hook it into her clothes and I would pull her up. Tuck went down again and without using the grapnel managed to bring her up to where I could reach her and pull her out of the water. Several onlookers were rushing out on the ice to recover the body. At that moment I could see all of us going through the ice. My only choice was to sling her body across the slick ice toward the oncoming group.

I really felt bad about treating the body in that manner. I am quite sure most of the crowd didn't understand my actions, but I don't think they misunderstood my Chief screaming and gesturing at them to get back off the ice.

That was a sad evening. I believe the girl was about 12 or 14. Everyone was very appreciative of our help and we were invited into the club. I know we had several drinks to sooth the bad experience.

During my tour at the tank, there were a lot of discussions about the value of the training we provided, and at what depth one could expect to escape from a crippled submarine. In 1959 Dr. Bond, who was now a full captain, and my friend Chief Cyril Tuckfield, released a buoy and ascended from the submarine Archerfish, from a depth of a little over 300 ft. In talking with Tuck, the hardest part had been getting their inflatable life-raft out of the escape trunk and released for its trip to the surface. I am sure they had a rescue boat ready to pick them up. The release of the raft was to demonstrate that they would have the use of one if needed when they reached the surface.

As to the value of the training, relatively few lives were saved because of it but it proved to be of inestimable value as a confidence builder among submariners who could be reassured that they could do it if they had to since they would have successfully done it before.

Although I have mentioned air embolism to some extent I believe it is important to point out that a rupture of the lungs, that can permit an air bubble to get to the heart or brain, is the most serious of all diving accidents and without immediate treatment, the diver will not recover.

Because we never had a case of *the bends* while I was at the tank, I have not said much about this supposedly common diver's disease. But I will briefly cover it to the best of my ability since it is of significant concern in diving. The fact is that this condition has been

Author and fellow diver recover casualty (bottom center). Navy Chief panics when bystanders surge out onto the dangerously thin ice.

well understood for a long time. Most divers are well aware of it and how to guard against it so it is actually quite rare.

SCUBA training would involve discussing the bends (technically known as *decompression sickness*) although in the limited and controlled environment of the tank it was not the issue divers would have to consider in later dives elsewhere.

Air is - for practical purposes - composed of 22% Oxygen and 78% Nitrogen. The Oxygen is needed and the Nitrogen is generally harmless. At the surface, body tissue will absorb the levels present in the surrounding air and excess is simply discarded in what is exhaled.

When the pressure is increased as in diving, and supplemental (tank) air - also under pressure - is used, the nitrogen (gas) present in solution in the body is compressed allowing more to be absorbed. The amount is increased by the pressure (depth) and the time under pressure, thus even a shallow dive can be harmful if prolonged.

Returning to the surface reverses the process and the excess nitrogen now in solution in body tissue must escape. Periodic stops (as determined by *diving decompression tables* are required to allow adequate time for the excess nitrogen to return to a gaseous state and be exhaled. If the ascent is too rapid the excess can form bubbles that can be trapped in various parts of the body. Sometimes a bubble lodges in a joint, such as the knee or elbow, and prevents the joint from being straightened, thus the word *bends*. Should these gas bubbles lodge in the central nerve column, the diver could become paralyzed. The interrupted return to atmospheric pressure allows time for the nitrogen bubbles to diminish in size and dissipate from the areas where they were trapped.

If the condition does occur, the treatment is to place the diver in a recompression chamber as quickly as possible and pressurize him to the depth at which pain is relieved to the equivalent depth of 165 feet if necessary, and follow the decompression treatment tables to return him slowly to atmospheric pressure. And if there is any doubt about the symptoms - do it!

In looking back on my naval career, I have always looked at my time at the submarine escape training tank as the best and most interesting of my tours of duty.

At the end of my tour at the tank, I received my orders to report to the USS Entemedor (SS340) on 3 Sept., 1958. The Entemedor was attached to Submarine Squadron 10, and was tied up to the submarine tender, USS Fulton (AS11), at State Pier in New London.

USS Entmedor: WWII configuration above, post war modificatins below

U.S.S. Entemedor (SS 340)

Reporting aboard the Entemedor was another culture shock. Since I was now a Chief Petty Officer, I received a lot more respect than I had been accustomed to.

I met the Captain, Executive Officer, Engineering Officer, Chief of the Boat, Chief Engineman in charge of the engine rooms, the Chief I would relieve, and all of the men in the two engine rooms who would be working for me.

Although this was the 4th submarine I served on it was my first with General Motor's diesel engines. All of the others had Fairbank's Morse engines. Chief Murphy, who I was relieving, was very helpful to me during the two weeks he remained aboard before transferring to shore duty.

The Entemedor had just returned from back to back secret operations and was not in the best of condition. She needed a lot of work but we were in port for 3 weeks of upkeep on the boat. One of our engines needed a complete overhaul. The tender Fulton didn't have the necessary facilities such as a gunk tank, or a space where work could be performed on the parts of the engine. Most of the work was being done in the passageway of the engine room itself. This created a complete mess. Across the river at the submarine base a facility known as the Engine Overhaul Shop was normally used for this purpose. It had a gunk tank to clean all of the engine parts, and equipment to grind valves and seats on the (16) heads of the engines. With a visit to the chief in charge of the shop - who I knew - and the use of their truck, this problem was quickly resolved and much appreciated by my men.

In my opinion, my job as a CPO was *not* to be hands-on in the engine rooms and take the tools out of the hands of the workers. The two first class petty officers in charge knew more about these engines than I did. During our three week upkeep I would check in to see if they needed anything or if there were any problems.

After the upkeep, we were scheduled for an operational readiness inspection and an administrative inspection. The ORI would be conducted at sea with a series of drills to see how the crew performed. These inspections would be conducted by the Squadron 10 officers. In checking the preventive maintenance books on our engines, I could see we were in deep do-do. It would have been nice if I could have raised my hands and said, "I'm not responsible - I wasn't aboard at that time," but that's not the way the Navy operates.

Every morning for over a week, when the crew's mess area was available after breakfast I took over one of the four tables in the compartment. On the table I had our Preventative Maintenance books (machinery history), dates, and work lists from previous upkeeps, and, armed with pens of various shades of blue, I doctored the books and brought them up to date. The result was an *outstanding* on our administration inspection. This was not the proper thing to do but I felt I had no choice. Our commanding officer, a highly admired captain, presented me with a letter of commendation on leaving for his next duty assignment on 16 July 1959. I hope it was for more than just doctoring the books for an inspection.

My boss, the Engineering Officer, was well liked by most members of our crew. However, I don't think he ever had a talk with me about what he expected from me as his chief engineman. I had the feeling that I was not in the loop. We had some sections of piping that needed to be replaced. Our engineer grabbed his favorite fireman from the engine room and said something like, "Come on Winsky, you little bastard, we have a job to do." This didn't bother Winsky any. He was a good kid and was working with the engineer. One day I approached the engineer and said, "Shouldn't I be taking care of this project? He replied, "Winsky and I have it under control."

In the Navy that I had served in for over 15 years, the engineer would have told me what needed to be done. Then, with the help of the two first class petty officers in charge of the engine rooms, we would assign the best qualified men to the job. Never in my Navy career had I seen the engineer wielding a tool on a job. Was he trying to impress the Captain - or just another Big John?

A couple of weeks later, when the Entemedor was back in port, our Engineering Officer was the Duty Officer and I was his Duty Chief. I wanted to have a few words with him so I waited until evening when everything was quiet in the Ward Room (Officers Country). I approached Mr. E, and in my blunt (and perhaps not too well chosen) words to him were, "It appears to me that you want to play Chief on this boat. Maybe you should have my hat," at which time I threw it on the ward room table. I also said maybe he should have me transferred to a boat that needs a Chief Engineman. I don't remember his answer but it took care of the problem on the piping job.

We had a third class petty officer in the engine room that had more time in the Navy than I did. He had a drinking problem and one day he was taken to Captain's Mast charged with being *over the hill* (absent without permission). My duty, I felt, was to say all the good things that I could about him regarding his knowledge and value at sea. Our Captain, who I had great respect for said, "Chief, I appreciate all the kind words you have to say about Lowery. I can only say it's too bad that the Entemedor doesn't spend 365 days at sea each year." He had me there.

At about this time we had a new XO report aboard. Without a doubt, Mr. Train would become the greatest officer I had the pleasure of working for in the Navy. He later became a 4 Star Admiral, and Commander in Chief of the Atlantic Fleet. One day he called me to his state room, which was nothing more than a small room with two bunks, a desk, and a curtain for a door. He asked me what I knew about the snorkel system. I told him I knew the system. He said he had never served on a submarine with one. He also felt that a lot of crew members probably didn't know the system and asked if I would prepare a lesson plan and give a series of presentations in the mess hall to the crew when they were off watch. He also told me he planned to attend. I knew the system quite well, except some of the safety circuits, and with some help from the electricians and my lesson plan, I must have done quite well. Mr. Train was quite pleased with the result.

One morning, while we were in upkeep, I made my usual inspection trip to the engine rooms. My FCPO in charge of the forward engine room (I will use the name Ham) was still feeling the effects of drinking the night before. He lived in one of the Navy housing projects and another member of our crew lived in the same project. He apparently had been spreading tales about Ham's wife and Ham told me he was going to *work him over* when he came through the engine room. I advised him not to do it on the boat or he'd be in *deep shit*. Before long the victim appeared before our Engineer and told him that Ham had beaten him up. Mr. E. had no love for Ham because Ham always gave him a bad time. The *sea lawyers* in the engine room had the case all figured out: "No witnesses; how can they convict him?" Meanwhile Mr. E. was overheard saying, "I've got the son of a bitch now." News travels fast on a submarine.

Ham was the best man I had in the engine rooms and had more time in the Navy and a more extensive war record than I did. He did great work for me. What could I do for him before he goes to Captain's Mast? I can't go to my boss Mr. E. - he had already expressed his feelings. My only shot was our XO, Mr. Train. I went up to his stateroom and knocked on the bulkhead next to his desk. He looked up at me and I asked him if he was busy. He pushed his chair back from his desk and said he was never busy - meaning, "I'm never too busy to talk to you." I asked him if he had planned to talk with me before Ham's Captain's mast. He said "By God, I should be talking to you." I told him that I was not present when the alleged attack took place and that my information was hearsay. And I also added that I believed in the chain of command and that I should be going through Mr. E. However, with his alleged statement about Ham and the hard feelings between the two, I thought it was necessary for me to come directly to him in Ham's best interest. I mentioned his war record, and told Mr. Train that he was my best first class and that his working relationship with me had been outstanding since I came aboard the Entemedor. Mr. Train thanked me for my input. I knew the Captain and Mr. Train would be discussing the upcoming Captain's Mast and hoped that my endorsement would be of some help to Ham.

On the day of Captain's Mast, the wardroom was full. Captain Nicklas, Mr. Train, the EO (Mr. E), I, Ham, the alleged victim, and the three men from the engine room were present. The captain questioned Ham about the alleged fight and Ham suggested the victim must have hit his head on the hatch to cause the bruises. The three men from the engine room, when questioned, "Didn't see anything happen." Captain Nicklas gave Ham a temporary reduction in rate to second class, meaning that in 6 months - if he kept out of trouble - he would be reinstated to FC. For Ham this was a severe punishment. Since he had only a short period of time remaining before his retirement from the Navy, he would not have a chance of making Chief and retiring at a higher rate. The *sea lawyers* had called it wrong.

A few days later, Captain Nicklas called me to come to his state room. His asked me, "Do you know why I busted Ham?" For the lack of a better word, I had to answer no. He told me that it had been one of the most difficult things he had had to do in his Navy career. He said, "If you remember, I specifically asked him three times if he had hit the victim. He lied to me each time." He went on to explain that as Captain of the Entemedor he could not permit a member of his crew to lie to him and that was the main reason he reduced him in rank. I thanked him and told him I understood.

With his tour of duty up on the Entemedor, Mr. E. was transferred to another ship and I was not sorry to see him leave. In all fairness, Mr. E. was a smart officer and generally well liked. In my opinion, had he been better at delegating operations in the engine rooms, he would have been an outstanding officer.

Shortly before the transfer the Entemedor took the wives of the crew to sea for a day for a *petticoat cruise*. Virginia had a chance to look through the periscope, operate the planes, and steer the boat. She really enjoyed her day at sea, and also the good food prepared by our cooks.

Our new EO, Mr. Carriway, moved up from a lesser position on the Entemedor, to become the engineer. He had been in the Seaman to Admiral Program in which a seaman in the Navy could be selected to attend the Naval Academy. I liked him very much and enjoyed working for him.

We also received a new Commanding Officer, Captain Walsh, who relieved Captain Nicklas. I was sorry to see Captain Nicklas leave; he was a great captain to work for. However, I never had a problem with Captain Walsh.

We had developed a high pressure air leak from a valve seat in the air manifold in our control room. The repair was scheduled to be performed at the shipyard, in Kittery, Maine. The yard workers were unable to shut the stop valve to this system because it was jammed in the open position. To apply enough force to close it could rupture the valve and expose the worker attempting it to an explosive and possibly fatal blast of air pressure. The EO explained the problem to me and said the Entemedor would have to be placed in dry dock (a very expensive and time consuming operation). With that done, a worker could enter the ballast tank and close the stop valve on the affected high pressure air tank. This would make it safe to work on the stuck valve and the manifold. I told him that with the shallow water diving gear we carried aboard, I could enter the flooded ballast tank and shut the stop valve. He said he would check with the Captain. In no time at all the Captain was on deck to talk to me. He wanted to know if it was safe to do it. I told him I could do it with a facemask, but without knowing the quality of the air in the tank I would prefer to use the diving gear to insure a good quality air supply. He was quite pleased with this alternative and gave me the OK. With my Engineer as my tender, my life line, and air hose, I had no problem diving to the underside (keel) of the boat and entering the ballast tank. I carried a waterproof battle lantern for light in the tank and had also brought along a large pipe wrench, should it be needed. This was actually a very simple job. I returned to the surface to find everyone happy and smiling. The following day after the work was completed on the manifold, I made a second dive to reopen the stop valve.

The captain was delighted. He was now able to notify his division commander that he was ready for sea and could meet his scheduled departure date.
A letter of commendation was entered in my service record for the achievement. In looking back to the escape tank and the much more complicated feat that George and I performed in renewing the leaky gasket and saving 250,000 gallons of treated water, without even a

thank you from our OIC, I was quite happy to be working for an officer I could support.

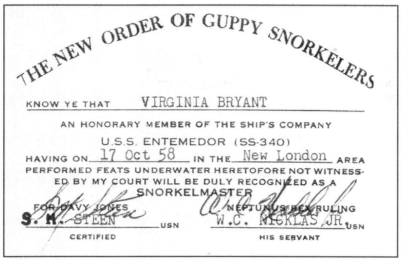

THE NEW ORDER OF GUPPY SNORKELERS

KNOW YE THAT   VIRGINIA BRYANT

AN HONORARY MEMBER OF THE SHIP'S COMPANY

U.S.S. ENTEMEDOR (SS-340)

HAVING ON 17 Oct 58 IN THE New London AREA

PERFORMED FEATS UNDERWATER HERETOFORE NOT WITNESS-

ED BY MY COURT WILL BE DULY RECOGNIZED AS A

SNORKELMASTER

FOR DAVY JONES   NEPTUNUS REX RULING

S. M. STEEN   W.C. NICKLAS JR.

_____USN   _____USN

CERTIFIED   HIS SERVANT

At this point I had no idea that I would eventually become an instructor in Leadership School - or that I would retell this story to every class as an example of good and bad leadership.

Shortly after leaving the shipyard and returning to tie up to our tender, the Fulton, we were ordered to join the 6th fleet in the Mediterranean.

This was at the height of the *Cold War* with the USSR. We did not have enough nuclear submarines to cover all of the Navy's secret missions. The Entemedor, equipped with a snorkel, was a front runner among the diesel submarines. She had completed a couple of operations before I reported aboard and we were fairly sure we would be involved in a secret operation while assigned to the 6th Fleet.

Crossing the Atlantic, we travelled mainly on the surface. When we were submerged we used our snorkel to supply air to continue to operate our diesel engines. The commanding officer of a submarine, when using the snorkel, prefers to travel as deep as possible so that less of it is visible on the surface. A head valve is mounted on top of the snorkel mast. When snorkeling at the maximum depth, if surface waves flowed over the head valve, it would close off the outside air supply to the engine rooms and prevent sea water from coming down the pipe. With the constant cycling of the valve because of the action of the waves the engines become starved for air. This also created an uncomfortable situation for crewmembers that had problems popping their ears during these irregular changes of the atmospheric pressure in the submarine. With an altimeter connected to the safety controls of the engines we could observe that we were operating in an atmospheric equivalent of about 3000 ft. If we should lose control of our depth, and the head valve remained closed, the altimeter would continually rise until at about the 8000 ft. equivalent the safety devices would shut down the engines. Operating at 5000 ft. (atmosphere) or more, the air supply has a reduced level of oxygen in it. The engines continue to run but rely on the air within the boat, and fuel consumption increases. Added to the back pressure on the exhaust system (because the exhaust is released underwater) the individual cylinder exhaust temperatures run much higher than normal, potentially resulting in burnt valves, cracked cylinder heads, and damage to other internal engine parts. The longer the head valve remains closed, the higher the exhaust temperatures will climb.

Our first stop was at Gibraltar to take on fuel. Although this was my third trip to the Mediterranean, I never went ashore there. Our next port of call was Malta where we tied up to a British repair ship for a minor repair.

We continued on to Naples. I had been there a couple of times before when I was aboard the Sea Owl. Naples was not my most favorite port. This time in Naples, a couple of my shipmates and I, while drinking in a bar on Saturday evening, met a friendly English speaking cab driver. We hired him to take us to Rome the next day. It was a beautiful trip and I really enjoyed the sights, especially the Coliseum. The only bad part was the hangover from the night of partying.

Our next stop was Messina, Sicily. This was not a very exciting city but perhaps I should have taken a guided tour of the area rather than drinking with my shipmates.

Shortly after departing from Messina our Captain informed us that we would be on a secret mission off the coast of Albania. Soviet war ships at times operated out of a port there. Our assignment was to remain undetected and observe the type of ships that were entering and leaving. Our priority was to determine whether the USSR had any nuclear submarines at that time. This was an uneventful trip and we remained in those waters for about 30 days without being discovered.

It was then time to return to the States. We pulled into Naples for a few days to take on fuel and stores. Our trip across the Atlantic was again on the surface with a few drills and dives to keep the crew in shape.

Virginia, my daughter Susan, now 8 years old and wearing crutches and leg braces, and my daughter Maureen, 3, were all at the pier when we arrived at the base, and as always extremely happy to see each other after the long separation.

Susan had been going to school at a special education facility run by the Catholic Church. She had been fitted for her braces at the hospital brace shop in 1958 at about the time I had been assigned to the Entemedor. They were very expensive and we were concerned about paying for them but the United Cerebral Palsy Association of New London covered the cost.

By now my friend Ham had been promoted back to first class and had received his orders to shore duty. Before our trip, we took on two new first class enginemen. They were both very talented men, and I am still friendly with one, Dennis Grace, today. They both made me look good and made my job much easier.

After a three week upkeep in port, we had a few months of local operations. One evening while in port, when I was the Duty Chief, a Chief Engineman reported aboard for duty at about 11 pm. He came into the Chief's quarters. I was in my top bunk reading a book; he was feeling no pain. He introduced himself, Dave Ross, and although I had never met Dave before, I had heard a lot of stories about him. He asked me if I was in charge in the engine rooms or the auxiliary gang. I told him I had the engine rooms and he said he had no problem with either gang. Dave was a very large man, over 250 pounds. The only light on in the Chief quarters was my reading lamp. Dave noticed a man in khakis sleeping in the bottom bunk. Dave could see that the man was too young to be a chief petty officer and said, "Who the fuck is in that bunk?" I told him it was an officer that the COB had put in there temporarily. Dave said "who the fuck is the COB here?" He went on saying, "No fucking officer will be sleeping in the Chief's quarters while I'm on this submarine!" Sometime during the night the officer moved out. He must have found a place to sleep in Officer's Country. Dave, for all his bluster, turned out to be a great shipmate and he really knew his job. We also had a Chief Commissary man (cook), Mike, report aboard who was a great baker. What an asset to a meal. More on Mike later in this chapter.

Virginia was saddened when I told her we would be leaving for another trip in a couple of weeks. She did have close Navy-family friends that she could call on if necessary. We also had a decent car and Virginia was a good driver. Part of my pay was in an allotment that went to her every month. With careful planning, she would have enough money to live on for the 3 or 4 months I would be away.

Our destination for this trip was Portland, England. In crossing the North Atlantic at this time of the year, we sustained a lot of damage to the deck surfaces (superstructure) of the boat. Use of the snorkel was impossible in the heavy seas. Portland was a small naval base but they did a great job in repairing our damage.

Our XO, Mr. Train, made arrangements for members of the crew who wished to could visit London for a couple of days. I visited Bond Street where I bought a nice Harris Tweed sport coat and a pair of pants to go with it. I was with my friend Dennis from the Engine room. After the clothes shopping, we did some drinking and saw a couple of shows.
Virginia said I made a good choice.

My picture appeared in Life magazine, at Buckingham Palace, at the time of the birth of Queen Elizabeth's second son. I encountered a crowd waiting outside the palace for news of the birth - just at the moment that a Life photographer clicked on the crowd from quite a distance away.

Detail from LIFE photo Feb. 29, 1960; Doug lower right.
Crowd awaits announcement of birth of Prince Andrew.

Returning to the Entemedor, now fully loaded with fuel and supplies, we left England and headed north. Once clear of the shipping channels, we submerged the boat and ran our diesel engines with the snorkel.

This was another secret operation. We were looking for Soviet Nuclear submarines, in Russian waters, and were again to remain undetected. Little did we know at that time it would be over two months before we would surface the submarine. Because we carried extra surveillance equipment on this trip, that needed to be monitored by officers, we required two Diving Officers of the Watch to handle the job. The Chief of the Boat and I were selected fill the two spots. A letter was later entered in our service records stating that we were fully qualified to perform the duties of Diving Office of the Watch.

The captain wanted to set up some competition among our three watch- sections. He planned to give points to the section, or sections that made first contact with a Russian ship. There were several other ways to earn points. The winning section was to be rewarded with a long (3 day) weekend liberty on our return to the submarine base. Sounded great. The problem: While at sea we operated with a three section watch to accommodate the duty schedule of 4 hours on, eight hours off for each man. Each section thus covered two watches in every 24 hour period. (There were no *days off* while on board.)

In port however we used a four section liberty policy that increased the time off for those not in the duty section.

Since the award was based on three sections it seriously complicated the four section rotation, and was unfair to those men who would normally have been scheduled for liberty but now had to forgo it and remain aboard in the absence of men from the winning section. Granting an award was one thing but penalizing someone else in order to provide it was something else again.

I was wild. I went to the Chief of the Boat and he understood the problem. However, since it was an order from the Captain, he didn't have any luck talking to our XO. I expressed my opinion to my Engineering Officer, Mr. Caraway who had no better luck. Using the chain of command, I told Mr. Caraway that I was going to see the XO myself. With my usual knock on the bulkhead next to his desk, I asked Mr. Train if he was busy. His answer (as always to me) was, "I'm never busy." I told him that I had talked to the COB and my Engineering Officer about the unfairness of the *rewards* program, but without getting any satisfaction on it. I added that rewarding some members of the crew by taking something away from others was simply not right. I could now see that Mr. Train was getting angry. He asked what the hell I was talking about. I explained in detail the unfairness of the plan. We both looked at each other and I finally asked, "Will I get an answer from you?" He asked, "Did you ever talk to me without getting an answer?" I answered no, and he said I would get my answer. But I knew he was upset. I returned to the chief's quarters. In the meantime the XO and the COB had put a plan together that allowed the winning section to be rewarded with their long weekend over a 4 week period and the crew could return to port in their normal 4 section liberty rotation.

A few days later, during one of my trips through the wardroom area, Mr. Train called me into his stateroom. He asked if I thought he had been angry at me during our previous conversation. I said I certainly did, but I thought I was supposed to stick up for my men. He went on to say, "I was. The reason was, you came to me with a complaint but you didn't have a solution." I said, "Mr. Train I had a solution but you didn't ask for it." Mr. Train, said, "By God you're right. I didn't." As I said before he was a great officer.

Our new Chief Cook, Mike (the baker), could make great bread, rolls and doughnuts. He was quite a bit older than most of us Chiefs and a real *suck ass* around the officers. One evening when I was on watch in the control room, Mike came in with fresh doughnuts that he took to the officers in the conning tower. He later returned with one for me. Once I had it in my hand, I said, "Thank you, you suck ass. I noticed that you took care of the officers before your fellow Chief." I thought this would be the end of my treats from Mike, but one day his mixer broke down. I had a very talented man in the engine room who was able to fix it and I was back in his good graces again.

A couple of times during this trip, we were detected by the Russians. At those times we would secure from snorkeling and operate on our batteries at a deep depth hoping to evade them. On one occasion they kept us down for 24 hours before we could evade them. We were of the opinion that they would not drop charges on us thinking they would prefer to force us to surface and escort us out of their waters which would be an embarrassing situation for us - and the country.

Because of a serious problem that developed with the generator on number one main engine, we could no longer use it. We were also burning valves and cracking a lot of cylinder heads because of the high exhaust temperatures on our engines as mentioned earlier. I told Mr. Caraway on more than one occasion that we could not continue snorkeling at this depth because we were running out of spare parts. I believe he understood the situation but was afraid to approach the captain. But with one of our three main engines now out of commission, I had had enough.

I went to the ward room area to see Mr. Caraway. I said to him, "Goddammit Mr. Caraway, we can't continue to snorkel at this depth." He raised his hand - I assumed for me to lower my voice, and said, "You don't understand Chief." "What the hell don't I understand?" He said, "You don't understand how embarrassing it would be to the Captain if they see our snorkel." I told the engineer, that the *old man* will be a hell of a lot more embarrassed if he has to call the Russians for a tow out of here. The Captain, nearby in his stateroom, came out into the passageway and asked, "What's the problem Chief?" I assume he must have heard my conversation with Mr. Caraway. I told him we were running out of spare parts and the damage to the engines was because we were snorkeling too deep. He immediately brought the depth of the submarine up a couple of feet. By doing so, he took care of our high exhaust temperatures. The Captain said, "If you have any problems, come and see me." For the remainder of the trip, when we crossed paths, he would always ask me, "Any problems aft?"

This was a long trip. We had spent only about 30 days in our patrol area but considerably more time in travel to our area and on our return home. Because of the secrecy of the operation, we did not surface until we were off the coast of Iceland.

After returning to the base, I took a few days leave. While on leave, but not at home, Virginia received a phone call from Mr. Train saying he would like to see me on the Entemedor. I had no idea why.

When I met with him, he informed me that the Personnel Officer of Commander Submarine Forces, Atlantic Fleet (located on the submarine base) was looking for a Chief Petty Officer to assist in teaching a course in leadership. He told me that he had mentioned me for the job and if I was interested, I should set up an interview with Commander Smith, the Personnel Officer. I thanked Mr. Train for his recommendation.

My interview with Commander Smith went very well. I was told that I might expect my orders in a month or less. Back from leave and on the boat, I found out we were getting a new XO and Mr. Train was leaving. I also found out that our new XO was to be Mr. Harkness, my old Engineer from the Sea Owl. One afternoon on returning from sea we were met by a tug boat from the base. Mr. Harkness was aboard. Like many officers, he wished to report aboard his new ship at sea. In talking with our Captain and XO he must have asked who the Chief Engineman was. When my name was mentioned, he came down below from the bridge to see me in the Chief's quarters. We were both happy to see each other. He was still as cocky as ever. He said, "Who the hell is the COB on this boat? I want you as my COB." I told him that I would like to be but I was being transferred in just a couple of weeks. "You bastard," he said, smiling. But I did tell him that he had a good reliable COB on the Entemedor.

In saying good bye to Mr. Train when he left the ship, I thanked him again for steering me to the leadership job. I also told him that I had enjoyed working for him, and had learned a few things. His replied, "Chief, I also learned a few things working with you."

Over the years I have often wondered why he recommended me for teaching leadership. Was it because I had two letters of commendation or possibly because I had a handicapped daughter and would be home from sea to help with her care? Maybe that I took care of my men - maybe all of the above.

I believed Mr. Train was a great officer and apparently others shared that opinion as he eventually retired from the Navy as a Four Star Admiral.

I couldn't complete this chapter on the Entemedor without relating this story about our new XO.

One day while cruising on the surface with our 3 diesel engines, the word was passed from the bridge, "Chief Bryant to the bridge." I knew there must be some *heavy shit* going down. I never had business on the bridge. I climbed the ladder to the conning tower, and as customary asked, "Permission to come on the bridge sir," answered with, "Permission granted." I climbed the second ladder to the bridge. Our new XO was the Officer of the Deck and was conning the boat. Also on the bridge, with a smirk on his face, was our Captain. He was sitting in his fold down chair. Mr. Harkness had a very stern look on his face. I now knew he was going to pull some shit on me. He pointed his finger to the after part of the boat, where the exhaust from our diesel engines could clearly be seen and said, "What's the problem back there?" I took a quick look aft and said, "I don't see any problem." He said, "Don't you see the smoke from the engines?" (I knew his preference for Fairbanks Morse

Diesel Engines over our General Motors versions). I said, "Mr. Harkness, if this was a Fairbanks boat, we would be in deep do-do. However, on this boat with General Motors Diesel Engines, we call that smoke *efficiency haze*." The Captain looked at his XO and laughed. Mr. Harkness looked at me and said "Chief you better go below decks. Your brain is getting too much oxygen up here in the fresh air."

My submariner readers may be wondering if I was the only Chief on the Entemedor. Actually we had a very good Chief of the Boat, as were all of the several other Chiefs on board. The few problems I had when reporting aboard, I hope I handled the way Chief Coover would have handled them. My friend Vinnie (of the Shoe story, age 96 as of this writing) on occasion will ask me, "Doug, what kind of Chief were you in the Navy?" My answer to him has always been, "I don't believe in self-evaluation. You'd have to ask someone who worked for me."

USS ENTEMEDOR (SS-340)

28 OCT 59:   Commended this date by the Commanding Officer, USS ENTEMEDOR (SS-340) for displaying special skills on 21 August 1959, at which time ENTEMEDOR was undergoing restricted availability at the U.S. Naval Shipyard, Kittery, Maine. On this date ENTEMEDOR experienced a stuck high pressure air hull stop valve. Before this valve could be removed for repair it was necessary to bleed off the air in the connecting air bottles which, at the time, contained air at a pressure of 2,500 lbs. In addition to your ENGINEMAN rating you are also a qualified Navy diver, and utilized your talents in this field to submerge beneath the water, enter the main ballast tank, and bleed off the air bottles under discussion. Having successfully performed this difficult and hazardous task you saved the Navy considerable money, which would have been spent for docking the ship, and assisted the ENTEMEDOR in meeting her departure date.

H. D. TRAIN II, LCDR, USN
Executive Officer

RECORD OF TRANSFER

DATE TRANSFERRED	ACTIVITY TO WHICH TRANSFERRED		
PURPOSE OF TRANSFER (DUTY, INSTRUCTION, ETC.)		AUTHORITY	
PRIMARY JOB CODE	SECONDARY OR SPECIAL PROGRAM JOB CODE	SIGNATURE AND RANK	

FOR USE OF INTERMEDIATE REPORTING STATIONS (*if necessary*)

RECORD OF RECEIPT

REPORTED AT (*ultimate destination*)	DATE REPORTED
	SIGNATURE AND RANK

Last, first, middle)	RATE	SERVICE NO.	BRANCH AND CLASS
BRYANT, Douglas A	ENC(SS)	573 25 09	USN

ADMINISTRATIVE REMARKS NAVPERS-601 (REV 10-58)   U. S. GOVERNMENT PRINTING OFFICE 1958—O-364725   13

Submariner Draws Praise

Douglas A. Bryant, chief engineman, USN, son of Mr. and Mrs. Almon H. Bryant of Madison and husband of the former Miss Virginia Ward of Lynn, Mass., is commended by his commanding officer for his outstanding performance of duty during the Entemedor's recent operations with the U.S. Sixth Fleet in the Mediterranean. Bryant received his commendation July 16 while serving aboard the Atlantic Fleet submarine USS Entemedor, operating in the New London area. He entered the Navy in August 1943.

Leadership School

On 3 Sept. 1960, I reported to Commander, Submarine Force's Atlantic Fleet Headquarters at Groton to join a Leadership Program being taught to submarine crews in the Atlantic Fleet. This school was under the direction of the Fleet Personnel Officer.

The course was well laid out with lesson plans and training aids. It was organized by Bud Porter, a very talented First Class Petty Officer. My job was to assist in teaching the course.

Most of the attendees were from the crews of the boats attached to the base at Groton. To present the class to the crews of other submarines in the fleet, we traveled at times to the bases at: Key West, Fla., Charleston, South Carolina, Norfolk, VA., and the Portsmouth Naval Shipyard, Kittery, ME.

Although it was called Leadership School, we covered more than just leadership. For example, we held group discussions that could bring out some of the actual problems that might exist on attendee's submarines. Should officers be among the class members, they could be made aware of these issues on their boats.

At this time some of our submarines had 3 section liberty while others had 4 section liberty. We would make sure that this subject was brought up in our group discussions: Which submarine would you rather serve on? Why can some of our submarines give the crew 4 section liberty, while others only gave 3? I believe we were responsible in our discussions for persuading some of the 3 section boats to change their policy and grant 4 section liberty. Another big problem we discussed was the grading system. The Navy marked on the 400 system with 4.0 (400) being the top mark for quarterly evaluations. These marks were very important when taking examinations for advancement in rate because a multiple based on other factors was used to add points to the final exam. The higher quarterly marks produced a higher multiple to be added to the final exam score.

I once gave an outstanding petty officer a 4.0 in professional performance. My boss, the engineer, told me he didn't believe in 4.0, saying that no one was perfect. I told him I would advise the man - who I felt was a top notch petty officer - to request a transfer to a submarine that gave more honest evaluations to improve his chances of advancing to Chief.

By focusing on the marking system explained in the Navy's Bureau of Personnel manual we hoped that officers responsible for evaluations would apply the same uniform standards.

And yes, my outstanding petty officer received his 4.0.

Another problem that was always discussed in these sessions was that when submarines returned to port after a long cruise, and with the wives and children waiting on the pier, why the COB on one could start liberty for the crew without any delay, while on another the COB was not allowed to start liberty until the captain visited the squadron office and paid his respects to the squadron and division commanders. This choice was at the discretion of the captains but we hoped to develop a greater consideration for the men and their waiting families among future leaders.

We had a highly motivational sound tape on Salesmanship. The story was about a salesman who, during WWII traveled from New York to Chicago by train every week for meetings connected to his job. He talked about his dress, the importance of arriving early, and arriving the night before his meeting if possible in order to have a good night's sleep. The most important thing that I remember about the tape was his comment about the train. I think he used the word priorities. He said he was not interested in the train, the engineer, or the conductor; he was only interested in the porter. The porter was the only man on the train who could provide him with a place to sleep. How many times in civilian life I have thought about that tape. The person that impressed me wherever I worked was the one who could give me a raise.

There are many different aspects to leadership. In my opinion, the most important of these in the Navy (or anywhere) is to take care of your men. I hope that message was conveyed in our course.

After a year on this job, I was ready to get back to sea. After working for the force personnel officer, I could almost pick my boat. I requested a school boat at the base - a school boat takes students from submarine school to sea and returns to port every evening - and was assigned to another former Hellcat, the USS Crevalle (SS291).

Crevalle at Kittery (Portsmouth Naval Shipyard)

USS Crevalle (SS291)

Following my orders to report aboard the Crevalle was an easy task. I only had to walk down to the lower base where the boat was tied up to the pier and turn in my papers.

The Crevalle was veteran of World War II where she made seven war patrols and had been credited with sinking 10 Japanese ships. She was one of the nine *Hellcats* in Operation Barney (along with the Sea Dog) where she sank 3 ships. This was not the first time I had walked on her deck. She was in the original configuration of a submarine from WWII. She had not been updated with a snorkel and was being used as a school boat, taking students from the submarine school to sea for training. We normally got underway at 0800 in the morning and returned from sea at about 1600 in the afternoon. With six Chiefs aboard, I only had the duty as the Chief of the Watch every sixth day, when I had to stay aboard overnight. On occasion when we were training officers from the submarine school, we would stay at sea for a week and return on Friday afternoon.

The engine rooms were in good condition with two excellent First Class Enginemen in charge. I had it pretty easy on the Crevalle. I also got along well with the Engineering Officer. The Assistant Engineer was - to be blunt - a *pain in the ass*. He drove a Mercedes convertible and supposedly came from money. He was always telling the men in the engine room what to do. On one occasion the First Class Petty Officer in charge of one of the engine rooms gave him some *guff*. Shortly afterward the Engineer asked me how well I got along with the Assistant Engineer. I told him about as well as anyone else on the boat. The Engineer, being very stern, said to me, "It doesn't matter what you or I think of Mr. J, someday he will be the Engineer on this or some other submarine, and it is our job to train him." He then asked me if I was willing to sit down and have a man to man conversation with him and indicated that Mr. J was agreeable. I told I would be more than happy to. A time and place was set up for our meeting the next day. With a day to prepare I decided I would get my oar in the water first. My first comment was that my men in the engine rooms tell me they feel you are standing on a soap box when you talk to them. Mr. J's reply was, "Chief, I have been told that before." Mr. J went on to tell me that one of my men always gave him a hard time when he told him to do something. I told Mr. J. that he didn't belong in the engine rooms telling the men what to do. If he had an occasion to be in the engine rooms and noticed something that needed attention, he should come to me about it, and if I agreed with him, I would see that it was taken care of. However, if I was not in agreement, I would have a discussion with the Engineer and we would make a decision on what you would like to see done. (I was trying to handle the situation the way Chief Coover on the Sea Owl would have done it.) I really don't remember if he was satisfied with our meeting or not. He did stay out of the engine rooms after that, but his demeanor remained unchanged. In fairness to Mr. J., I think we became friends; we both liked cars. At my next duty station, he would drop in to see me occasionally.

Overall I was quite happy on board the Crevalle. As I recall, the XO was not well liked by the crew. However, within a short period of time we received a new XO and he got on well with everyone.

The Engineer Overhaul Shop that I wrote about briefly when I was on the Entemedor was the most coveted berth on the base for a Chief Engineman. Sometime after WWII somebody recognized the need for a shop where crews overhauling their engines would have a place to clean the parts of their engines, grind the valves and seats of the cylinder heads, and receive technical support when necessary from the Chiefs who ran the shop.

The shop was run by Submarine Squadrons 2 and 8 under the direction of the two Squadron Engineers. Because there were no billets for these positions an Operations Officer of Squadron 2 or 8 would inform the XO of any submarine involved, that they had a need for Chief so and so at the squadron. The XO of the submarine does not argue with a Squadron Operations Officer. He says, "Yes Sir," and Chief so and so reports for duty. Meanwhile his records are kept aboard the submarine. His name is on their roster and he receives submarine and sea pay as a member of the staff of the squadron he is assigned to.

Frequently senior officers on the staff would bring their cars to the shop for tune-ups and repairs. Unbeknownst to me at this time, a Chief Petty Officer friend of mine worked for the Operations Officer in Squadron 2. The subject of working on cars in the overhaul shop came up. The Operations Officer said to his Chief that it seemed as if the officers in Squadron 8 have repairs performed on their cars because their Chief in the shop had a lot of talent with cars. My friend told his boss, we need a Chief from Squadron 2 in the shop who is also good with cars. My friend knew that I worked part time in a repair shop in town and also at home on customer's cars. He told the Operations Officer about me and recommended me for the job. He also reminded him I was stationed aboard the Crevalle, a submarine in his Squadron.

I was quite surprised when our new XO called me to his state room and told me that the Squadron would like to have me at the Engine Overhaul Shop. He asked me if I would be interested and my immediate answer was yes. I asked him if I needed a set or orders. He said no, pack up your clothes, go home and report to the shop in the morning.

I thought I had died and gone to heaven.

Submarine Base New London c.1957

Engine Overhaul Shop

Reporting to the shop the next day was awkward for me because of the way I had been brought into the job. Although I knew the four Chiefs in the shop, it was not until later in the day that my friend, the Chief who worked for the Operations Office, came to the shop to tell me the story. He brought me up to his office to meet his boss, the Operations Officer. My friend told me he had planned to see me and explain the situation but didn't realize I would be released from the Crevalle so quickly.

The way that news travels so fast in the Navy, I'm quite sure the Chiefs in the shop had already heard that Chief Bryant from the Crevalle was being assigned to the shop.

The Chief in charge of the shop, Henry Reid, was a very skillful man and we became close friends during the time I worked for him. Whenever an engineering problem developed on one of the submarines in Squadrons 2 or 8, and the Squadron Engineer was called for assistance, he would immediately go to Chief Reid for advice. In many cases this would involve a visit to the submarine by Chief Reid. Whenever possible I would go with him and in doing so I learned a lot.

Henry was a *shit-kicker* (as I was) but from Ohio. I believe he had a couple years of college. When WWII broke out, he left school to join the Navy and never went back. He was a Senior Chief Engineman and as I said, very talented. As a result had been at the shop for several years.

One day the engineer from one of our squadron boats, thinking to *do something* for his Chief Engineman, paid a visit to our boss, the

Squadron Engineer. He told him he had a very talented E9 Master Chief Engineman (Henry was an E8, Senior Chief) that he would be interested in trading for Henry. He implied that Chief Reid had been at the shop for a long time and it might be time for a change. Our boss politely thanked him but went on to say that it would not be fair to have all of Henry's skill on one boat and it would likely be better to keep him at the shop where his talents could be shared among the 16 boats in the two squadrons.

The young and downcast engineer put his tail between his legs and left. I would love to have known what he told his Chief.

At that time, a lot of First Class and Chief Petty Officers were recommended for commissions as Officers, most being LDO (Limited Duty Officers) in their specialty area. For example, if I had been advanced to LDO my specialty would have been engineering.

Henry had a dry sense of humor. On the day of his interview at the Squadron Offices for possibly becoming an Officer (that he was not interested in *a-tall*) he returned to the shop and commented to me, "Doug, you can't put a pig in a parlor."

When Henry retired from the Navy, he became a technical writer for Electric Boat in Groton where submarines were being built. On one of his days off from work at E.B. (Electric Boat), he came to the shop to visit us. He said, "Doug, you know that stuff you guys in the Navy call ass kissing? At E.B. it is called *job protection*."

Many Chiefs who retired from the Navy at the base were hired at E.B. There was a saying at the base that the rate structure was: E7 - Chief, E8 - Senior Chief, E9 - Master Chief, and EB.

Another Chief at the shop was very helpful to me and although I had known him for quite some time, we were not close friends. His name was Chester Cargil. One of our responsibilities at the shop was to make sure the piers where the submarines tied up, were kept clean. Occasionally after an upkeep replaced parts would be left on the pier and if we failed to notice it before the submarine returned to sea we would have to clean up the mess. We made a daily check of the piers in our pickup truck to avoid that.

Each of the submarines at the base had a wire enclosed cage assigned in the basement of Building 106. These cages were used by the submarines to store equipment not always needed on the boat. Each submarine had a key for their cage and a second key was required to enter the basement. That one was kept at the engine overhaul shop and to get it a member of the crew was required to sign a log book with the identification of the boat, time out, and time returned. The person picking up the key - which was attached to a 3 foot length of 2x4 lumber by a chain - would be told by our Chief, John (who loved this job) that he must go directly to Building 106 and not take it to the boat, and to follow the same procedure when retuning it. By doing so, if a crew member from another boat had need of it, he could easily see the sailor carrying the 2x4 with the key. If he failed to spot the 2x4 at least he would know the path of the key.

Why not give all of the boats a key to the building? It was tried at one time and some of the cages were broken into. Expensive new jackets were stolen and on one occasion, the door to the building was left open on a cold winter night and pipes froze and caused a water leak. Although our system was not perfect, we at least had a record of who had been in the building.

But - *the rest of the story.* John, who had been the COB on a submarine, knew how to deliver an ass chewing to a young sailor and was not unwilling to do the same to a Junior Officer. One day a young officer came into the shop for the key. John gave him the same lecture that he gave everyone. The Officer felt it was degrading to carry the 2x4 with the key attached to it and asked that it be removed. John went into his long spiel. He told him that the key had once been taken aboard a submarine that went to the Portsmouth Navy Yard and once left in the car of a sailor who had pulled a

265

liberty in New York City. He continued telling him the shop was in the process of making a round disc with a diameter greater than any opening on a submarine hatch so the key would not see any more sea duty. By this time, the young Officer had enough and left carrying the 2x4.

During my time at the shop I was fortunate enough to be advanced to Senior Chief. This added a star to my rating badge. At about this time the Texaco Company used a big star on their gas pumps and on the uniforms of the attendants at their stations. Their motto was, "You can always trust your car with the man who wears the star." One day while I was working on a senior officer's car, a Chief from one of the boats came into the shop, and in a real loud voice, said, "Yes, you can trust your car to the man who wears the star." Some guys can't be jealous without making some noise about it.

After WWII many of our submarines (as well as surface ships) were de-commissioned and placed in the Reserve Fleet. Some of these submarines were put back into commission during the Korean War. Over time, the boats in the Reserve Fleet became obsolete and the government sold them for scrap. While I was in the shop (1961-1964), a newer model torpedo was developed and was going to be tested on a submarine - the USS Guardfish (SS217) - from the Reserve Fleet. The engine overhaul shop was given the job of getting the propulsion system up and running so that it would be a live target. It had been several years since the diesel engines had been in use. Working for Henry, we were able to get one of the main engines running to propel this moving target. Because a submarine of this type was a diesel-electric drive, we needed an electrician from one of the boats in the squadron to operate the controls to provide power to the main motors that turned the screws to propel the boat. On the day of the test we thought we had a well-coordinated plan. Henry and I put the amount of diesel fuel in the clean fuel oil tank that would be enough for the test. With a couple of our squadron officers on the bridge, Henry and I to start the engine, and our electrician to put propulsion to the boat, we proceeded. We were towed to the test area in Long Island Sound by my old ship the Sun Bird. Once on station with our rudder locked amidships, and our diesel engine running, our two officers and Henry and I were picked up by the Sun Bird's whale boat. The electrician was required to stay aboard the boat until it was under way.

With the submarine carrying the test torpedo on station, and propulsion on the Guardfish, the electrician left the Guardfish in a rubber boat tied to its side. The submarine fired the test torpedo - and missed. The now unmanned target traveled much further than had been predicted and it was quite some time before the Sun Bird could corral the runaway and return it to the base. The poor Chief Torpedoman from the submarine that missed never heard the end of the story for the remainder of his Naval career.

Sometime during the early spring of 1962, I and another Chief from our shop were sent to Bayonne, New Jersey, to be members of the Security Crew of the Submarine Tender Apollo (AS 25) during its tow to the Submarine Base by one of our Submarine Rescue Vessels. I believe it was the USS Trigger (ASR 14).

The Apollo was in out-of-commission status in the Reserve Fleet and carried a lot of spare parts for submarines on board. With working parties detailed from the submarines in port to off load these spare parts, it was estimated that several hundreds of thousands of dollars were saved in spare parts for our Atlantic Fleet submarines.

Once the ship was unloaded, we rode it under tow to Jones Point, New York, where it was delivered to the Maritime Administration of the Department of Commerce.

For this, and the Guardfish (torpedo) operation, I received citation letters in my service record. I have to wonder if Mr. M, my old boss from the training tank, had been in charge of these operations, would he have done that?

I was happy with my job at Submarine Refitting and Training Group; the official name of our group at the shop. But I knew the job would come to an end at some point - just not when it would be. Our personnel man from the Squadron came over to the shop to see me and told me I was about due for shore duty. He recommended that I put in a request for the type of duty I preferred, otherwise I might receive orders to some place I might not wish to go. I asked if he had any suggestions. He suggested a reserve boat, a training aid for Naval Reserve personnel. In other words, a submarine that never went to sea. He told me the locations around the country of the available boats and when he mentioned Salem, MA. I thought that would be good option. Virginia's mother and family lived in Lynn, next door to Salem, and my brother and his family also lived in the area. That was my request and they must have been waiting for me. Within a month, I received my orders to the Sea Dog at Salem, my old submarine from WWII. With about a month before reporting to Salem, I had to find a place to live.

Our primary concern was finding the town that had the best special education school for Susan's needs. In checking with my brother Jack and his wife Olga, they recommended Danvers. On our first available weekend, Virginia and I, with Susan and Maureen, went to Lynn where we dropped off the girls at her grandmother's house.

We visited a real estate office in downtown Danvers. We told the Agent, Ray Webster, that we were looking for an apartment to rent. He said it would be very doubtful that we could find a place to rent in Danvers. He went on to suggest that we consider buying a house. We told him that we owned a house in Connecticut and would not have a down payment for another. Ray said, "Take a ride with me. I have one I would like to show you." It was a beautiful 3 bedroom, 1½ bath house and the asking price was $17,000.00. He said the bank would require a down payment of $1000.00 but by lowering his price to $16,000 he could give us credit for the down payment of $1000. Virginia and I were very pleased with this, and our mortgage payments would be less than the rent on an apartment. I asked that my brother Jack be allowed to inspect the house before we passed papers on the property as he knew a lot more about houses than I did. Things went very well and we were able to pass papers before I was scheduled to report to the Sea Dog.

Shortly before my leaving the engine overhaul shop for Salem I had a visitor. He was an Officer from one of the boats on the river. I knew him slightly from conducting an operational readiness and administrative inspection on the submarine he was attached to.

Mr. L. introduced himself to me and he told me that he also had orders to the Naval Reserve Center in Salem where he would be Officer in Charge of the station as well as the Sea Dog. He said he had heard that I had orders to the Sea Dog and went on to tell me that the Navy had a new concept for the Naval Reserve Program. He said members would have to *cut the mustard* or they could not stay in the program. He added that he was relying on me to achieve that goal. What could I say except, "Yes Sir," and shake his hand?

I was lucky and found a Chief I knew who was looking for a place to rent and this worked well for several years until we sold the property in Connecticut.

The movers contracted by the Navy came to our house the day before our move and packed everything except the beds. Early the next morning they picked up the final items and we were on our way to Danvers. Virginia, with Susan, drove the family car and I drove our second car with Maureen for company. We all arrived at our new house where the movers delivered our goods. Our first night in town was spent at my brother Jack and Olga's place.

Sea Dog at Salem about 1965; former Pequot Mills in rear

Return to USS Sea Dog (AG SS 401)

It was a pleasure to report to the Sea Dog at the Navy Reserve Training Center on Derby Street in Salem. This was the first time I had seen her since 1946.

The crew welcomed me aboard in the afternoon after I had completed my check-in routine. I had met the Officer in Charge of both the boat and Division 1-11 at the 1-11 Center that morning.

The first order of business was to introduce me to the preferred drinking establishments along Derby Street where I learned that some caution was required with the generous pourings in Salem compared to the closely measured shots around the base at New London.

We had a crew of eight Regular navy Petty Officers assigned to the boat that included the Chief of the Boat who at that time was Ray Hackett, a Senior Chief Radioman. Our job, as Shipkeeper Instructors was to maintain the equipment used for training the Navy Reserve personnel assigned there to insure it was in proper order for their once-monthly weekend drills.

Although we were all First Class and Chief Petty Officers we were responsible for keeping the interior compartments clean and painted as necessary, and painting the exterior when needed.

Our work day hours were from 8:00 AM to 1:00 PM on weekdays plus the weekend of the Reserve drills. One member of the crew would have 24 hour duty each day to provide security for the boat. In addition he would receive visitors from the general public and conduct tours during the afternoon hours of 1:00 to 4:00. Salem was (and is) a big tourist town and we had many visitors especially in the summer.

A lot of time was spent during the week to keep our lesson plans up to date in preparation for the weekend drills. Naval Reserve Petty Officers handled about 60% of the instruction and we handled the rest.

Attendance of the Reserve personnel was not held to the same standard as the Regular Navy and we had to be prepared to cover if a Reserve instructor should fail to appear. Generally they were reliable and would at least notify us in advance if they were to be absent to allow us to prepare.

When I reported aboard Mr. L. (and by now readers will recognize someone who would be a problem thus remains un-named) who was also assigned, had not checked in.

As soon as Virginia and I were settled in our new home we got in touch with the Cerebral Palsy Center in Salem and with their assistance arranged an appointment at the North Shore Children's Hospital to have Susan evaluated by Dr. Hugenberger, an orthopedic surgeon.

Dr. Hugenberger was a very compassionate man who donated a lot of his time to assisting *crippled children,* as they were called at the time. His diagnosis was that she was *spastic* (had exaggerated tendon reflexes) and he recommended surgery to relieve some of the tension on the tendons involved. Arrangements were made with Children's Hospital in Boston for him to perform the operation there. Following the surgery Susan was immobilized in a full body cast that kept her legs extended and straight. She had been expected to remain at Children's for about six weeks, but her recovery was very slow and it extended to three months. We visited her every evening except for two when a storm prevented travel into Boston. On the days when I had the duty on the Sea Dog, Virginia drove in alone.

After a few weeks the cast was split on the sides to allow it to be removed for bathing and performing the stretching exercises we had been doing for several years. At Christmas (1964) we were allowed to bring her home for the day. Because of the body cast the only way I could transport her in the car was to make a plywood bed across the back seat where she could be placed on her back.

When she was finally able to return home permanently she was still required to use the cast for several months. It was such an obvious relief

to her to have it removed periodically that it was heartbreaking to put her back into it.

The doctors and nurses who cared for her in Boston were outstanding and we could never thank them enough. The costs were in the thousands, money we did not have, but were covered by the Crippled Children's Association.

We had faith in the recommendations of the doctors. Unfortunately there is no way to tell how much was really gained by their efforts. Despite all that was done she was destined to lead a difficult life.

Virginia's mother had moved in with us. We had plenty of room and it was a great help to Virginia to have her there. Maureen loved her. Virginia's sister Gail and her family still lived in Lynn so we had a lot of company.

Maureen was now in the second grade and between school and our neighborhood had many friends to play with - unlike at the home in Connecticut.

At the Reserve Center, our new Officer in Charge, Mr. L., had relieved the previous OIC. On his initial tour of the Sea Dog he pointed out a number of areas that needed cleaning and painting, and stressed the need for properly maintaining the training equipment.

While making task assignments, one of the Chiefs suggested to the COB that we all work together doing one compartment at a time and work through the boat. I had already noted however that Chief O. was not much of a worker, so told the COB to just assign my compartments to me and they would be taken care of. His duty assignment was at the station so he had little direct control of the crew. Most were good workers, but not Chief O. and I had little interest in picking up his slack.

Occasionally Mr. L. would have me monitor a training class and if I noted that an instructor had done poorly - as I would report on his evaluation sheet - he would order that one of our men take over the class. I quickly realized it was in our best interest to grade all the instructors highly or we would be doing all of the instruction.

I don't recall that Mr. L. ever made reference to his pep talk at the sub base about "cutting the mustard." His new priorities seemed to be "Recruit, Retain, Advance" - things that would have the most beneficial effect on his own fitness report.

One day he called me to his office and told me he had been unaware of my part time job and that he thought there should be enough work in my Navy job to keep me busy. I told him I always had a part time job when I was in port and that I felt it was necessary to provide the lifestyle to my family I thought they should have. I did not choose to remind him of other financial obligations I faced.

I suspect I made no points with my response.

In less than a year our COB retired from the Navy. With only one other Chief on board - who was junior to me - I became the COB under Mr. L. Within a couple of weeks I began giving the man who had the duty and stayed aboard overnight the next day off. A short time later Mr. L. had a need to see the man I had given liberty to, and when he found he was not there informed me that he had not authorized the absence.

I got the message; my wings had been clipped. I was to be only a messenger.

On another occasion he asked me to stop by his office before I *went ashore*. I arrived at his office about 30 minutes before my normal liberty time. His office door was closed which told me he was either in a meeting with someone or had left the building. After waiting about an hour, I went home. The next morning he called me in and said, "I thought I told you I wanted to see you before you went home." I explained what had happened but had the feeling I was digging a deeper hole for myself. I thought of my XO from the Entemedor who would have had the courtesy to open his door and acknowledge me.

I had to doubt that Mr. L. had ever attended Leadership School. He certainly did not have the best interests of his men at heart.

Our routine in getting going in the morning was low key. If a crewmember was occasionally late it was not a big deal. We had coffee together in the wardroom while we were getting organized. One morning I arrived to find the whole crew on time sitting in the wardroom and I knew something was going on.

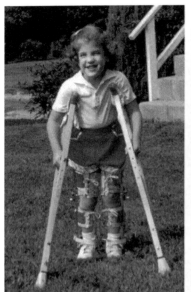

Top: Susan (b. Sept. 10, 1952) in 1958 and about 1960.
Bottom: Doug, Maureen, Susan, Virginia – Danvers, MA, 1964.

Chief O. was the spokesman, and he opened saying that we were all Firsts and Chiefs here and used to running our own gangs, but I seemed to be running the whole show. (Did he somehow forget that I was the Chief in Charge?) He felt they all should have a say in how things were to be done.

I told him I was of the opinion that Mr. L. was running things and he was the man who told me what he wanted done. I suggested he might want to set up a meeting with Mr. L. to let him know how he thought things should be done. I also mentioned to him that if he could get himself here on time for a week I would be willing to listen to his suggestions. There were none.

When I had been transferred to the Sea Dog - for the usual 3 year tour - I had been planning to remain in the Navy for 30 years. I was now eligible to take the exam for E9 (Master Chief Engineman). Although I had not been selected I planned on taking the exam the next year. Shortly before the time arrived, Mr. L. told me I would not be eligible as I needed to do some public relations work to qualify. When the exam was being given at the station I remained on the Sea Dog. The yeoman called me and said he had my exam and I told him Mr. L. had told me I was ineligible. A couple of minutes later the phone rang again and the yeoman told me Mr. L. said it would be OK. I told him to tell Mr. L. I had taken his word on it - and did not take the exam.

The air conditioning on the Sea Dog had not been working for some time. When I asked the enginemen about it I was told the system had leaks and wouldn't hold a charge of Freon. A lot of classes were held on board and it became oppressively hot during the summer. Mr. L. wanted it fixed.

At that time I had no idea about what was wrong with the system. Ordering spare parts or materials at a Reserve Center took forever. I took our pickup truck down to the repair shop at new London. I needed a bottle of dry nitrogen to locate the leaks and a bottle of

Freon to charge the system if I was able to repair them. I had connections there and they took care of me. After charging with the nitrogen I could not detect any leaks, and over time there was no loss of pressure in the system. I had to conclude there were none. After charging with the Freon, it produced cold air but only for a few hours before it would freeze up and stop working. This suggested there was moisture in the system, but there were two dryer cartridges installed that were supposed to prevent that. By alternately removing the cartridges and baking out the moisture they had become saturated with, over several cycles and a couple of weeks we were consistently producing cold air.

At our next meeting, and it happened to be a hot weekend, we were very comfortable on the boat. Mr. L. came aboard and was quite pleased. Although he had lowered my quarterly marks from the time he took command he bumped them up on the next marking period - but not to the 4.0 level I had usually achieved. He and Mr. M. at the escape tank were the only ones to ever mark me lower.

I lived on a fairly busy street in Danvers, and one morning as I was getting into my car to head for work a Navy sedan stopped in the street and the Navy officer driving called me over. He asked me where I was stationed. I told him and he asked, "What the hell is wrong with your CO? – what the hell is he trying to prove?" This officer was the CO of the Reserve unit in Lynn. All I could say was that I had to work for him.

So it wasn't "just me."

Through the grapevine I learned we were going to get a surplus Coast Guard 36 ft. Rescue Boat. Apparently Mr. L. had discussed the benefits of acquiring it with a Chief Torpedoman who worked for me and the two of them had gone into Boston to inspect it. The paperwork was done and we were to take delivery in a few days.

I went to Mr. L's office and told him I had heard we were getting the boat. He told me the value of it and how he planned to use it to teach seamanship to the reservists. I had a question: who was to take care of the vessel? He said the Chief Torpedoman had volunteered to do it. I mentioned to him that the Chief had problems enough doing his own work on the Sea Dog. I also asked him how he came to ask the Chief to check out the boat, and he said he thought he would know the most about small boats. My temperature was rising, but I was trying to control myself. I asked him if it had sails - he said no, that it had a diesel engine. I asked who was to take care of the engine, and, by the way, was I still the COB and if so why had I not been in the loop?

He did apologize; I think the only one made during his time at Salem.

As much as I had hoped to remain in the Navy for 30 years I had to consider Virginia and the girls. I was not qualified for nuclear submarines and most of the diesels were now decommissioned. I would have no way of knowing where I might be sent when my tour at Salem ended. So I submitted my papers for retirement effective in six months.

My tour at Salem was definitely not my best although things were about to change for the better there. Mr. L's tour was also coming to an end and he had orders to report to a submarine as its XO.

Our new CO, Mr. Goode, liked the condition of the Sea Dog. He told me to continue as I had been doing and if he had any thoughts about changes he would discuss them with me. He also told me his door was always open if I had any problems.

When the next quarterly marks came out I was back at 4.0.

Mr. Goode was a much better man to work for; my attitude improved, and Virginia could see the change in me.

He called me into his office one day and told me he had a set of orders for me to report to a minesweeper in Viet Nam. I really wanted to go but was feeling more that I could not leave Virginia and the girls. And my separation date had been approved.

In fairness to Mr. L., I have to give him credit for raising the standards of Division 1-11. Under his leadership the division won efficiency awards in two consecutive years. He also presented me with two letters of commendation during the time I worked for him.

Shortly before I retired I had a conversation with Frank Gage one of the reservists assigned to the Seadog. Frank was a Chief Machinist Mate and had survived the sinking of his ship during the war. He was known as a *squared away* CPO. He asked me what my plans were for retirement and I told him I had nothing lined up. Frank was the foreman of the machine shop at "Ion Physics" in Burlington, MA, and invited me to visit him there. He introduced me to a few people at the plant and I was told by the personnel department to come in when my separation was final - only a matter of a couple of weeks from then.

At my retirement ceremony I was transferred to the Fleet Reserve, and at the expiration of 30 years of service received my certificate of retirement from the Armed Forces of the United States in 1973. During my time in the Fleet Reserve I was subject to recall if the Navy had need of my services.

After the ceremony we adjourned to one of the Derby Street water holes where I probably had more to drink than I should have.

Epilogue

I retired from the Navy on a Friday and was at "Ion Physics" on the following Monday. I was hired as a vacuum technician on a project involving high voltage testing in a vacuum chamber. At that time (1967) there was a lot of government money available for projects like that, but they didn't usually last too long.

My father passed away in 1968. With the loss of his Social Security my mother could no longer afford to live in her home in New Hampshire. Virginia and I bought a larger house in Danvers and my mother moved in with us. We now had both of the girl's grandmothers living with us. Was Virginia a saint? - Yes, she was. It was tough for her at times, however my mother was a great cook, and with Virginia's mother working they both did their share.

With two baby sitters and the extra money from my Navy pension we took several trips and sometimes took Susan and Maureen along with us.

When the project at Ion Physics came to a close a buddy from the Entemedor, Dennis Grace, and I were hired by a Boston company to do maintenance work and I remained there for about seven years. Realizing that I wouldn't be able to do that kind of work for the rest of my life I found a position with "International Materials" testing crude oil for a few years and later was hired at "Varian Associates" in Beverly, where I remained until my second retirement at age 62.

I realized in less than a week that I was not ready for retirement. I knew the chief engineer at the Danvers State Hospital and since I had a license to operate high pressure steam boilers, he hired me. I planned to remain there until I reached 65 and take my Social Security but the job and benefits were so good I reached 72 before I finally pulled the plug. I guess I took after my father who always loved to work.

Even in retirement I worked on the Salem to Boston Ferry for a few trips each week in the summertime.

One day in the fall of 2013, at age 87 and looking for some excitement, I drove out to Orange, Mass. - October 20 to be exact - and did a tandem jump from an airplane from 13,500 feet. What a thrill!

Next on the agenda - with a birthday gift-certificate from my special friend - I will be doing three laps flat out with a NASCAR racing instructor at the New Hampshire Motor Speedway.

I keep moving - now I've written a book.

I am not a *hero*. At least I don't consider myself to be one.

I've said that publicly, and repeat it here to avoid anyone thinking I am claiming to be one in presenting my story. My motive is simply to tell it - because I think it's worth telling - and to preserve it. If all of us veterans did it, there would be more stories told than anyone could read or listen to, but the simple fact is very few do so. Some of us must. Famous admirals and generals always produce accounts of their great victories, but those of us who simply answered, "Aye, aye, sir," when the captain called out, "All ahead full," need to get our two-cents worth in.

Roughly sixteen million American men and women served in the Armed Forces during World War II - and there were less millions of us in those days than now. Nearly all played small parts in very large events, some smaller, some larger, and many in fact were true heroes.

Regrettably many of those were never allowed to record their stories as they gave everything they had in carrying out the duties they had sworn to perform.

The thinking today seems to be, "Well, you were there, therefore you're a hero." My feeling on that - and I am not alone in it - is that, "When everyone is a hero, no one is a hero."

I joined the Navy to escape the economic privations of the Depression. Was I influenced by the demands of the war? Of course. There was no getting around that, but the war provided an economic opportunity. And, to steal another expression, "My Mama didn't raise no fool!"

The Submarine Service was *high risk* and higher paid because of it. I followed the money. Why not try to get the best return for my time on the job? We all need to provide for ourselves and those who depend on us and there are very few who would not wish to "do a bit better" in order to drive a better car, or get the color TV or the backyard pool - or the house with the backyard to have a pool in.

So we use the skills we have to do the best we can. Hoeing beans on a hardscrabble farm in northern New Hampshire doesn't give a lot to work with. The Navy gave me an opportunity to advance in a way that would not have been otherwise available to me. Despite the risks of the work I was engaged in - aside from the increased hazards of the war itself - I experienced an interesting and at times exciting career that left me with a wide range of experience and skills that carried me forward in my later life.

Many jobs have risks that must be accepted for the rewards that (sometimes) come from them. That's not heroic, it's just life.

1 April 1966

Chief Bryant
USS SEA DOG (SS401)
U.S. Naval Reserve Training Center
Derby Street at Central Wharf
Salem, Massachusetts

Dear Chief Bryant,

Thank you so very much for sending me the SEA DOG
patch. It certainly brings back many fond memories of the
days I spent aboard that fine submarine as well as memories
of the wonderful shipmates aboard SEA DOG.

With warm personal regards,

Sincerely,

V. L. LOWRANCE
Vice Admiral, U.S. Navy

Jacket Patches related to the author's Naval Service.

(note: Seadog on cover is later version designed by author during final tour in Salem 1964-67)

US SUBMARINES LOST DURING WORLD WAR II

USS Sealion (SS-195)	25 December 1941	USS Grayback (SS-208)	26 February 1944
USS S-36 (SS-141)	20 January 1943	USS Trout (SS-202)	29 February 1944
USS S-26 (SS-131)	24 January 1942	USS Tullibee (SS-284)	26 March 1944
USS Shark (SS-174)	11 February 1942	USS Gudgeon (SS-211)	18 April 1944
USS Perch (SS-176)	03 March 1942	USS Herring (SS-233)	01 June 1944
USS S-27 (SS-132)	19 June 1942	USS Golet (SS-361)	14 June 1944
USS Grunion (SS-216)	01 August 1942	USS S-28 (SS-133)	04 July 1944
USS S-39 (SS-144)	14 August 1942	USS Robalo (SS-273)	26 July 1944
USS Argonaut (SS-166)	10 January 1943	USS Flier (SS-250)	13 August 1944
USS Amberjack (SS-219)	16 February 1943	USS Harder (SS-257)	24 August 1944
USS Grampus (SS-207)	05 March 1943	USS Seawolf (SS-197)	03 October 1944
USS Triton (SS-201)	15 March 1943	USS Escolar (SS-294)	17 October 1944
USS Pickerel (SS-177)	03 April 1943	USS Shark (SS-314)	24 October 1944
USS Grenadier (SS-210)	22 April 1943	USS Darter (SS-227)	24 October 1944
USS R-12 (SS-89)	12 June 1943	USS Tang (SS-306)	25 October 1944
USS Runner (SS-275)	01 July 1943	USS Albacore (SS-218)	07 November 1944
USS Pompano (SS-181)	01 September 1943	USS Growler (SS-215)	08 November 1944
USS Grayling (SS-209)	09 September 1943	USS Scamp (SS-277)	16 November 1944
USS Cisco (SS-290)	28 September 1943	USS Swordfish (SS-193)	12 January 1945
USS S-44 (SS-155)	07 October 1943	USS Barbel (SS-316)	04 February 1945
USS Wahoo (SS-238)	11 October 1943	USS Kete (SS-369)	Ab 20 March 1945
USS Dorado (SS-248)	12 October 1943	USS Trigger (SS-237)	28 March 1945
USS Corvina (SS-226)	16 November 1943	USS Snook (SS-279)	08 April 1945
USS Sculpin (SS-191)	19 November 1943	USS Lagarto (SS-371)	04 May 1945
USS Capelin (SS-289)	01 December 1943	USS Bonefish (SS-223)	18 June 1945
USS Scorpion (SS-278)	01 February 1944	USS Bullhead (SS-332)	06 August 1945

On Eternal Patrol

Author Doug Bryant, USN (Ret) with transcriber Joanne Frate in Chief's Quarters on USS San Juan 2012

Co-author Jeff Wignall, PNC 80th Infantry Division Veterans Association, author of *Farebersviller 1944* (2010)

Bryant Service Awards:

Good Conduct	American Campaign	Asia-Pacific Theater
WWII Victory	WWII Occupation	National Defense
Combat Action	PI Liberation	PI Presidential Citation

74687069R00166

Made in the USA
Middletown, DE
29 May 2018